THE
RED
FOLDER

Private
Lessons
on the
Practice of Hoodoo

edited by
catherine yronwode

Missionary Independent
Spiritual Church

→ 2019 ←

The Red Folder:
Private Lessons on the Practice of Hoodoo
Edited by catherine yronwode

© 2019 Missionary Independent Spiritual Church

Texts used by permission of the following authors,
who retain co-copyright to their individual contributions and have granted
Missionary Independent Spiritual Church (MISC) the right to print and reprint their contributions:

Pages 4-7, 18, 21, 25, 35, 38-39, 40-41, 47-48, 104, 109, 129-130, 131-134, 135-136, © 2014, 2015, 2016, 2017, 2018, 2019 catherine yronwode and MISC; page 11, © 2019 catherine yronwode and Deacon Millett and MISC; pages 8-9, 10, © 2016, 2018 Jon Saint Germain and MISC; pages 12, 13-14, © 2014, 2016 Michele Jackson and MISC; pages 15-18, © 2016 Kast Excelsior and MISC; pages 19-20, © 2017 Chas Bogan and MISC; page 22, © 2017 Grey Townsend and MISC; pages 23-24, © 2017 Susan Diamond and MISC; pages 26-29, © 2014 Madame Nadia and MISC; page 30, 46, © 2018 Valentina Burton and MISC; page 31, 92-93, © 2017, 2019 Dr. Jeremy Weiss and MISC; page 32, 110, © 2015, 2018 Phœnix LeFæ and MISC; pages 33-34, © 2016 Madame Pamita and MISC; pages 36-37, 99, 113-114, © 2014, 2015, 2016 Professor Charles Porterfield and MISC; pages 42-43, 96-97, 105-106, 121-122, © 2015, 2016, 2018, 2019, Ms. Robin York and MISC; pages 44-45, © 2016 Gabrielle Swain and MISC; pages 49-50, © 2015 Papa Michæl Bautista and MISC; pages 51-52, © 2019 Papa Gee and MISC; pages 53-54, © 2017 Co. Meadows and MISC; page 55, © 2018 Mama E. and Clayton James and MISC; pages 56-57, © 2017 Beverley Smith and MISC; pages 58-59, © 2015 Susan Barnes, Madame Pamita, Miss Michæle, Valentina Burton, and Marin Graves and MISC; pages 60-64, © 2018 Angela Marie Horner and MISC; pages 65-66, © 2015 Miss Elvyra Curcuruto-Love and MISC; pages 67-68, 69-70, © 2018, 2019 Papa Newt and MISC; pages 71-72, © 2017 Candelo Kimbisa and Mama E. and MISC; page 73, © 2016 David Borji Shi and MISC; pages 74-75, © 2018 Devi Spring and MISC; pages 76-77, © 2017 Storm Færywolf and MISC; pages 78-79, © 2017 Madame Nadia and Jaiye Dania and MISC; page 80, 83, © 2014, 2016, Aura Laforest and MISC; pages 81-82, © 2016 Ambrozine LeGare and MISC; page 84, © 2014 Miss Michæle and Professor Charles Porterfield and MISC; page 85, © 2015 Khi Armand and MISC; pages 86-87, 116, © 2014, 2015 Dr. Johannes Gårdbäck and MISC; pages 88-89, © 2015 Candelo Kimbisa and MISC; pages 90-91, © 2014 ConjureMan Ali and MISC; pages 94-95, © 2014 Madame Nadia and Madame Pamita and MISC; page 98, 100-101, © 2015, 2019 Deacon Millett and MISC; pages 102-103, © 2019 Lady Muse and MISC; pages 107-108, © 2014 Ms. Melanie, Kast Excelsior, Miss Elvyra Curcuruto-Love, Lou Florez, Miss Phœnix LeFæ, and Ms. Robin York and MISC; pages 111-112, © 2019 Ms. Robin York, Angela Marie Horner, Mama E., Papa Newt, Elle DuVall, and catherine yronwode and MISC; page 115, 118 © 2017, 2018 Miss Aida and MISC; page 117, © 2014 Ladies Auxiliary of MISC; pages 119-120, © 2017 Ms. Robin York, Miss Michæle, Angela Marie Horner, Co. Meadows, Candelo Kimbisa, Ambrozine LeGare, and MISC; pages 123-124, © 2016 Beverley Smith, Sister Girl, Miss Michæle, Papa Lou, Candelo Kimbisa, Angela Marie Horner, Professor Charles Porterfield and MISC; pages 127-128, © 2014 Apollo Dark and MISC; Plate I © 2016 catherine yronwode and MISC; Plate II © 2018 Angela Marie Horner and MISC.

Artwork:
Grey Townsend, nagasiva yronwode, Deacon Millett

Typesetting and Production:
catherine yronwode, nagasiva yronwode

First Printing 2019

Published by
Missionary Independent Spiritual Church
6632 Covey Road
Forestville, California 95436
MissionaryIndependent.org

ISBN: 978-0-9960523-6-8

Printed in Canada.

THE RED FOLDER
Table of Contents

INTRODUCTION
catherine yronwode

My, my, how time flies. It seems like only yesterday that we assembled and published *The Black Folder, "an omnium-gatherum for the ages,"* comprising 20 years' worth of Lucky Mojo shop flyers and hand-outs for workshops at Missionary Independent Spiritual Church's annual Hoodoo Heritage Festivals from 2008 through 2013. And yet here we are, a mere six years later, with another 136-page book. This one is a companion to the MISC Festival workshops of 2014 through 2019, reprinting all the flyers, plus extracts from the books we gave to attendees in those years.

Looking back, it is amazing and gratifying to see how many friends, colleagues, and associates have joined in this work to present African-American folk magic, as well as the magic and spirituality of other cultures, to the world. The Festivals could not have brought their wonder and joy to participants had not a stalwart staff of volunteers, workers, and presenters mobilized themselves every year to put on the annual show. Meanwhile, the small publishing company that my husband nagasiva and i founded in 2002 now has a back-list of three dozen titles, and this would not have been possible without the enthusiasm and effort of a loving band of authors, illustrators, typesetters, editors, designers, and production workers who want to preserve and popularize the beautiful treasures of folk magic, folk religion, and the divinatory arts.

By 2013, organizing the yearly Hoodoo Heritage Festival was a major mission of the Association of Independent Readers and Rootworkers. AIRR had sprung to life in 2008 and gone online in 2009 as a directory of ethical psychics who were also trained in the practice of hoodoo, rootwork, and conjure. Both AIRR and the annual Festivals were the brain-children of Ms. Robin, a well-known Bay Area psychic.

As the AIRR roster grew, more informational topics were added to the ReadersAndRootworkers.com site. Those who wrote and illustrated AIRR's hundreds of helpful web pages felt the need for regular meetings, and so the AIRR Tech Team came into being. At first we just envisioned having a little chat-space where folks with IT skills could link up every Tuesday via Skype and discuss proposed site updates. However, with a fairly stable membership and a tendency to stay in the background, the Tech Team soon became the secret engine that powered the MISC Festivals.

It was at the weekly Tech Team meetings that we discussed the offers that AIRR members had made to present workshops on spirituality and magic. It was at the Tech Team meetings that we laid out the web pages for each year's Festival. And it was Tech Team members who rode herd on the presenters, their flyers, the materials they would distribute at their workshops, and all the other thousand deadline-sensitive details of putting on a yearly convention.

In January 2014, while we were preparing for the annual May event, we suffered a terrible personal and organizational blow. Just hours after putting the finishing touches on our 2014 Festival web site and designing the year's postcard announcing the event, our dear friend and colleague Dr. E. — Eddy Gutierrez — died of a heart attack. His loss was tragic. He was young, and greatly loved, and he had been in good spirits at that very day's Tech Team meeting. He will never be replaced in our hearts, but we feel his spirit near.

Only a few weeks later, we lost another AIRR member, Rukiah Shamon, a gifted healer and crystal ball scryer, who was taken from us by cancer. Again we were devastated.

We soldiered on with plans for the 2014 Festival, and, with the help of many hands, we pulled it all together, just in time. A total of 15 psychics shared the reader's tent, which was sponsored by the good folks at the Hoodoo Psychics telephone reading line, under the direction of Deacon Millett. Tarot cards, crystal balls, and candles decorated the space, and in the back, the HP crew hosted two Vacant Chairs, for Eddy and Rukiah.

We opened Saturday morning with a Quimbanda ceremony for Exu led by ConjureMan Ali, who gave each attendee an Exu amulet he had made by hand. "Wildcrafting Herbs Around the Home" featured me leading folks around our property with the help of Kast Excelsior, teaching how to identify and gather herbs. Then, back at the tents, everyone learned to dry and vacuum pack their herbs, under the guidance of Professor Porterfield. Madame Pamita entertained us, telling fortunes in song, and lunch was catered by Mother Katrina Mead of Missionary Independent Spiritual Church.

Aura Laforest's new book *Hoodoo Spiritual Baths* made its debut that year. Aura could not attend, so Miss Phœnix LeFæ, Lou Florez, and Professor Porterfield did the honours at her workshop, and everyone got the book and a packet of House Blessing Bath Crystals. The Panel Discussion was "Our Favourite Money Spells," with Miss Elvyra, Lou Florez, Kast Excelsior, Miss Phœinix LeFæ, Ms. Melanie, and Ms. Robin. Madame Nadia then taught how to use tarot, Lenormand, and playing cards to divine someone's future, diagnose a client, and decide which spells to cast. In addition to her flyer, participants received a deck of playing cards.

Dr. Johannes Gårdbäck's "A Norse Trollknytte for Protection" class introduced us to the traditional folk magic of Sweden, Norway, and Denmark. We learned to make a troll bundle, and participants took home a special preview of *Trolldom: Spells and Methods of the Norse Folk Magic Tradition,* with our promise to mail them a free copy upon publication of the finished work!

Sunday began with a Spiritualist Candle Service for "Overcoming Obstacles and Opposition" with Apollo Dark; and each attendee got a flyer, a candle, a dressing oil, and a packet of our new Block Buster herb mix. Madame Pamita and Madame Nadia teamed up to present "Love and Glamour Magic" with a flyer, a packet of Love Herbs blend, and a packet of Look Me Over Sachet Powder.

At the 2010, 2011, 2012, and 2013 Festivals, we had held a Conjure Cook-Off featuring magical recipes, under the direction of Sister Robin Petersen. Everyone who took part in those events received one of our annual 16-page recipe booklets. In 2014, the four booklets, with additional recipes, were collected in *Hoodoo Food! The Best of the Conjure Cook-Off and Rootwork Recipe Round-Up*, and attendees at the Sunday buffet lunch each got a copy of the new book.

"Contemporary Bone Reading" led by Michele Jackson, featured her new book *Bones, Shells and Curios,* and participants received a small carved shell to add to their bone sets. At "Bible Magic: Blessing and Cursing with Holy Scripture" Miss Michæle and Professor Porterfield; distributed their new book, *Hoodoo Bible Magic,* a 23rd Psalm prayer card, and a Missionary Independent Spiritual Church fan.

"Defending Yourself Against the Dark Arts" was ConjureMan Ali's presentation on defensive and protective magic, and we each made own personal guardian fetish under his direction.

The 2015 Hoodoo Heritage Festival opened with "Voices of Hyatt: A Tribute to Rootworkers of the Past." Professor Porterfield, Ambrozine LeGare, Sister Girl, and Khi Armand brought to life the informants interviewed by Harry M. Hyatt in the early part of the 20th century. The handout was "How Can We Remember?: Harry Hyatt and Hoodoo." Miss Phœnix LeFæ followed, with *Hoodoo Shrines and Altars,* her new book, and gave each participant an altar cloth to take home. Madame Pamita again serenaded us with her ukelele and lunch was catered by Mother Katrina Mead of Missionary Independent Spiritual Church.

I conducted a workshop on petition papers at which i gave away copies of my new book *Paper in My Shoe,* along with a pew pencil and an assortment of fancy and plain papers for writing. "Afro-Caribbean Protection Magic" by Candelo Kimbisa was next, and featured a flyer, plus a macuto charm.

"Money Magic" was led by Ms. Robin York, and everyone got a packet of Money Herb Mix, a packet of money magic sachet powders, a crisp one-dollar bill, and a two-page handout. Then came *A Deck of Spells,* Professor Porterfield new book, and attendees also received a deck of playing cards.That evening, after the workshops, we held our first Saturday Presenters' Banquet.

Miss Elvyra brought us the Sunday morning program on "Angels and Archangels," and distributed bottles of 7-11 Holy Oil, white candles, and a two-page handout. Next up was "How to Make Your Own Sachet Powders" by Papa Michæl, where we each created a sachet powder to take home. And Mother Katrina again catered the buffet lunch.

Hoodoo Return and Reconciliation Spells was Deacon Millett's new book, and his opportunity to give a copy to each attendee, along with a packet of Return To Me Sachet Powder. The panel talk, "Our Favourite Lodestone Spells" featured Valentina Burton, Susan Barnes, Marin Graves, Miss Michæle, Madame Pamita, and Apollo Dark — and everyone got a pair of matched Lodestones and a packet of Magnetic Sand.

At Khi Armand's workshop, his brand new book *Deliverance!: Hoodoo Spells of Uncrossing, Healing, and Protection,* was given to all participants, along with Cast Off Evil Bath Crystals. We ended the day with "A Closing Circle," at which all the professionals exchanged business cards while i urged them on to greater success, fame, and financial security.

The 2016 Festival brought us "Voices of Hyatt II" with Kast Excelsior, Ambrozine LeGare, and Professor Porterfield, plus a flyer i wrote on Harry M. Hyatt's books. "Dem Dry Bones: Working with Osteomantic and Necromantic Curios" by Kast Excelsior was about the power of zoological remains. Kast then switched gears and performed a lunch concert with Madame Pamita. The food was catered by the Ladies Auxiliary of Missionary Independent Spiritual Church.

"Sew Much Hoodoo: Textiles and Needlework in the Domestic Conjure Arts" by Gabrielle Swain brought fiber arts to the fore, and each attendee received a pattern and a sewing kit. Ambrozine LeGare then shared tips for "Blessing and Protecting Your Home," as we made herbal cleansing washes. "Amulets and Talismans: The Art of Consecrated Curios" was Ms. Robin's offering and everyone took home a collection of nine lucky charms. Professor Porterfield gave us his book, *The Sporting Life: How to Help Yourself with Hoodoo and Rootwork, from the Streets to the Sheets,* and each participant also got a packet of Jezebel Bath Crystals. Throughout the day, we had 18 readers on site, courtesy of Hoodoo Psychics, and after the reading tent closed down, we celebrated at the Presenters' Banquet.

Sunday morning opened with distribution of *North Asian Magic: Spellcraft from Manchuria, Mongolia, and Siberia,* a new book by David Borji Shi, who led us in a shamanic ritual around the oboo, or sacred pole. At "Teas and Tisanes: Making Magical Potions and Infusions" with Madame Pamita, everyone made an herb tea and took home a souvenir cup and saucer. Lunch was again provided by the Ladies Auxiliary.

At "Our Hoodoo History: The Revival of the Occult Shop Pamphlet" i distributed the restored book *Legends of Incense, Herb, and Oil Magic* by Lewis de Claremont, plus seals from *The Sixth and Seventh Books of Moses.* "Our Favourite Social Justice Spells" was our panel talk, with Beverley Smith, Miss Michæle, Candelo Kimbisa, Angela Marie Horner, and Sister Girl. Michele Jackson led "Bone Reading: Mastering Groupings and Configurations," and gave us each a flyer, a bottle of cleansing spray, miniature handcuffs, and a Cougar bone.

Jon Saint Germain, "The Voice of the Crystal Silence League," introduced his new book *Crystal Magic: Divination, Healing, and Spellcraft with Gems and Minerals,* and each person also got two lucky gemstones. And again we held "A Closing Circle" and business card exchange for the success of all.

For 2017 the opening ceremony was Pagan. Storm Færywolf & Company gave us "Witchcraft and the Færy Tradition," and we danced with be-ribboned and belled Færy Wands. *This Amazing Book: Hoodoo Herb and Root Medicine,* was my second book restoration as part of the Lucky Mojo Library of Occult Classics, and in addition to the book, folks also went home with a traditional medical herb mix. Madame Pamita and Jon Nelson entertained us at lunch with hoodoo songs, and food was provided by the Ladies Auxiliary of Missionary Independent Spiritual Church.

Madame Nadia and Jaiye Dania brought us "Fit and Foxy: The Magic of Attraction," and in addition to their flyer, they also distributed Attraction spiritual supplies. "Ouija Revelations: Conjuring Spirits and Other Sorceries" by Chas Bogan gave us a history of spirit board divination, and everyone got a pocket tin of Ouija Mints and a pair of Ouija or Fortune Teller socks.

The new book *Cursing and Crossing: Hoodoo Spells to Torment, Jinx, and Take Revenge on Your Enemies,* plus a vial of Tarantula exoskeletons, was Miss Aida's gift to her workshop's attendees. Susan Diamond was up next, with "The Potent Power of the Pendulum," and everyone took home her flyer and two pendulums. We had 20 readers on site, and when the tents closed, we enjoyed our Presenter's Banquet.

"A Dominican Mesa Blanca" in the Sanse tradition, with Candelo Kimbisa and Mama E. began our Sunday program. Beverley Smith then gave us "The Moving Flame," a two-page flyer, plus candles to burn at home. Lunch was catered by the Ladies Auxiliary, and Professor Porterfield presented a live version of "The Now You Know Show," his variety podcast.

Vulvamancy was the new book written by Dr. Jeremy Weiss, introducing a little-known but ancient technique of body-reading. Attendees received the book and a sampler vial of Lucky Clover Vulva Oil. The panel talk was "Our Favourite Court Case Spells," led By Ms. Robin York, with Miss Michæle, Ambrozine LeGare, Candelo Kimbisa, Angela Marie Horner, and Co. Meadows.

Women's Work: Home-Style Hoodoo Spells for Marriage, Sex, and Motherhood was Aura Laforest's introduction to her book of the same name, and participants also got Queen Elizabeth Root spiritual supplies. Co. Meadows taught us "How to Load Soaps and Beauty Products," with lotion, shampoo, and soap as swag. And we closed with "The Closing Circle" and business card exchange.

The 2018 Festival was unusual in several ways. The MISC church had burned down in July 2017, our entire county was hard hit by wild-fires in October 2017, and a local psychic fair was cancelled while the fires raged. In solidarity with the Santa Rosa Mystic Fair, and to raise money for fire victims, we teamed up with the show's promoter, Alan Scott, moved our show to the Santa Rosa Veteran's Memorial Building, and held it in April, in conjunction with the Fair, as we were rebuilding the MISC church to re-open in July 2018 under the auspices of the Association of Independent Spiritual Churches (AISC).

Saturday began with "Patron Saints" and a Saint Joseph altar for the rebuilding fund, led by Papa Newt. Attendees received a flyer and a collection of Catholic holy cards — and donated generously to help rebuild Santa Rosa. *Lithomancy* was Jon Saint Germain's new book. Participants got the book and a pouch with three coloured stones to use in divination. Lunch was available from the Mystic Fair food booth.

The Art of Making Mojos was my new book for the year, and attendees made a mojo hand. "Sigil Magic" with Angela Marie Horner was a crafty class, as we cut out seals and sigils from diverse cultures and pasted them on a central Spell Star, to create an altar piece. "Figural Candle Magic" with Mama E. and Clayton James introduced Clayton's new line of candles, and workshop participants prepared and dressed a candle to take home and burn.

Sunday gave us "Working With Asian Deities" with Devi Spring, who led us in an altar call to Ganesh the Elephant-headed Hindu god of obstacle removal. Phœnix LeFæ's new *Cash Box Conjure: Hoodoo Spells for Luck and Money* book was the feature of her workshop, and attendees took home money drawing spiritual supplies to try for themselves.

Miss Aida's new book, *Destroying Relationships* was presented with panache by Deacon Millett, who took us through the creation of a fiery Lemon spell to drive away enemies. The show closed with "Get What You Want in Love and Marriage," by Ms. Robin York, and her two-page flyer was accompanied by spiritual supplies for drawing and keeping sexual love.

And now it is 2019. This book, *The Red Folder,* contains all the flyers for the year's events, and sample pages from all of this year's new books. Our Saturday opening ceremony features Lady Muse and Company in a gospel ministry with sermon, songs, and blessing with Holy Anointing Oil.

Genuine Black and White Magic of Marie Laveau is my presentation of a book that restores a treasured text by Zora Neale Hurston. Participants will make a Yard Sprinkle to Control Evil Neighbours. Lunchtime entertainment with Master Mind-Bender Jon Saint Germain is an homage to the crystal gazing act performed by Alexander, The Man Who Knows. Lunch is courtesy of Heidi Simpson and the Ladies Auxiliary.

"How to Attract New Love" with Deacon Millett offers nine love potions to make. "Jewish Spell Bowls for Protection" with Dr. Jeremy Weiss is a crafts class where we inscribe our own demon-divorcing bowl. The panel talk on "Our Favourite Good Luck Spells" is led by Ms. Robin, with Mama E., Angela Marie Horner, Elle Duvall, Papa Newt, and myself. "The Nine Stages of Court Case and Legal Work" with Ms. Robin features a flyer and a custom-blended herb mix. And after that comes the annual Presenters' Banquet.

Sunday opens with "Catholic Folk Magic and Saints" by Papa Newt; attendees receive chromo prints to frame. Papa Gee then presents "Dirts, Dusts, and Powders in Folk Magic," and the take-home is … a powder, of course. Our buffet-style lunch is provided by the Ladies Auxiliary, and for entertainment, we bring you The Shock Doc Show, featuring Dr. Jeremy Weiss in a death-defying straitjacket escape!

"Ten Little Fingers, Ten Little Toes" leads us through the magic of fertility, pregnancy, and childbirth with Lady Muse, and we create a blessing gift for a baby. *The Secret of Numbers Revealed* by Dr. Roy Page Walton, Godfrey Spencer, and me is a half-old-half-new numerology book; attendees also get a novel set of cards so they can do their own work-outs.

Jon Saint Germain presents *Secrets of the Crystal Silence League* by Claude Alexander Conlin, our compilation of two rare pamphlets on crystal gazing and Silent Influence. In addition to the book, attendees receive a small quartz sphere. We close with advice to the professionals, a copy of *The Fortune Teller's Guide to Success* by Valentina Burton, and our traditional flyer on "The Closing Circle."

2019 marks the end of an era. In my 72nd year, i am stepping down from hosting the Festival. Of course i'll keep the shop open, teach my course, write books, run the Lucky Mojo Forum, and hold apprenticeships, but the days of the big tents and crowds of people on my lawn have now concluded.

— catherine yronwode

LITHOMANCY: CASTING YOUR FIRST STONES
Rev. Dr. Jon Saint Germain

YOUR FIRST THREE ORACLE STONES

Here's an easy method of casting, using three stones, one white, one black, and one brown. These can be stones collected on the beach, on walks, or purchased from a shop, but they should be round, flattish, and about the size of a quarter. They can be oval in shape. The most important thing about them is that they should be of three different colours, and easy to tell apart. You may prefer to use crystals of various colours. Quartz, Obsidian, and Jasper would make a nice set, as would Moonstone, Black Tourmaline, and Carnelian, or three simple river rocks of white, black, and brown.

How you select these stones is important. You'll want stones that are personal, intimate, and that speak to you alone. Over a lifetime of practice, I have come into the wisdom that your tools choose you, every bit as much as you choose them. If you call out for them, they'll find you. This I promise.

The quest for your tools, preparing them for work, and training them for the job are important steps that infuse life into your divinatory tools and bind them to you.

There are two schools of thought about whether or not you should magically prepare divinatory tools. Some practitioners buy a tarot deck or set of runes from a shop and put them to work immediately. Others ritually prepare them for work.

I fall into the latter group. All I can say is that my connection with my oracles, and consequently my readings, took a quantum leap for the better when I began ritualistically preparing my tools. I can read a new tarot deck or cast with borrowed coins or stones I just gathered from the ground, but these readings are a shadow of what I can do with my prepared, familiar, trained tools.

The more effort you put into selecting and preparing your stones, the more of "you" is infused into them. Yes, you could buy some glass beads at a crafts store and draw glyphs on them with a Sharpie, but putting days and weeks into polishing, anointing, and smudging your stones does charge them with your essence in a way that you can really feel.

CLEANSING YOUR STONES

Stones and crystals have memory. They remember what you tell them. They also store, transmute, and transmit energy events that occur in their vicinity. Therefore It's important to discharge any lingering psychic impressions they may have absorbed before you made their acquaintance. New Age workers call this cleansing, but in the older traditions that formed my practice, the process is called discharging.

Discharging can be done by leaving your stones in a bowl of blessed salt or white rice overnight. You can hold them under running water for a few minutes, and if you use this method with crystals, it's most efficient to hold them point-downward. Hoodoo workers like to clean stones in Hoyt's Cologne or whiskey, or smoke them in Uncrossing Incense.

When you divine for people, your stones connect with their vibrations and act as interlocutors or intermediaries to the Powers from whom you're seeking advice. Furthermore, you act as a third point in this spiritual circuit, so a lot of energy is passed through those stones. Therefore, many practitioners like to discharge their stones after each divination.

CHARGING YOUR STONES

The simplest way to charge your stones, as well as teach them to act together as a group, is to arrange them in a circle in the Sun for a day, and then under the Moon for a night. I have a simple rule: Charge crystals under the Sun for healing. Charge them under the Moon for magic. Since divination can be both a healing and a magical act, I do both.

Charging stones can be quite enjoyable. I "sing" to mine. I play a Tibetan singing bowl over them and allow the gentle harmonics to restore the crystalline energy matrices. They can also be tapped with a chakra wand, to both charge and discharge them.

TRAINING YOUR STONES

Training not only makes your tools more intelligent, but also binds them to you. They learn to work for you, and you alone. If you loan them to someone else they will need to be discharged and retrained.

A SUFFUMIGATION FOR YOUR STONES

I smoke all new stones with incense over the course of five days, using five different magical preparations and five corresponding prayers.

- **Day One:** Uncrossing Incense; Proverbs 2:6. *"For the Lord giveth wisdom: out of his mouth cometh knowledge and understanding."*
- **Day Two:** Frankincense; Psalms 119:34. *"Give me understanding, and I shall keep thy law; yea, I shall observe it with my whole heart."*
- **Day Three:** Clarity Incense; Proverbs 18:15. *"The heart of the prudent getteth knowledge; and the ear of the wise seeketh knowledge."*
- **Day Four:** King Solomon Wisdom Incense; 1 Kings 3:9. *"Give thy servant an understanding heart to judge thy people, that I may discern between good and bad: for who is able to judge this thy great people?"*
- **Day Five:** Spirit Guide Incense; Psalms 119:104. *"Through thy precepts I get understanding: therefore I hate every false way."*

INSTRUCTING YOUR STONES

Because stones are living things with memory, I instruct each one in its purpose. This is most important. If your oracle doesn't understand clearly what it's supposed to do, how can it do its job? Teach your stones well, and they will serve you well.

Once you've gathered, prepared, and trained your stones, carry them in a small bag so you won't lose them.

OPENING TO THE WORLD OF SPIRIT

I usually prepare for each divination by rubbing a drop of Psychic Vision Oil over my third eye, sometimes followed by a drop of King Solomon Wisdom Oil. I may prepare for difficult divinations, such as those involving necromancy, by burning Psychic Vision Incense, smoking my hands in the fumes, and covering my face with my hands as I pray for guidance.

CASTING THE STONES

Now you have collected three stones, they've been trained, and you're ready to cast! Start with these three simple methods, and you will be able to gradually add stones as your skills grow.

ONE STONE: HEADS OR TAILS

Although more commonly used with coins than stones, the one-stone "heads or tails" method, known as a binary toss, is very handy. You will need one stone, your white one. One side of the stone is designated "Yes," the other "No." Perhaps one side is lighter than the other, or you can mark one side. The stone is shaken, tossed, dropped, or flipped in the air, as you call upon Divine Guidance. Whichever side lands upright provides your answer.

TWO STONES: CASTING LOTS

Casting lots in its simplest traditional form consists of placing two items, designated "Yes" and "No" into a container, mixing them up, and asking for divine guidance to answer your question. You reach into the container and select one of the items. The item that you select provides your answer.

Use your black and white stones for casting lots. Ask a simple question, such as, "Should I meet with my boss today about requesting a raise?" Reach into the bag and if you draw the white stone, go for it.

By the way, I have a suggestion for you about "Yes-No" type questions. I've learned it's better to not ask "Should I do this thing?" but rather to phrase the question as "Is now a good time to do this thing?"

THREE STONES: A PERSONAL CASTING

Let the brown stone represent you. The black stone is "No," and the white stone will represent "Yes." Concentrate on a question that can be answered "Yes" or "No."

Ask the question, and shake the three stones in your cupped hands as if they were dice. Gently toss or drop them on a soft surface, like your carpet or a folded towel, from a distance of about one foot.

If the white stone lands closest to the brown stone, the answer is "Yes." if the black is closest to the brown, the answer is "No." If your stones end up under your couch, you threw them too hard.

"Lithomancy: Divination and Spellcraft with Stones, Crystals, and Coins" is a 96 page book by Rev. Dr. Jon Saint Germain, published for his 2018 HHF workshop. This sample provides a taste of the contents; the entire book is available from Lucky Mojo. Jon is a member of AIRR and can be contacted at his web site, JonSaintGermain.com.

HOW TO MAKE A MAGICAL SCRYING RING
Rev. Dr. Jon Saint Germain

THE BEST CRYSTAL POINTS AND STONES FOR GAZING

Crystallomancy or stone scrying is a form of visionary work that involves gazing into a crystal, or any shiny or translucent surface, for the purpose of seeing images, which are interpreted for divinatory purposes. Scrying is an advanced mystical art that few truly master — but many can become quite proficient with practice. While any transparent or shiny medium yields itself to scrying, certain crystals are believed to enhance clairvoyant talents. These are:

• Amethyst	• Aquamarine	• Azurite
• Beryl	• Carnelian	• Citrine
• Clear Quartz	• Emerald	• Flint
• Heliodor	• Hematite	• Jet
• Lapis Lazuli	• Moonstone	• Morganite
• Obsidian	• Opal	• Rose Quartz
• Sapphire	• Tiger's Eye	• White Calcite

GEMSTONE JEWELRY FOR SCRYING

Some of the above stones and crystals are available as roughs, points, tumbles, or spheres, but others — especially the brightly transparent crystal gemstones — are better worn in rings or necklaces for scrying purposes. There are three reasons for this.

First, the availability of certain crystals in the form of palm stones, points, or gazing spheres is limited by their mineralogical growth pattern. There are no 2-inch diameter Pyrope Garnet spheres, for instance, because the crystals simply do not grow to that size.

Second, in many cases, the cost of genuine gemstone spheres is too high; few individuals will be able to afford a substantial table-size Amethyst sphere, even if it did come on the market.

Third, crystals are heavy, and if you are a traveller, a small scrying stone — especially one that looks like jewelry and can unobtrusively double as a protective charm or lucky talisman — will serve you very well. Whether worn on the finger or on a chain, the gemstone can be used to gaze into and can also double as a pendulum for quick yes / no answers.

HOW TO FIX A GEMSTONE RING FOR SCRYING

Since ancient times, small gemstones set in silver, gold, or a combination of the two, have filled the need for portable scrying tools. One way to wear such a scrying stone is to have it set in a ring. Depending on the stone, it can be a smoothly domed cabochon or a sparkling faceted gem. Scrying stones of the Beryl family, all quite costly in the larger sizes, are well within the range of most people when worn as rings. A necklace pendant in an open setting makes a great portable scrying stone too, and it can double as a divinatory pendulum. Or you can simply wear it to match your scrying ring, and folks will comment favourably on your fashion sense.

Start by selecting a ring in which is set one of the many scrying stones listed above. It should fit comfortably and be well made. Gemstones are powerful in and of themselves, but magicians know that when working with a gem for scrying or divination, you will get faster results if you attune or "fix" the stone to yourself before putting it to use.

For seven days and nights, do not wear the ring on your finger or try to scry with it, but carry it in contact with your skin, talk to it, and sleep with it. Ask it if it has a name, and if it replies, address it by that name.

You may, if you wish, attempt to draw a spirit of divination into your ring. To do so, you must first have contact with that spirit. Burying a piece of jewelry in a grave is one way invite a familiar spirit of the dead to take up residence within. Ceremonially invoking a spirit and commanding or inviting it to dwell in the stone is another ancient method.a

After seven days, or after a familiar spirit is brought into the ring, hang it on a cord and test its accuracy by using it as a pendulum. If the answers prove out, the ring is ready to wear on your finger as a scrying stone.

"How To Make a Magical Scrying Ring" is an extract from "Crystal Magic," a 96-page book by Rev. Dr. Jon Saint Germain that was distributed at his 2016 HHF workshop on spell-casting with crystals. Jon is a member of AIRR and the author of numerous books on the divinatory arts.

CRYSTAL GAZING: MEDITATION FOR CLAIRVOYANCE
Claude Alexander Conlin

DEVELOPING YOUR INNER FORCES

The Crystal as a Tool: The Crystal Sphere, when properly used, is second to none for projective, transmissional, and psycho-visional purposes. It does not disturb the nervous system, injure the brain, nor cause any unhealthy conditions. The Crystal Seer is wide-awake, intelligent, and in possession of every sense. There is no tension on the nerves. In sensitive lucidity the visions rapidly pass away, but in the Crystal any given place, face, scene, or locality can be, by an effort of the will, made to remain fixed, stationary, and solid as long as the seer chooses. More people are able to see in a Crystal than by any other method.

Sit comfortably and breathe. Select some place where you will be free from all possible interruptions. Sit in an easy position, the neck chest and the head in a straight line. The Crystal should be placed before you, about three inches below the chin and 24 to 36 inches from the face. Dim your room slightly, though do not have it absolutely dark. Either artificial or natural light may be used; preferably the latter. Close your eyes and roll the eyeballs upward. Thoroughly relax; become as limp as you can, having no tension on the nerves. Now practice a few rhythmical breathing exercises. When your breath is easy, sit perfectly quietly, and look steadily — but do not stare — into the Crystal, and see what thoughts come to you.

Observe the thoughts. Very likely you will be surprised at the many thoughts that chase one another in your brain. You do not know how restless a mind is until you try to quiet it. Continue to breathe and to observe. Soon it will quiet down, looking to you for orders.

Observe your body. Now think of yourself as something separate from your own body. Consider it the temple you dwell in. Think of yourself as existing outside of it. Think of pleasure, hunger, thirst, painful sensations, and cravings, and consider them but as events of the past or as present processes of human evolution, to be discarded as the eye becomes perfected and reaches the spiritual heights of evolution. In time the ego is clad in a "body of pure energy," and you will notice that neither food nor drink is needed to sustain life while the body is in a state of quiet meditation.

You, Your Emotions, and Your Intellect: Your emotions, such as fear, greed, selfishness, anger, love, and hate, are not you, because you can stand aside and analyze them. If you have allowed yourself to be identified with them, you have been made to suffer. Realize that you need not be affected by the painful emotions, and cultivate the finer ones. Now study your intellect and see how you are independent of it as well. Observation will reveal how the complex processes of intellect are made amenable to control. You and your mind are not the same. Even while you are engaged in the deepest state of concentrated thought action, you can stand aside and watch the play of thought. You are able to think how you are immortal, invulnerable, part of the essence of Eternity.

Liberation: We now come to an important stage. Shut out all external and internal thoughts, and think of that only which leaves the body at the time of death, that which is called the soul. Focus all your mental energy inwardly on your soul, and a veritable blaze of illumination will rise within you. This is a wonderful experience — this bathing in the great ocean of soul-force. It will develop startling powers in any one. It is capable of charging your being with powerful energy, Dynamic Thought. It will brighten your intellect, lighten your physical weight, and may even give a sensation of rising in the air or astral liberation. You will develop a kind of clairvoyant power and open your vision on the subtle planes. You will be a transformed being.

The way has now been pointed for you: The task is solemn and sacred. Talk never of it, try to put the teachings into practice, live them and think them. If you do, you will gain the power of externalizing spirit strength in thought, word, and action. But never debase this art or science; if you do, it would be far better you had never heard of it. Live up to it, make it a part of your very life. Be perfectly pure, and you have nothing to fear as your Guardian of the Threshold will guide you and see that you reap your just dues.

"Crystal Gazing: Meditation for Clairvoyance" is an extract from "Secrets of the Crystal Silence League," a 96-page book containing material originally written by Claude Alexander Conlin, "The Man Who Knows," between 1919 and 1921. Rev. Dr. Jon Saint Germain of Divine Harmony Spiritual Church presented a workshop on the Crystal Silence League at the 2019 Hoodoo Heritage Festival.

AN INTRODUCTION TO BONE READING
Michele Jackson

THE STARTER SET OF BONES

The easiest way to acquire bones is to order a set from a vendor. Bone sets as currently sold are what I call "starter sets," and they are usually labelled as such. You will receive several bones and other pieces to get you started. Individual readers personalize their sets by adding different items. In fact, every reader I know has added something to the basic set.

Another way to acquire a set of bones is to gather the pieces you need from scratch. Several shops carry a variety of animal bones and curios. You can even procure entire skeletons. Those who spend time outdoors may come across bones already cleaned by nature. It can be difficult to determine the source species for found bones, but occasionally the skeleton is complete enough for the species to be identified. If knowing the species is important to you it may be best to buy bones from a reputable dealer.

THE CONTAINER

You will need some type of container for your bones when they are not in use. Some online vendors sell containers, such as large Abalone shells, baskets, or boxes, but you can find one locally as well. I use a basket with a lid for my main set and I use the basket lid to toss the bones onto the cloth. I use a smaller basket for my travel set. It also has a lid, but I throw this set from the basket itself.

Any type of small container that you find æsthetically pleasing can be used. I prefer natural materials. I have used a carved wooden bowl with a lid for a container. I have seen readers who use ceramic containers and readers who use baskets without a lid. I have seen readers who store their bones in the cloth bag their starter set came in.

Use anything you feel is suitable and attractive and if you find that you can cast from it as well, so much the better.

Whichever container you choose should be spiritually cleansed before use. Likewise any portable reading surface you decide to use should be cleansed.

HOW MANY PIECES?

Starting out, you want to keep the number of pieces you are working with rather small to avoid feeling overwhelmed, while still having enough pieces to cover the situations you are likely to be asked about. Certain topics frequently come up in readings. You can assign them to pieces in your starter set.

- **A piece to represent yourself or the client:** Having a piece specifically for this purpose gives me a focal point or starting point for the reading. The piece does not have to be a figure. It can be anything at all — a sea shell, a curio, or even a human bone. Your Client Piece may have an up-side and a down-side. This can provide additional insight into the client's state of mind.
- **A piece to represent financial issues:** Coins are an obvious choice, but I have also used a carved Peach pit with the Chinese symbol for good fortune. Money and finances touch almost every area of our lives and people whose issues seem to have nothing to do with money on the surface often end up asking about the financial aspects of it before the reading is over.
- **Two pieces to represent a couple:** These can be any two things that are distinguishable from one another. I use two pieces of sea shell, one short and light, the other long and dark. Readers who do a lot of relationship readings pairs for different kinds of relationships, but the two pieces for a couple are a good beginning.
- **A piece to represent "now":** This helps to gauge when things are taking place. Things closer to this piece are current and things farther out are less current.
- **A piece to represent home:** This piece can shed further light on domestic issues. Many of the situations we are concerned about happen in or around the home.
- **An "action" piece:** I use a Garnet Bracelet for this. Things falling within the Bracelet are actions to be undertaken by the client. It is rare that nothing falls inside the Bracelet.

"Introduction to Bone Reading" is an extract from "Bones, Shells, and Curios," a 96-page book by Michele Jackson that was distributed at her 2014 HHF workshop.

BONE READING: INTERPRETING GROUPS
Michele Jackson

WHAT ARE GROUPS?

Many bone readers tell me they are overwhelmed by the number of possible interpretations when they cast a large set of bones, say 30 or more. Assuming that you have a set of bones and have assigned meanings to the pieces that you have memorized and found effective, reading groups is a way to break the interpretation down into manageable narratives.

Why interpret groups? If your bone reading set has expanded beyond 30 pieces or so, you may be finding it difficult to interpret every piece individually on its own. Even if you have a smaller set, you may find that reading naturally-falling groups of pieces together adds a nuanced layer to your readings. For example, instead of saying a female will affect the client's life, you may be able to provide more information about that female by reading the pieces grouped around her as descriptive adjectives. Pieces tend to fall in small groupings and interpreting those groups as a whole instead of as individual pieces will enhance your reading skills. I demonstrate reading groups in my book *Bones, Shells, and Curios: A Contemporary Method of Casting the Bones.* This handout will cover the topic in a bit more depth and provide an additional example.

Most throws naturally fall with pieces grouping together to some degree. There are also solitary pieces, or outliers, but usually the majority of pieces end up falling into one or more groups. Interpreting a group of pieces can seem daunting at first, but with practice, it can become one of the most valuable reading skills in your toolbox.

When you throw the pieces, take a moment to look the spread over and see what groupings appear and where they are in proximity to the piece that represents your client. In my readings, I like to start with the client piece and I usually interpret the pieces closest to the client first. Likewise to me, groups closest to the client piece are of more immediacy, and are more likely to manifest than groups further out in the spread. Unless led to do otherwise, starting with the group closest to the client piece will probably provide the most pertinent information. Then move outward as groupings are further and further away.

GROUP INTERPRETATION BASICS

If you don't keep a Bone Reading Journal, this may be an excellent time to start one. There are several ways you can approach this practice – you can do a short reading for yourself, or you can just pick some random pieces to interpret outside of an actual reading just for practice. Record these practice interpretations in your journal. You can draw a quick sketch or take a photo for printout and pasting in your journal if you are a visual learner.

For many folks just writing down the pieces involved and their positions will be fine. Then write down your interpretation. Writing helps reinforce your knowledge. Over time you might find that some pieces appear together frequently and your journal will be useful in discerning these patterns.

Smaller groups are easier, so let's start with two pieces. Go to your bone set and pick two random pieces. Drop them on your reading surface. See which piece catches your attention first and start with its meaning. How does the second piece you chose affect your original piece's interpretation? Does it enhance or make the meaning stronger? Does it change the meaning slightly? Does it provide additional or descriptive information about the first piece? Perhaps it adds a caveat. Or does it change the meaning drastically?

Now pull another random piece and add it to the group. Does this piece seem to draw your attention more than the other two, or does it just seem to add another bit of information to the piece that originally caught your eye? Either way, how does it change your interpretation?

You're on a roll now — add an additional piece, bringing the grouping to four pieces. Again, how does this piece change your understanding of the group?

In my personal numerology five is often a number of strife and discord and, true to form, looking at a group of five or more pieces can be quite daunting at first glance, but we have built up our understanding of this grouping gradually. At this point the additional piece should not throw us off of our game.

Ask yourself, does adding a fifth piece to the group change the focus of the group? Does it strengthen the previous interpretation? Does it weaken it? Does it change the group interpretation altogether?

Done this way, a five or more piece grouping is quite manageable. You can apply this approach to all groupings. See which piece draws your attention first in the group, then determine how each nearby piece modifies your interpretation of that piece. With practice you will be able to grasp the meaning of a group without consciously going through these steps individually. It will seem smooth and seamless.

SAMPLE GROUP INTERPRETATION

I asked the question: "What do I need to know today?" The pieces I picked at random were:

1. **Lion Bone** – Courage, power, pride
2. **Scorpion** – Negative energy
3. **Metal Head** – Thoughts or thinking
4. **Carved Skull** – Ancestors or spirits
5. **Turtle Bone** – Things moving slowly

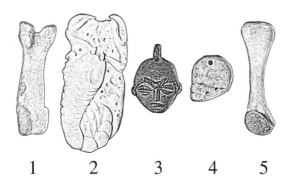

1   2   3   4   5

When I dropped them onto my cloth, they fell in a diagonal straight line, like this:

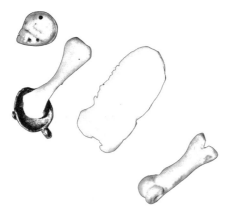

The first thing that caught my eye was the Scorpion – negative energy. However, it is face down, which is a good position for this piece. There is no negative energy, or negative energy is being blocked. Good news! So what else is going on around this piece?

The skull representing the ancestors or spirits is at the top. I interpret this as a message from them. The metal head signifying thoughts is face down — not thinking, or, better still, not worrying. The turtle bone in the head represents thoughts moving slowly. In this position, I interpret it as telling me to slow my thoughts down, or "Don't worry — don't give it any thought." The Lion bone is telling me to be brave, proud, and stand in my power. Together these pieces seem to be reassuring me that my ancestors have my back. I shouldn't waste time thinking about, or worrying about negative energy, or work being done against me. This is timely and reassuring to me because there happens to be a lot of turmoil right now in one of the communities of which I am a member.

By selecting the piece that caught my eye first and building the interpretations of the surrounding pieces around it, I got a clear message that things are going to be all right. This seems more useful to me than just knowing that there is no negative energy around me now. It provides the "who" and the "how," instead of merely giving me the "what," or several unconnected "whats." Take your own bones out and try it!

In this example the pieces fell into a linear group, suggesting a linear narrative — ancestors speaking, don't worry, no negative energy, go forward bravely. Other groupings may not be linear; pieces may surround a central piece, or the central piece may lay on top of — or under — other pieces. Take these things into account in your interpretation.

This is a skill that will become easier with practice. If you look at a grouping and just feel stumped, take it back to interpreting the piece that seems most prominent and building onto it piece by piece. Also, while working with the mechanics of interpreting groups, don't discount intuitive or spiritually-inspired guidance in your interpretation. Happy Bone Reading!

This hand-out accompanied Michele Jackson's 2016 Hoodoo Heritage Festival workshop. For further lessons on divination with bones, see her book, "Bones, Shells, and Curios," and also "Throwing the Bones" by catherine yronwode. Michele can be reached via her BonesShellsAndCurios.com web site.

DEM DRY BONES: OSTEOMANTIC READINGS
Kast Excelsior

WHY USE NECROMANTIC CURIOS?

In conjure and other spiritualistic practices, we commonly incorporate collaborative work with previously incarnate spirits. Whether for divination, spiritual communion, or active spellwork, this may take the form of setting up a memorial shrine, buying grave dirt to connect more closely with someone in particular who has gone to the other side, or working with curios that were once parts of the bodies of living beings. These latter items I call necromantic curios.

The use of necromantic curios as a source of constructing tools for spirit-work can be traced at least as far back as the first shamanic ancient burial sites that contain shells, feathers, pelts, and bones. Many traditional practices today continue to prominently include the use of bones and other animal remains as central items in spiritual rites.

Initiated priesthood members of the Kongolese-based Afro-Cuban religion of Palo Mayombe will have a nganga (or spirit pot) which often contains a human skull and other various bones and houses a spirit who can be summoned and worked with.

In some tantric traditions in Asia, bones have been used to make prayer bead necklaces and other sacred jewelry. In the Himalayan regions of Tibet and Nepal, ceremonial drums and flutes have combined the magical forces of both bones and music. One such instrument is the Kangling or "leg flute" made from the femur bone of someone whose death came under certain specific conditions of violence or disease, thus imbuing the bone flute with specialized powers to transform or transmute malevolent spirits, to perform healing, or to control violent weather.

The kapala or ritual skull bowl plays an important role in the initiation process of the Aghori, an ascetic Hindu sect, and in Tibetan Buddhism. Obtaining ownership of a human skull-bowl for ceremonial use identifies the dedicant with the wrathful deities of India and Tibet (who are often depicted holding skull-bowls), and can assist in invoking the force of those deities into the initiate.

In Thai sorcery we find the Kuman Thong, or "Golden Boy," in which necromantic elements are connected to a young or fetal corpse that has been ritually charged into a fetish item by monks to create a magical ally from the child's spirit. Thai workers also produce the infamous Nam Man Prai, or "Corpse Oil," made from the rotting chin of a pregnant corpse.

But bones, in particular, provide unique and intimate keys to the spirits because, whether human or otherwise, almost all flesh and blood organisms are closely dependent on their skeletal bone structure throughout their entire incarnate lives. And, like a poetic display, when almost all the elements of these lifeforms have faded away, the skull and bones remain as a permanent remnant of the specific mind and life that once animated them. What better curio to utilize as a link and bridge to the spirit we seek to contact and work with?

MATCHING CONDITIONS

As with the correspondences used in divinatory bone casting, each bone has a specialty in magical use. Totemic principles and the classical magical Doctrine of Signatures also come into play in deciding which bone is best suited for particular magical work. Think of the qualities of the animal species and how they would be helpful to manifest the magical goal you have in mind. Intuition is useful in determining which animal is best for your goals, but here is a general list of body parts that match particular conditions.

CATEGORIES OF POWER

- **Legs, Ankles, Feet:** To open or close roads and pathways.
- **Hands, Fingers, Claws:** To take proactive steps to accomplish a specific result.
- **Fangs, Jaws:** To issue warnings, to gossip, and to attack.
- **Vertebræ:** To give overall support and powerful re-enforcement from within.
- **Skulls:** To strengthen mental powers and expand awareness or to communicate with other spirits.

CONSECRATING AND FIXING

Once a particular bone or item is obtained, you can make preliminary preparations to consecrate it, focusing on its upcoming magical alliance with you. Here are a few steps to provide an intentionally empowered contact with every manifestation of the elements and ready the piece for increased activity.

BY EARTH AND SOIL

This is the step of providing a formal burial. The bone or item can be wrapped in a bit of cloth or placed directly into the earth; then it is dug up again after a period of time spent fully buried. The length of time should be at least 24 hours, providing one full night of burial. Some may choose to make the duration 3 nights, 9 nights, or another sacred number that best corresponds to your practice or intent.

Planetary days and Moon phases can also be aligned to play a part in this Earth empowerment. For instance, planning to dig up a bone on a Tuesday (aligned with Mars and military prowess) for protection or warfare, on a Sunday (aligned with the Sun) for success and personal power, or a bone resurrected on a Friday (which is aligned with the planet Venus) can be geared toward workings of love, lust, luxury, and domestic harmony. The Waxing Moon phase will also be best to resurrect an item for the building up and accumulation of power; the Waning Moon will be best for uncrossing, removal of things, and also for enemy work.

If you don't have direct access to a secure area of open ground to bury the piece, you can also bury it in the soil of a potted plant. It will still have contact with the elemental force and burial rite, albeit in a smaller environment. For skulls or larger bones of a size that may make full burial impractical, place the piece on a dish or mat that has been covered in graveyard dirt.

BY AIR AND SMOKE

Pass the item through the smoke of incense that matches the condition that the bone will specialize in or one for general activation that would be well-matched for a necromantic curio, like Power or Spirit Guide Incense Powder. An alternate incense to use is the resin of Frankincense and Myrrh burned on charcoal with pinches of Acacia and Life Everlasting added. Make sure all of the item's surface area comes into direct contact with the rising smoke.

BY WATER AND OIL

Prepare an herbal wash in the form of a light tea made by boiling a small bit of Acacia, Bay Laurel, and Life Everlasting (all of which are associated with the resurrection of the dead) and, after cooling, you can also add a few dashes of Florida Water Cologne or, if preferred, Holy Water. Sprinkle the bone or other item on all its sides; no need to overly saturate it; you will merely asperge the overall surface area. You can then anoint your hands with the essential oils of Frankincense and Myrrh (both of which are also traditionally associated with the raising of the dead back to life) and transfer just enough to make contact with the item's surface. Be careful to not use too much and get the bone too oily or stained.

BY FIRE AND FLAME

Pass the piece quickly over the open flame of a candle. Make sure it's a quick enough pass to not scorch or fire-stain the bone, unless you plan to intentionally fire-mark it for a certain purpose. The colour of the candle wax can correspond to the category of power that you intend for the bone, and you can, finally, set the piece next to the the candle as a charging vigil. Another option is the use of pyrography. A wood burning tool can be used to add images or sigils to the bone, and the personalization of a consecrated bone via pyrography is a unique way of consecration by the fire-element in its electric form.

HEBREW SCRIPTURAL RESURRECTION SPELL

Here is a simple spell to further imbue the bone with living force and to resurrect it into heightened magical activity using the method of Scriptural Magic.

Recite the Biblical scripture of Ezekiel 37:1-10 aloud over the bone. This is the famous "Valley of Dry Bones" passage in which the Prophet is instructed to speak to the bones in God's name, and the bones are renewed with life.

While concentrating on the inner force of your own vitality, repeat the portion of verse 5 that states, "Behold, I will cause breath to enter into you, and ye shall live." Do this three times and then exhale a stream of vital force (as breath) out of your mouth and transfer it directly into the bone. Envision and, more importantly, allow yourself to feel the concentrated vital force that is now housed in the bone.

Ezekiel 37:1- The hand of the Lord was on me, and he brought me out by the Spirit of the Lord and set me in the middle of a valley; it was full of bones. 2 He led me back and forth among them, and I saw a great many bones on the floor of the valley, bones that were very dry. 3 He asked me, "Son of man, can these bones live?" I said, "Sovereign Lord, you alone know." 4 Then he said to me, "Prophesy to these bones and say to them, 'Dry bones, hear the word of the Lord! 5 This is what the Sovereign Lord says to these bones: I will make breath[a] enter you, and you will come to life. 6 I will attach tendons to you and make flesh come upon you and cover you with skin; I will put breath in you, and you will come to life. Then you will know that I am the Lord.'" 7 So I prophesied as I was commanded. And as I was prophesying, there was a noise, a rattling sound, and the bones came together, bone to bone. 8 I looked, and tendons and flesh appeared on them and skin covered them, but there was no breath in them. 9 Then he said to me, "Prophesy to the breath; prophesy, son of man, and say to it, 'This is what the Sovereign Lord says: Come, breath, from the four winds and breathe into these slain, that they may live.'" 10 So I prophesied as he commanded me, and breath entered them; they came to life and stood up on their feet—a vast army.

א הָיְתָה עָלַי יַד־יְהֹוָה וַיּוֹצִאֵנִי בְרוּחַ יְהֹוָה וַיְנִיחֵנִי בְּתוֹךְ הַבִּקְעָה וְהִיא מְלֵאָה עֲצָמוֹת: ב וְהֶעֱבִירַנִי עֲלֵיהֶם סָבִיב | סָבִיב וְהִנֵּה רַבּוֹת מְאֹד עַל פְּנֵי הַבִּקְעָה וְהִנֵּה יְבֵשׁוֹת מְאֹד: ג וַיֹּאמֶר אֵלַי בֶּן אָדָם הֲתִחְיֶינָה הָעֲצָמוֹת הָאֵלֶּה וָאֹמַר אֲדֹנָי יֱהֹוִה אַתָּה יָדָעְתָּ: ד וַיֹּאמֶר אֵלַי הִנָּבֵא עַל הָעֲצָמוֹת הָאֵלֶּה וְאָמַרְתָּ אֲלֵיהֶם הָעֲצָמוֹת הַיְבֵשׁוֹת שִׁמְעוּ דְּבַר יְהֹוָה: ה כֹּה אָמַר אֲדֹנָי יֱהֹוִה לָעֲצָמוֹת הָאֵלֶּה הִנֵּה אֲנִי מֵבִיא בָכֶם רוּחַ וִחְיִיתֶם: ו וְנָתַתִּי עֲלֵיכֶם גִּדִים וְהַעֲלֵתִי עֲלֵיכֶם עֲלֵיכֶם עוֹר וְנָתַתִּי בָכֶם רוּחַ וִחְיִיתֶם וִידַעְתֶּם כִּי אֲנִי יְהֹוָה: ז וְנִבֵּאתִי כַּאֲשֶׁר צֻוֵּיתִי וַיְהִי קוֹל כְּהִנָּבְאִי וְהִנֵּה רַעַשׁ וַתִּקְרְבוּ עֲצָמוֹת עֶצֶם אֶל עַצְמוֹ: ח וְרָאִיתִי וְהִנֵּה עֲלֵיהֶם גִּדִים וּבָשָׂר עָלָה וַיִּקְרַם עֲלֵיהֶם עוֹר מִלְמָעְלָה וְרוּחַ אֵין בָּהֶם: ט וַיֹּאמֶר אֵלַי הִנָּבֵא אֶל הָרוּחַ הִנָּבֵא בֶן אָדָם וְאָמַרְתָּ אֶל הָרוּחַ כֹּה אָמַר | אֲדֹנָי יֱהֹוִה מֵאַרְבַּע רוּחוֹת בֹּאִי הָרוּחַ וּפְחִי בַּהֲרוּגִים הָאֵלֶּה וְיִחְיוּ: י וְהִנַּבֵּאתִי כַּאֲשֶׁר צִוָּנִי וַתָּבוֹא בָהֶם הָרוּחַ וַיִּחְיוּ וַיַּעַמְדוּ עַל רַגְלֵיהֶם חַיִל גָּדוֹל מְאֹד מְאֹד:

EZEKIEL IN THE VALLEY OF BONES

A print-out of the text of Ezekiel 37:1-10 (shown above in English and in Hebrew) can be used as a petition paper to write your request for what the bone will work to manifest. You may fold it and use a string to fasten the paper to the bone. For a small bone, write your petition on the back of (or across) the square of scripture, then fold it into a seed-packet container to hold the bone; see catherine yronwode's instructions from *Paper In My Shoe* on the next page.

Alternatively, you may burn and transmute fixed petition papers (or Solomonic planetary seals) into ash and then apply and rub the charged ashes onto the bone, to enhance the spell by the spirit-force within the bone. The bone can be added to a mojo bag, or it can be the central focal point of a dedicated totemic animal shrine or an altar to the category or condition of power aligned with the chosen bone.

OTHER NECROMANTIC ITEMS

PELTS

Animal skins have been used to invoke totem powers for millennia. From the shaman's ritual garb to the legendary Norse Berserkers calling upon the strength of Bears and Wolves in battle, the pelts of animal allies provide unique variations of necromancy. They can be worn, added to ritual tools, or provide a canvas to enshrine bones or items aligned with the animal's totemic powers.

REPLICAS

For those with taboos against working with bones, or who want to obtain a bone that is unavailable or not legally obtainable, modern technology provides bone replicas cast from real specimens. While the spirit-force of the specific person or animal will not have been in direct contact, a magically fixed replica is a powerful symbol that can still approximate similar conjurations in the hands of a skilled worker.

THE ETHICAL BONE TRADE

Magical work with bones and other necromantic materials has an infamous reputation for being gruesome and unethical, and in some cultures and traditions there are taboos against working with necromantic materials of any kind. It's also no secret that, since ancient times, high demand for rare animal parts has led to poaching; I highly suggest a whole-hearted rejection of such materials for practical, legal, ethical, and metaphysical reasons.

Unbeknownst to most people, bones (even human bones) can be obtained through legal and ethical means. This is definitely true for the U.S.A.; check your local laws and policies in other countries. Human bones enter into the ethical and legal bone trade via those who have donated their cadavers for research or for spiritual relics. Medical and research institutions release a portion of their bone donations to the bone trade as do certain spiritual lineages that create sacred relics from bone parts.

SOURCING BONES

Legal and ethically-obtained bones of animals often enter the trade through roadkill, as corpses found in nature, or through the food industry. Common bones, especially those of dogs and cats, may be acquired through animal control agencies which, unfortunately, are forced to reduce the population of urban animals that do not reach adoption. While this is a sad reality, there is a way to honour and respect these species.

For rare and endangered species the conditions are urgent. According to a recent report by CITES (the Convention on International Trade in Endangered Species), there are 673 species near extinction, with an additional 4,835 in danger of entering that category under current conditions. Be sure to become aware of which animals are endangered, since owning or trading in their parts is illegal even if they were found as corpses in nature. By increasing our awareness of the need to protect endangered species, we can maintain respect and honour for the animals with which we seek spiritual alliances. In doing so, we also can extinguish the branches of the bone trade that participate in poaching and inhumane forms of killing.

Even for human bones, we must be vigilant in not trafficking with sources who may be suspect of participation in the theft and desecration of graves or the exploitation of prisoners or the homeless (who have all been said to be sources for the unethical harvesting of body parts and bones).

By only dealing and trading with vendors and suppliers who refuse to do business with poachers or cruelty-oriented harvesters, we can honour the animals with whom we seek magical alliances.

EXPRESSING GRATITUDE

As a gesture of honourable ethics and magical gratitude to a spiritual ally, bone-workers can donate to animal shelters, conservation groups, funerary services, charities, or human rights advocacy groups. Such contributions will expand spaying and neutering resources in urban areas so that high-kill institutions can eventually become no-kill shelters, assist the protection of truly endangered species, and, in human society, reduce the conditions that lead to the unethical exploitation of human remains in the bone trade. Considering the symbiotic and collaborative nature of spirituality, efforts like these will be sure to strengthen your bone work on multiple levels.

Ultimately, it is your responsibility to get as much information as possible from your bone sources to confirm that they also adhere to ethical and legal standards. While not every practitioner will want to delve into working with bones, those of us who do can rest assured that we need not support unethical traders in the process, especially when, with just a bit of research, we can secure ethical sources.

These online resources may be of help to you:

Cites.org
FWS.gov
BatCon.org
FreeTheSlaves.net
BoneClones.com

"Dem Dry Bones" was written by Kast Excelsior for distribution at his 2016 MISC workshop. A bone reader, rootworker, and member of AIRR, he can be reached at ConjureHaus.com.

HOW TO FOLD A SEED-PACKET
catherine yronwode

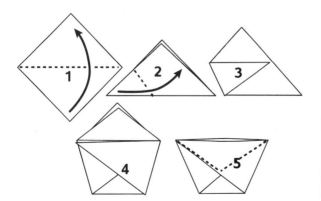

Here's how to make a seed-packet out of a 3-inch square Post-It note or a Nepalese prayer paper:
1. After you write on the paper, fold it in half on the diagonal.
2. Fold the left corner up so that its top is parallel to the bottom edge.
3. Fold the right corner up to the left, also parallel to the bottom edge.
4. Fill the envelope with herbs, powders, curios, or personal concerns.
5. Fold the two free tips into the pocket formed by the outside flap.

OUIJA REVELATIONS
Chas Bogan

HISTORY OF THE OUIJA

Both a venerated Spiritualist instrument and the Devil's favourite plaything, the Ouija board is an often maligned and under-utilized tool of divination. However, when looking into the history of the Ouija board, you will find that it is not as old as you might have imagined.

Mid-19th century Europeans and North Americans were fascinated with the idea of communicating with the dead. The doctrines of Spiritualism, which stated that the dead could and were inclined to communicate with the living, had captured the imagination of war-torn Europe, and on March 31, 1848 found fertile soil in Hydesville, New York. It was there that the Fox sisters, Kate and Margaret, claimed to communicate with the dead through a series of rapping noises. Their table rapping inspired a culture that drew in many adherents who would soon find themselves struggling from the casualties and losses of Civil War.

Associated with political movements like abolition, female suffrage, and temperance, Spiritualism gained popularity throughout the latter 19th century until its peak in the 1920s. This period was also a time for great inventions, when new tools such as the telegraph and telephone first permitted communication from great distances. With the advent of these devices, it was not hard to imagine that other innovations, such as the Ouija board, might allow for communication between the living and the dead.

Spirit communication was at first cumbersome, as it relied on someone announcing the letters of the alphabet while others engaged in table tipping, whereby the rapping of the table leg chose letter after letter. Improvement came in the form of a planchette, a heart-shaped plank of wood supported by two rear casters and a pencil at its narrow end. The scribbling of the planchette was sometimes indecipherable, which eventually led to the idea of the planchette serving as a pointer. Various alphanumeric platforms were developed, such as printed disks that turned in relation a fixed pointer. Not until 1886 do we first read a description resembling the Ouija board which we now recognize, for which the pointer — still referred to as a planchette — moves independently across a board.

ENTER THE "OUIJA BOARD"

In 1890 Elijah Bond, Charles Kennard, and their associate patented what we recognize as the modern Ouija board. The name OUIJA was spelled out by the board when Kennard and Bond's sister-in-law, Helen Peters, asked what it ought to be called. Kennard believed Ouija to mean "good luck." Years later, William Fuld, who took over production of the Ouija board, claimed that the name meant "yes, yes," combined from the French word "Oui" and German "Ja," a legend that persists to this day.

For an instrument so focused on language, it is little wonder that its own proper name must be stressed. Hasbro, Inc. currently holds the trademark for the name "Ouija." While all manner of alphabet boards are commonly referred to by the name Ouija, they are more accurately referred to as talking boards or spirit boards.

However you refer to it, the Ouija board remains an iconic fixture in North American culture, where even today being spooked by its uncanny powers serves as a rite of passage for many young people.

HOW IT WORKS

For some Ouija is just a game, and for others it is a valued spiritual tool. Much depends on approach, and whether one attributes a scientific or supernatural reason for its functioning. Secular minds define its success to the ideomotor response, suggesting that the mind of whoever manipulates the planchette controls movement through subconscious muscular reflexes. These enthusiasts are able to successfully use the Ouija without relying on occult powers, using it instead to uncover their own inner truths, such as their desires, fears, and motivations. Others imagine the Ouija opening a portal between the living and the dead, allowing the ghostly hands of spirit to vibrate the planchette, pushing it to spell messages from beyond the grave. The marriage of these two paradigms suggests that spirits communicate through an individual's mind and body, expressing themselves by manipulating the hands positioned upon the planchette.

TALKING WITH THE DEAD

The first step in starting a conversation is deciding who you wish to talk with. This is where many folks find trouble. Rather than contacting one of their ancestors, loved ones, or someone they have researched, many instead begin by inquiring if there is a spirit nearby who wishes to speak. This is like texting a random stranger and expecting them to tell you the secrets of the universe. This practice is not entirely discouraged, and it can sometimes lead to very productive relationships with spirit helpers. Nevertheless, I advise starting out by working with known ancestors or spirit guides.

Choosing your setting is important, particularly with regard to time and place. The veil between the worlds of the living and the dead is thinnest at certain times, such as twilight and midnight, and harsh daylight is uncomfortable for spirits. Pay attention to the mood being set, as this will influence the experience. Ideally you should feel secure in your environment.

Some folks set protective boundaries to work in, such as a circle of salt. This is often done to protect against evil spirits. I am more concerned with the meddling of unwanted mortals than with bothersome spirits, but for many, protection against evil spirits is a concern. Leaving your Bible open to Psalms 91 is a simple way to avoid trouble. A silver coin placed on the board is also said to protect against bad spirits.

Like the living, spirits appreciate hospitality. If you plan to call on your grandpa and you know that he enjoyed chicory coffee and cornbread, then those would make a splendid offering. Other common hoodoo offerings, such as flowers, incense, candies, tobacco, coffee, tea, or whiskey also suffice. I favour using an upside-down shot glass in place of a pointer, then filling it with whiskey as a thank you after the session is completed.

Offerings are often placed beyond the top of the board. Be sure they will not get knocked over, especially if you are working as a group with people positioned around the board. You can work on the floor or on a table, whichever you prefer.

Along with offerings, if you have a personal concern belonging to the spirit being invoked, then place it with your offerings. Additionally, I always set out a glass of water, which is said to draw spirits and help them manifest in the realm of the living.

Once your space is prepared and everything is in place, verbally call the name of the spirit you wish to invoke. I like to use my own energy to get the pointer started by moving it continuously as a sideways figure 8, or lemniscate pattern, but you may prefer another method. When the spirit is ready to speak, the pointer will waver from the pattern and begin spelling messages. It is useful to keep a recording device turned on and to speak aloud each letter, as this helps later to decipher longer messages. For those engaged in magical work, spirit boards offer unique methods for sorcery.

OUIJASTITIONS

When inquiring about what practices to avoid while working with a Ouija board, one finds that there are numerous practices deemed as harmful. Taboos of this type often arise from a mistrust of the Ouija or from fears about interacting with the spirit world. Hoodoo practitioners tend to have a favourable attitude toward working with the dead, and therefore engage in some of the supposedly "forbidden" practices. Consider the admonishment against using a Ouija board in a graveyard; people who work among the tombstones collecting dirt or burying bundles are unlikely to heed such a prohibition. Here are some other "Ouijastitions":

- **Never use the board alone.**
- **Never ask when someone will die.**
- **Never ask questions about the nature of God.**
- **Never let the pointer fall from the board.**
- **Never leave the pointer alone on the board.**
- **A bedevilled pointer makes figure 8s.**
- **When finished, use your own effort to move the pointer to the word Goodbye.**

Your attitude toward these beliefs will likely be informed by what you have learned from your family, friends, community, culture, and personal experiences.

FURTHER RESOURCES

A bibliography on spirit boards can be found here: **Yronwode.org/spirit-board-bibliography**

This hand-out was prepared for the 2017 Hoodoo Heritage Festival. Chas Bogan designs and crafts spirit boards and other occult arts for his company Carnivalia. A professional rootworker and member of AIRR, Chas is part owner of The Mystic Dream, a spiritual and magical supply store. He also teaches classes on various occult subjects.

THE BASICS OF DOWSING
catherine yronwode

METHODS

Some methods used in dowsing:

- **Field Dowsing:** Walking the field or physical location in a grid pattern is a common method when one is engaged in hard-target dowsing.
- **Scanning:** The dowser walks the edge of a field, using L-Rods to triangulate where to enter, saving time that might otherwise be spent walking the field.
- **Map Dowsing:** The dowser uses a map as a proxy for the field or location to be dowsed.
- **Remote Dowsing:** The dowser either mentally or astrally visualizes the area to be dowsed.
- **The Matacia Method:** Face North, drink water, write a list, touch the map and list, and say, "Show me."
- **Body Dowsing:** This consists of dowsing over a living human, animal, or plant or a representation of the entity for the purposes of diagnosis and treatment.
- **Chart Dowsing:** The use of a pre-determined layout, board, or chart for informational dowsing; the work is usually performed while seated at a table.
- **Free-Form Dowsing:** Engaging in Informational dowsing with a pendulum but no chart or layout.
- **Hand Dowsing:** No tools are used; the dowser simply extends a hand and reads the energy directly.

INDICATORS OR TOOLS

Some of the indicators or tools used in dowsing:

- **Y-Rod:** This is a forked tree branch, often cut fresh for the occasion. Artificial Y-Rods are also used.
- **L-Rods:** A pair of L-shaped metal angle-rods with handles or "jackets" that allow free rotation of the rods.
- **Mosaic Rod, Rod of Aaron, Bobber:** A single wand or rod. If weighted at the tip, it is called a bobber.
- **Cameron Aurameter:** This is a single L-Rod containing a coiled spring and a weighted bobber tip; it is highly sensitive to motions.
- **Plumb-Bob Pendulum:** This is a metal, stone, or glass bob weight suspended on a string or chain.
- **Witness Sample Pendulum:** This is a hollow or chambered pendulum into which a small specimen of the item for which one is searching can be inserted.
- **Impromptu Pendulum:** This can be a ring, key, button, root, holed stone, jack ball, or any convenient object suspended on a string, thread, or chain.

OBJECTIVES

Some reasons one might wish to dowse:

- **Hard-Target Dowsing:** This is the search for verifiable physical substances, such as water, oil, minerals, missing persons, or lost possessions.
- **Soft-Target Dowsing:** This is the search for subtle energies, like ley lines or geopathic stress fields, or for spiritual entities, such as ghosts.
- **Informational Dowsing:** This is the search for answers to questions, including "Yes / No" questions and complex queries such as, "Which puppy in this litter will make the best herding dog?"

FOUNDATIONAL BELIEFS

Dowsers base their work on a variety of beliefs:

- **Active Dowser Theory:** The belief that dowsing tools or indicators can be trained to work for the dowser, who is the active participant and relates to the indicators through personal "codes" by which stated movement patterns have specific meanings.
- **Passive Dowser Theory:** The belief that higher forces or divine spirits guide the tools and the dowser's main task is to be submissively receptive to spirit.
- **Psychological Theory:** The belief that dowsing consists of us asking our own brains for knowledge which we are not conscious that we possess.
- **Bio-Electrical Theory:** The belief that dowsing consists of using indicators to magnify real but minute electro-magnetic anomalies or molecular frequency resonances to a biologically perceptible threshold.
- **Selectivity Theory:** The belief that "energy follows attention," so our mental focus helps us find what we seek, whether objects, depths, volumes, or answers.
- **Natural Ability Theory:** The belief that naive children make excellent natural dowsers until and unless they absorb societal condemnations that cause them to consider dowsing to be unrealistic.

"The Basics of Dowsing" was written by cat yronwode in 2017 as a hand-out for customers who purchased divination supplies at the Lucky Mojo Curio Co. The reverse side, drawn by Grey Townsend, shows "Four Ways to Read a Pendulum" and was distributed at the 2017 Hoodoo Heritage Festival.

FOUR WAYS TO READ A PENDULUM
Grey Townsend

CIRCULAR PENDULUM MOTION

Clockwise rotation is "Yes." Counterclockwise or a straight line is "No," depending on the operator.

8-WAY PENDULUM PATTERN

To-and-fro is "Yes." Crossways is "No." "Maybe" and "I don't know" are diagonal. Circular doesn't count.

4-WAY PENDULUM PATTERN

To-and-fro is "Yes." Crossways bars the path and is "No." A clockwise circle indicates "Maybe" and a counterclockwise circle means "I don't know."

ALPHABETIC PENDULUM BOARD

To-and-fro is "Yes." Crossways is "No." Diagonals spell out words and numbers or indicate zodiac signs, according to the question. Circular doesn't count.

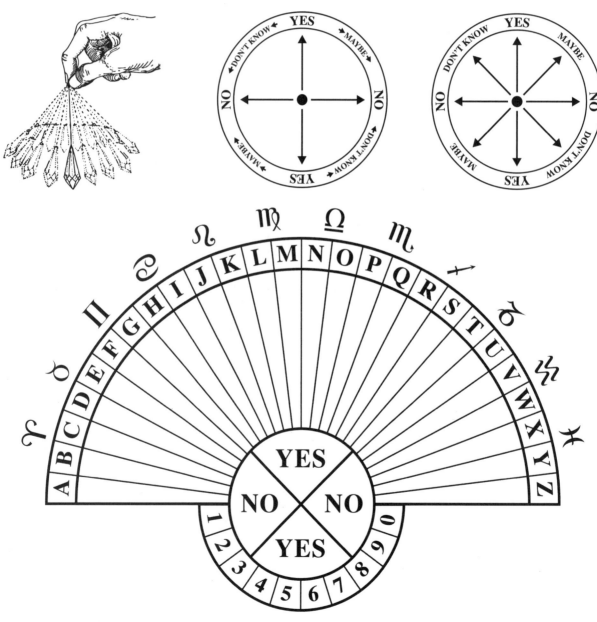

THE POTENT POWER OF THE PENDULUM
Susan Diamond

DOWSING BEYOND DIVINATION

Dowsing with pendulums, in their many forms, has long been a practice in folk magic. Too often mentioned as a side note or minimized as a minor tool, they are actually a major tool with a broad array of applications:

- **Dowsing for water and minerals**
- **Seeking lost objects and persons**
- **Diagnosis and healing**
- **Divining or truth-seeking**
- **Prescribing remedies**
- **Communing with the dead**
- **Communing with plants, animals, and stones**
- **Increasing magical potency**
- **Drawing in and casting out energies**
- **Discerning progress on spell work**

THE DOWSER'S TOOLS

Y-ROD

Y-shaped sticks or tree branches have been used throughout history to detect water, minerals, and unmarked graves. You grasp the two "handles" of the Y-shaped branch, then walk slowly along waiting for a twitch or dip that indicates where the item is that you are seeking. Hazel wood is a preferred medium in Europe; in the United States, Willow or Peach are more common. Flexible plastic Y-rods are also used.

L-RODS AND AURAMETER

L-Rods are simply two bent metal rods. They are available commercially or they can easily be made from coat hangers. The dowser holds the short end of one rod loosely in each hand. The long ends are trained to point in the direction of the desired object or energy field or to open or cross when the dowser is over it. The Cameron Aurameter is a single L-Rod with coiled springs and a bobber tip to increase sensitivity.

WAND, MOSAIC ROD, AND BOBBER

Wands can be made of a flexible rod, branch, or wire. Some have a coiled wire like an aurameter and some have a weighted bobber tip. They bob up and down to indicate an answer or a location.

PENDULUM

By far the most popular dowsing tool is the pendulum. There are many types of pendulums and many ways to employ them in your conjure work.

Our old time rootwork predecessors tended to use regular surveyor's plumb bobs for dowsing. These can be found in any hardware store in America. There is also a tradition of using small objects with personal meaning, such as a key, button, wedding ring, earring, cross, locket, bone from a pet or other animal, or a curio root. Depending on weight, the object can be suspended from a horse hair, human hair, sewing thread, crochet cotton, mop string, or necklace chain.

Jack balls, prepared as a type of container spell or mojo, contain herbs, roots, curios, and personal concerns. They are an extension of the person for whom they have been made and they are used both as divinatory pendulums and to perform spell work.

A pendulum is an excellent tool to determine if your rootwork is succeeding or not. Let's say you just completed a money drawing spell. You can ask the pendulum, "Will my spell succeed as I wished?" If the answer is "No," you can then ask other questions, such as, "Is someone blocking me?" or, "Should I continue with another form of spell?" or, "Do I need to take an entirely different approach to money drawing?"

If you are new to pendulum magic, you must first determine your "codes," that is, what is a "Yes" and what is a "No" for you and your pendulum. Codes vary from person to person. For me a circular motion is "Yes" and a straight line or back-and-forth motion, is "No." Your "Yes" and "No" may look entirely different.

The pendulum can also be used in conjunction with a pendulum board. The board allows for complex answers that range from choosing a colour or selecting a health remedy to spelling out full names and dates.

LEARN MORE ABOUT DOWSING

Read the Y.I.P.P.I.E. Dowsing Bibliography here:
Yronwode.org/dowsing-bibliograpjy
Join the American Society of Dowsers here:
Dowsers.org

HOUSE CLEARING WITH A PENDULUM

Here's how I use a pendulum to discover negative energies or entities and clear them from a home. My preferred method involves two pendulums — one for clearing out negativity and one for blessing the home.

CRYSTAL AND MINERAL PENDULUMS

While almost any stone or crystal may be used, for this particular work, I recommend these minerals:

To discover, draw out, and remove negativity:

- **Hematite:** Discovers and deflects negative energy.
- **Jet:** Attracts the sorrowful and mourning dead.
- **Lodestone:** Attracts whatever you ask it to draw.
- **Malachite:** Discourages unwanted entities.
- **Obsidian:** Cuts attachments from harmful people.
- **Onyx, Black:** Accesses the dead or old energies.
- **Quartz, Smoky:** Absorbs negative energies.
- **Tourmaline, Black:** Reverses all magical attacks.

To bless and heal the location:

- **Agate, Blue Lace:** Encourages communication.
- **Amethyst:** Protects, removes fear, dispels poison.
- **Angelite:** Increases peace and contentment.
- **Aventurine:** Eases heartache and loss.
- **Celestite:** Brings feelings of peace and unity.
- **Fluorite:** Sustains mental order and truthfulness.
- **Pearl:** Powerful self-healer, especially for women.
- **Quartz, Rose:** Builds trust, love, and compassion.

Read about the spiritual uses of stones in this book: **"Crystal Magic" by Jon Saint Germain**

ROOT AND RESIN PENDULUMS

Whole root or resin chunk pendulums contribute their own energies to the task. To prepare resins and roots as pendulums, they may be tied with string, wrapped in wire, or hung in a bag with a drawstring.

- **Angelica Root:** For divine healing and blessing.
- **Camphor Resin:** To purify; for house cleaning.
- **Dragon's Blood Resin:** Attracts and protects.
- **High John Root:** For power and potency.
- **Lucky Hand Root:** For luck, skills, and cash.
- **Queen Elizabeth Root:** A female divining spirit.

Read about the spiritual uses of roots in this book: **"Hoodoo Herb and Root Magic" by C. Yronwode**

STEP ONE: IDENTIFY THE NEGATIVE ENERGY

Using your pendulum according to your own "Yes" and "No" codes, first determine if there is a negative entity or energy in the home. If you receive a "Yes" answer, continue asking questions to identify what kind: Elemental? Demonic? Human? Curse? Ghost? Geopathic Stress? Diagnosing the trouble helps you to determine which allies you will need in clearing it.

STEP TWO: ATTRACT IT AND ERADICATE IT

When I work with a pendulum or jack ball for magical works, I spin it counterclockwise to facilitate the capture of a negative condition and clockwise to cast good energies into an area or toward a client.

Slowly move through the home, spinning your "drawing" pendulum counterclockwise to pull the entity or energy out of the shadows. Address the unwanted entity and tell it to leave in no uncertain terms.

Once you have drawn out the unwanted spirit, dip your pendulum in a glass of salted water. You may add Camphor, Hyssop, Rue, or Florida Water to the glass.

Repeat this process, if necessary, in each room. Be sure to work into dark, cluttered, or shadowy areas.

Open all the windows and doors and move through the home with a brazier of Uncrossing or Banishing Incense. Alternatively, scrub out with Chinese Wash.

STEP THREE: BLESS AND SEAL THE HOME

Having removed the negativity, you will want to bring in that which you desire for the home. Use your "blessing" pendulum, and, spinning it clockwise, move through the rooms while calling in what you want the place to be filled with. For instance, you might call in helpful ancestors, prosperity, peace, healing, or love.

Light a blessing candle — a white tea light will do — in each room. Seal the entryways with salt, protective stones, Vicks VapoRub, Red Brick Dust, or Devil's Shoe Strings, according to your inclination and training.

Upon completion of the work, release the salted water to a flowing stream below the level of your home.

"The Potent Power of the Pendulum" was a 2017 MISC workshop presentation. Susan Diamond is a member of AIRR and the proprietor of Serpent's Kiss in Santa Cruz, California. Reach her online at Serpents-Kiss.com.

NUMEROLOGICAL NAME ANALYSIS
catherine yronwode, Dr. Roy page Walton, Lewis de Claremont, and Godfrey Spencer

THE ABC-123 NUMBER KEY

Here is the 123-ABC Key for working out names, along with a set of brief keywords for each number:

```
1 2 3 4 5 6 7 8 9
A B C D E F G H I
J K L M N O P Q R
S T U V W X Y Z
```

1 Adventurous, bold, brave, a leader, an innovator,
2 Receptive, gentle, diplomatic, peaceable, calm.
3 Expressive, enthusiastic, joyous, inspirational.
4 Practical, scientific, accumulative, hard-working.
5 Changeable, adaptable, intelligent, quick, dextrous.
6 Humanitarian, compassionate, helpful, intuitive.
7 Introspective, quiet, meditative, reclusive, poised.
8 Organized, acquisitive, successful, financial.
9 Universal, artistic, upright, virtuous, enduring.

ANALYSIS OF A SINGLE NAME

Knowing someone's name helps us evaluate our similarities and differences. Let us say that you, a man who goes by the name of BOB, which is your nickname and not your birth name, has struck up a casual conversation with a man who goes by the name of PETE, and whose surname you do not yet know. You have met at a tavern, you seem to have a lot of interests in common, and he seems to present the possibility of a real friendship, so now, before you even know him well enough to get his full name, you make a quick character sketch:

```
PETE      BOB
7 5 2 5   2 6 2
  19        10
  1         1
```

No wonder the two of you hit it off so well! You both prefer to be known by a short nickname, and both of your nicknames work out to the identical masculine, adventurous, do-and-dare number 1. This man speaks your language and you speak his, and so he may become your buddy in time.

You can do a deeper analysis later, when you get to know his full name, but for now, the road is open and the lights are green.

ANALYSIS OF A NAME AS PRESENTED

Assessing the degree of compatibility between yourself and another person is not the only reason to craft a numerical character analysis. Another reason, which finds particular value in schools and businesses, is to assist in treating each person with compassion. We are wiser helpers when we understand the self-presentation of a name.

For this we use the name exactly as it is presented — without an attempt to uncover the true birth name, the current legal name, or the birth date. In fact, we are directly assessing the character-impression the person brings to the social situation in which we meet.

Let us take as an example a man named CHUCK OWEN. This name is on his business card and in the telephone directory. For our purposes it does not matter whether his birth name is CHARLES DANIEL OWEN or CHARLEMAGNE JOHNSON JONES — to us he is clearly and simply CHUCK OWEN. We have known him thus for many years, and as such he has built his reputation with our business.

So who is he "being" for us? How does he present?

```
CHUCK       OWEN
3 8 3 3 2   6 5 5 5
   19         21
   10          3
        13
         4
```

He presents as a physical worker, an outdoorsman, and a collector with a bent for practical science and hard labour. We shall not offer him a desk job in quiet solitude, as we would if his birth name was a 7:

```
CHESTER       DAVOE     OWENSFORTH
3 8 5 1 2 5 9 4   4 1 4 6 5   6 5 5 5 1 6 6 9 2 8
     37            20              58
     10             2              13
      1             2               4
              7
```

This is a brief sample from the 96-page book "The Secret of Numbers Revealed" by catherine yronwode, Dr. Roy Page Walton, Lewis de Claremont, and Godfrey Spencer, presented as a workshop at the 2019 Festival. The full book is offered for sale through the Lucky Mojo Book Co.

BEYOND THE READING: DIAGNOSIS BY CARTOMANCY
Madame Nadia

HISTORY

Cartomancy is the art of divination with cards. We know that cards seem to originate in Italy, spreading through Spain, Germany, and France. By 1375, playing cards with 4 suits were well known in Europe. While the earliest record of cartomancy in Europe appeared in the year 1759, the practice of card reading probably existed long prior to this date.

Judging by the lovely paintings of Harry Herman Roseland (1867-1950), card reading was a popular form of divination among African-Americans during the 19th century. Playing cards — either piquet decks of 32-36 cards or 52-card poker decks — were the most common tool of hoodoo cartomancers. Gypsy oracle decks, Lenormand cards, and the tarot were accepted by down home practitioners as well.

DIAGNOSIS STRATEGIES

The first step in any magical case is proper diagnosis to uncover the root of a problem. For example, why can't Susie Q lose those couple of inches around her hips that she's been trying to take off for more than a year? Is it stubborn baby fat, did her ex-boyfriend tie and bind her love life, or has a jealous frenemy "traded" her own excess girth for Susie Q's? We need to know what is happening here.

The second step is being Spirit-led to prescribe the most effective magical treatment. Certainly, if your client has gotten the evil eye from a jealous co-worker, you'd want to treat the case differently than if an enemy had him goofered. However, for both of these conditions there are numerous possible prescriptive spells. So how will you know whether the client should bathe or burn a Reversing candle — or maybe both bathe *and* set a Reversing light?

Cartomancy helps us to diagnose and to prescribe. It illuminates the root of a magical malady, and it indicates the proper rootwork approach to facilitating spiritual healing. Whether you use playing cards, a Lenormand deck with playing card image inserts, or the major and minor arcana of a tarot deck, the following pointers will help you to successfully diagnose and prescribe.

GROUND RULES

These rules will stop you from doubting your own advice and help you deliver clear, Spirit-led solutions:

Pick and Stick: Practice does makes perfect, so focus on one system of cartomancy until you really know it. These ideas work equally well with a poker, piquet, tarocchi, or Lenormand deck, but you must know how to read that deck. If you are a beginner, I suggest you start with playing cards; if you know tarot or Lenormand, start with whichever you know best.

Keep It Simple: To approach the cards, make an assessment, decide upon an action, and cast a spell doesn't require complicated cartomantic maneuvers. On the contrary, some of most successful rootwork arises from basic divination and simple conjure work.

Set Parameters: Decide what means what, and stay within these parameters. For example, if you ask a Yes / No question and the spread is based on the ratio of Red to Black cards, count how many Red and how many Black cards you have, but don't be tempted to read the meaning of the individual cards.

Ask Clear Questions: Precise questions yield exact answers. The better you know your cartomantic system, the easier it is to ask sharp questions.

CARD-LED CONJURATION

In order to use the cards to formulate spells for clients, you will need to add a layer of meaning to each card beyond those you have already learned to read in a divination. Keep in mind as you do this that you are not to "interpret" the cards; rather, you are to look at them as a framework upon which to craft a spell, prepare an amulet, or perform a traditional hoodoo job of work. The deeper your knowledge of conjure, the easier this will be for you.

In addition to my own personal thoughts, the lists that follow reflect the practical rootwork experiences of a number of my peers. I would like to extend my thanks to Khi Armand, ConjureMan Ali, nagasiva yronwode, Professor Charles Porterfield, and Miss Cat for contributing to this compilation.

PLAYING CARD COLOURS

Black: No, night, negative, dense, heavy, hidden, dark.
Red: Yes, day, positive, light, uplifting, revealed, bright.

PLAYING CARD AND TAROT NUMBERS

Since numbers are associated with cards in all three of the card systems, you can use numerology as a reference tool.

1: Individualistic, one item, a circle, a coin, an arrow, a point.
2: Cooperative, paired items, two items tied together.
3: Communicative, three ingredients, three days, a triangle.
4: Stable, four corners, four directions, cross, crossroads.
5: Expansive, five-spot pattern, pentagram, five senses.
6: Harmonious, six-pointed star, hexagon, cube, box.
7: Philosophical, seven items, seven knots, seven days.
8: Powerful, eight rays, infinity symbol, eight-pointed star.
9: Selfless, nine items, nine knots, nine days.

PLAYING CARD CLASSES

Pips: Read them by numeral or by tarot image equivalent.
Court Cards: Read them as signifying types of people.

SUITS FOR PLAYING CARDS AND TAROT

Clubs   Wands: Fire   South   Noon   Summer
Candles, lamps, fire in a cauldron, burning items to ash.

Diamonds Coins: Earth   North   Midnight Winter
Talismans, sigils, minerals, dirts, powders, salts, stones.

Spades   Swords: Air   East   Sunrise   Spring
Incense, needles, nails, scissors, knives, pins, weather.

Hearts   Cups: Water   West   Sunset   Autumn
Waters, washes, oils, colognes, baths, teas, rivers, oceans.

PLAYING CARD CALENDAR AND ALMANAC

52 cards in a deck: The number of weeks in a year.
13 tricks in a deck: The number of weeks in a season.
13 cards per suit: The number of New Moons in a year.
12 face cards: The number of months in a year.
4 suits of cards: The number of weeks in a month.

(See the entire Playing Card Almanac in the book "Hoodoo Bible Magic" by Miss Michæle and Prof. C. D. Porterfield.)

THE TAROT SUIT OF CUPS

Ace of Cups: Spiritual bathing, use the 23rd Psalm.
2 of Cups: Love Me, personal concerns in drink.
3 of Cups: Shared ritual, water on the altar, magic in drinks.
4 of Cups: A need to uncross love or to uncross nature.
5 of Cups: Lift off an ancestral, multi-generational curse.
6 of Cups: A tricked gift, Jasmine, crossroads disposal.
7 of Cups: Confusion, Bewitching, tricked items of all kinds.
8 of Cups: Restless, walk away and don't look back.
9 of Cups: Petition ancestors, offerings need to be made.
10 of Cups: Family spells, Dixie John Root, House Blessing.
Page of Cups: Sex magic, Stop Gossip, baths, colognes.
Knight of Cups: Teas, bathing, use of water-loving herbs.
Queen of Cups: Psychic Vision, Influence, scrying, baths.
King of Cups: Stay At Home, Restless, tricked alcohol.

THE TAROT SUIT OF COINS

Ace of Coins: Prosperity, coin talisman, foot-track work.
2 of Coins: Paired mojo bags or talismans, mizpah charm.
3 of Coins: Vow a gift to a church or non-profit organization.
4 of Coins: Uncross money, nail down coins, Money Stay.
5 of Coins: Prayer for a family in trouble.
6 of Coins: Coins for the poor, trained hunting money.
7 of Coins: Steady Work, Money House Blessing.
8 of Coins: Steady Work, dressed business cards or coins.
9 of Coins: Talismans for animals, ring of power.
10 of Coins: Money House Blessing, dress pets, Maximon.
Page of Coins: Lucky talisman, Road Opening.
Knight of Coins: Trained Lodestone for money.
Queen of Coins: Crystals, rocks, coin charms, red Roses.
King of Coins: Wine, tinctures, nail property down, Nature.

THE TAROT SUIT OF WANDS

Ace of Wands: Fire of Love, Healing, roots, sticks, herbs.
2 of Wands: Safe Travel, long distance work.
3 of Wands: Road Opener, tidal or Sunset spells.
4 of Wands: Harvest spells, offerings, Marriage.
5 of Wands: Spells to foster competition, Confusion.
6 of Wands: Victory, Commanding, Bay leaves.
7 of Wands: Protection, Fiery Wall of Protection.
8 of Wands: Communication spells, Saint Expedite.
9 of Wands: Live things, incarcerating enemies.
10 of Wands: Hag riding, tricked work tools.
Page of Wands: Creative journaling, fire, sacred geometry.
Knight of Wands: Hire a helping rootworker.
Queen of Wands: Defensive work, herbs, Black Cat.
King of Wands: Heating spells, Ginger, Cinnamon, Power.

THE TAROT SUIT OF SWORDS

Ace of Swords: Justified court case, Crown of Success.
2 of Swords: Uncrossing, work at the New Moon.
3 of Swords: Cut and Clear, cord cutting, black wax heart.
4 of Swords: Bury an item, coffin box spell.
5 of Swords: Pins, needles, knives, Hot Foot by the tides.
6 of Swords: Hot Foot, throw into running water.
7 of Swords: Ward off thieves and liars, sneaky tricks.
8 of Swords: Bind doll in mirror box, tie woman's nature.
9 of Swords: Instill paranoia, black skull candle, Influence.
10 of Swords: Stab doll-baby, burn on grave or at tide mark.
Page of Swords: Weather magic, storms, Confusion.
Knight of Swords: Inflammatory Confusion, storms.
Queen of Swords: Coffin nail, spirit of a child, justice work.
King of Swords: Knife spells, magical jewelry.

THE TAROT TRUMPS OR MAJOR ARCANA

The Fool: Foot-track magic, Clarity, white Roses.
The Magician: Spell-casting, the four elements.
The High Priestess: Psychic development, the use of Bibliomancy and Psalms.
The Empress: Love spells, fertility, Venus, feed your stuff.
The Emperor: Mastery, Protection, San Simon.
The Hierophant: Blessings, Holy Oil, Holy Water, crossroads and Road Opener work, use keys.
The Lovers: Come To Me, Marriage, Uriel, Chuparrosa.
The Chariot: Master, astrological timing, Black and White.
Justice: Court Case, a justified worker, don't seek revenge.
The Hermit: Lamp, Solomon's seals, freezer spells.
Strength: Love binding, Stop Gossip, Domination, Leo.
The Wheel of Fortune: Past life or ancestral issues, astrological remediation, the four elements.

The Hanged Man: Binding and tying a doll, client was tied.
Death: Initiatory rite, graveyard dirt, D.U.M.E.
Temperance: Tying for love, Crown of Success, Raphæl, Queen Elizabeth Root (Iris).
The Devil: Cut and Clear with fire, Uncrossing, bind dolls and set them on fire, lust magic.
The Tower: Destruction, Confusion, burning one doll and bathing another, Lightning Struck Wood, fire spells, sulphur.
The Star: Healing water, love bath, feed bath water to lover.
The Moon: Tides, maternal ancestors, Crab Shell Powder, skin-changing (lycanthropy), dream magic.
The Sun: Solar magic, protection of children, Safflower.
The Judgement: Gabriel, graveyard dirt of an ancestor.
The World: Victory, distance work, astrological magic, the four elements, internet magic.

THE LENORMAND CARDS

1 Cavalier: To bring a new lover, protection for vehicles, heating up work, Saint Expedite, work on the other man.
2 Clover: Fast Luck, Gambler's Gold, gambling spells, work with herbs, work with Clover herb or charm.
3 Ship: Safe Travel, wish fulfillment, business success, spiritual bathing, working with the Water element.
4 House: Peaceful Home, House Blessing, Money House Blessing, nailing down property, protection of the family.
5 Tree: Ancestor work, heal or cause disease, use roots and bark, Palo religion, Shamanism, dispose of remains by a strong tree, petition the spirit of a tree.
6 Clouds: Mind control, instill fear, cause depression, bring about madness, Confusion or Inflammatory Confusion, make use of the Air element.
7 Snake: Break Up, binding an enemy, eliminating a love rival, fidelity spells, tempting or working to prevent temptation, the other woman.
8 Coffin: Coffin box, mirror box, freezer spell, mock funeral, graveyard dirt, cemetery work with the dead, hag riding.
9 Bouquet: Use herbs and flowers in spell work, beauty and glamour spells, physical attraction spells, tricking a gift, spiritual bathing and teas.
10 Scythe: Cut and Clear, sharp herbs and curios, Break Up, sharp tools, cause an enemy to lose his or her teeth.
11 Whip: Spiritual cleansing, Law Keep Away, Stop Gossip, cause fights, whip foot-tracks, sexual bondage, sporting life.
12 Birds: Stop Gossip, communication spells, say prayers, use a Parrot feather, spells to conceive.
13 Child: New beginnings, alimony spells with Pay Me, new beginnings, protecting children.
14 Fox: Boss Fix, finding the truth, Clarity, giving or removing the evil eye, tricking objects, Master, Power, success in sports, a Cat.
15 Bear: Motherhood, Money Stay With Me, maternal ancestors, mother-in-law, financial success, make your partner generous with money, trick a bank.
16 Stars: Crown of Success, Master, Luck, astrological magic, astrological timing of spells, working by night, psychic development, charisma.

17 Stork: New beginnings, weight loss, adoption, fertility, keeping a pregnancy, promotion, moving house, new lover.
18 Dog: Friendship, fidelity, working on your co-workers, black Dog hair, Steady Work.
19 Tower: Visa, immigration, Court Case, Anima Sola, taxes, Boss Fix, incarceration, hang a doll upside-down.
20 Garden: Planting, burying items or ritual remains, tricking a large crowd, cheating or fidelity, Earth element.
21 Mountain: Block Buster, Road Opener, a major enemy, Lodestone work, immigration, crossing borders safely.
22 Crossroad: Crossroads spell, Road Opener, appeal to a crossroads deity.
23 Mice: Protect from theft, instill anxiety and fear, Money Stay With Me, pins and needles, protection against disease.
24 Heart: Love work, sex magic, using a heart.
25 Ring: Engagement, Marriage, binding work, fidelity, crafting a talisman, magical jewelry.
26 Book: The occult, the Bible, Psalms, religious texts, Crown of Success, keeping work hidden.
27 Letter: Dressed petition papers or documents, fixed money, communication spells.
28 Gentleman: A male client, a male love interest.
29 Lady: A female client, a female love interest.
30 Lilies: Sex magic, to find a spiritual guide, paternal ancestral line, justice and legal work, freezer spells.
31 Sun: Work by day, solar magic, Crown of Success, Mastery, Victory, the Fire element, charisma and self-confidence, heating up spell work.
32 Moon: Mirror box, work by Moon signs, Attraction, beauty, Bewitching, dream magic, hag riding, Reversing.
33 Key: Master Key, Road Opener, Victory, crossroads work, Block Buster, make a talisman, use a key.
34 Fish: Money spells, business success, spiritual bathing, personal concerns in food or drink, sex magic, fertility, male nature, disposing of remains in water, the Water element.
35 Anchor: Stay With Me, binding, Money Stay With Me.
36 Cross: Uncrossing, Crossing, graveyard dirt, cemetery magic, working at the house of God, religious amulets, Crule of Courage, working with saints, death spells.

LAYOUTS FOR SPELL ASSESSMENT

THE YES / NO 5-CARD SPREAD

This diagnostic spread works well with playing cards. It can be used with Lenormand cards too. Frame a clear question, appropriate for a Yes or No answer, and draw five cards. Many Red cards increase the chances for a Yes answer, while a majority of Black cards give a strong No.

- **All 5 Red** = 100% Yes, a predetermined situation.
- **1 Black 4 Red** = Most likely Yes, and the querent has an excellent chance to influence the matter.
- **2 Black 3 Red** = Probably Yes; the querent has a chance to influence the matter with conjure.
- **3 Black and 2 Red** = Probably No; a positive outcome may develop with aggressive rootwork.
- **4 Black and 1 Red** = Most likely No; not much chance, but the situation is not hopeless.
- **All 5 Black** = A solid No.

THE GOOD OL' 3-CARD CUT

- **What:** The first card describes the known circumstances; it is the 'What' card.
- **Why:** The second card stands for the hidden factors at play, revealing 'Why' this is happening.
- **How:** Ideas for remediating the situation are seen in the final card, telling 'How' to solve the problem.

SAMPLE SPELL WORK FROM CARDS

Let's go back to Susie Q, who thinks she may have been tied by an ex to prevent her from attracting a new lover by blocking her ability to lose weight.

TAROT CARD READING AND SPELL WORK

We;ll start with the 3-Card Cut for tarot. We draw 8 of Swords in the "What" position, the Devil in the "Why" position, and the Tower in the "How" position. 8 of Swords reveals the client to be tied and bound. The Devil reveals a perverse bond. The Tower shows crossed conditions; her situation is dangerous.

To remediate, we look at the Tower: It suggests a need to sever the bindings with swords of fire. Both the 8 of Swords and the Devil highlight doll-baby work, and the 8 of Swords also suggests a mirror box. This difficult combination emphasizes extreme magical measures. To completely and permanently remove Susie's ex's influences, graveyard work is advised.

PLAYING CARD READING AND SPELL WORK

We'll use the playing cards next, and the 5-card Yes / No Spread. We draw 8 of Spades + 9 of Diamonds + 8 of Diamonds + Queen of Hearts + 9 of Spades. The Red to Black ratio is 3 Red cards vs. 2 Black cards, suggesting a Yes. Now let's examine the cards for traditional combos: 8 of Spades + 9 of Spades + 9 of Diamonds + Queen of Hearts (significator) = a spiritual attack; 8 of Spades + 8 of Diamonds = an intentional jinx: The client has indeed been crossed. 9 of Spades speaks of loss and death. 8 of Spades is for breaking ties. 8 of Diamonds is associated with the evil eye, glass, and cutting. 9 of Diamonds is about speed, and when it is with Spades, it's a warning of danger.

Obviously, now Susie wants to know how this mess. Consider the elements: We have two Spades and two Diamonds — so we know to incorporate Air and Earth elements into the spell. Based on these meanings, I would instruct Susie Q to craft a mirror box with a doll-baby stuffed with and baptized for her ex. She could stab it and set it alight on a pile of incense, and then bury it in a cemetery. Or she could burn the whole thing directly on a grave.

LENORMAND READING AND SPELL WORK

Now let's view the same spread using Lenormand cards. We draw Scythe + Ring + Heart + Bouquet + Cross, a ratio is 3 Positive Cards to 2 Negative — suggesting a Yes. Examining the cards for important combos we find Scythe + Ring = forcing someone into a relationship; Scythe + Ring + Heart = cutting bonds and ties; Bouquet + Cross = crossed beauty. We also consider that Cross = cemetery work, Heart is an actual heart, and Bouquet = herbal magic.

Based on these combinations, I suggest that Susie Q is cursed; she should buy a Chicken heart, name it for the ex, stuff it with cursing herbs, stick it with pins and needles, set it on fire, and bury in a grave.

CONCLUSION

Cartomancy is a powerful tool that not only helps us predict the future and identify a person's spiritual condition; it also allows us to prescribe conjurations to help that individual. Truly, all is in the cards.

This was a hand-out at the 2014 workshops. Madame Nadia is a member of AIRR and Hoodoo Psychics, and can be reached at MadameNadia.com.

TAROT CARD TIPS: CHOOSING THE SIGNIFICATOR
Valentina Burton

COURT CARD METHOD

One way to choose a significator card to represent your client, is to select the court card that coordinates with your client's zodiac sign and age or station in life. I use the Golden Dawn system, so Wands are Fire, Cups are Water, Swords are Air, and Pentacles or Coins are Earth. This is the table of correspondences:

- **Aries:** Queen of Wands.
- **Taurus:** King of Coins.
- **Gemini:** Knight of Swords.
- **Cancer:** Queen of Cups.
- **Leo:** King of Wands.
- **Virgo:** Knight of Coins.
- **Libra:** Queen of Swords.
- **Scorpio:** King of Cups.
- **Sagittarius:** Knight of Wands.
- **Capricorn:** Queen of Coins.
- **Aquarius:** King of Swords.
- **Pisces:** Knight of Cups.

Ask for the date of birth to select the zodiac sign and its significator card and, before you even begin to read, you will know key things about your client.

If they are Gemini or Aries they are impatient and want ANSWERS, so I will start with noting the things they have come to address, assuring that we will get to those things in the reading. A Taurus or Capricorn wants to know that the reading will be useful, not a waste of time and money. Aquarius, Scorpio, or Virgo may want to know how or why you know these things. Virgo and Gemini will ask tons of questions about your process. Cancer or Pisces need to be understood emotionally to feel the reading is "good." Sagittarius or Leo want validation of their need for an authentic life, to know it is okay to want "more."

In my practice I use this system to select a significator card that can be placed into spellwork to represent the client, and I also make it the significator in the reading to help me understand what the client can use, can hear, and will consider "good." And let me just add that the importance of the client considering the reading to be "good" or "accurate" is about much more than the ego of the reader. If a client thinks you are "right on" they are more likely to listen, take heed, and implement your suggestions.

BIRTH AND YEAR CARD METHODS

These ways to select a significator were originally written about by Angeles Arrien and Mary K. Greer.

To calculate the Birth Card, add the client's month, day, and year of birth. Keep all numbers from 1 to 22, and reduce all others. The number relates to a Major Arcana card. This can be used as the significator or to point out the client's life purpose.

To calculate the Year Card, add up the birth month and day plus the **current** year, and reduce to twenty-two or lower. Mary K. Greer suggests that the inner effects of this card run from birthday-to-birthday, the outer effects are after the New Year.

KEYWORDS FOR EACH YEAR

1 and 2: Magician and High Priestess: not seen until 9957 and 9958, respectively.
3: Empress: Creative and Prolific.
4: Emperor: Authority and Rules.
5: Hierophant: Study, Stress, Values, Beliefs.
6: Lovers: Relationships and Choices.
7: Chariot: Goals, Mastery, Self Control.
8: Strength: Desires, Perseverance, Courage.
9: Hermit: Introspection, Find or Become a Guide.
10: Wheel Of Fortune: Changing Circumstance.
11: Justice: Decision, Adjustment, Responsibility.
12: Hanged Man: Releasing, Suspended, Trust.
13: Death: Transformation, Liberation.
14: Temperance: Patience, Healing, Blending.
15: Devil: Compulsion, Power, Attachments.
16: Tower: Revolution, Change.
17: Star: Goals, Hope, Achievement.
18: Moon: Imagination, Unseen Patterns.
19: Sun: Success, Reward.
20: Judgement: Restructuring, Awakening.
21: World: Completion, Success.
22: Fool: Risk, Inspiration, a Move.

Because these cards are never just "good" or "bad" they are terrific for showing a client how to work with the energy of their particular year.

Valentina Burton, The Dallas Psychic, is a member of AIRR; this flyer was prepared for her 2018 workshop. Find her at ValentinaBurton.com.

AN INTRODUCTION TO VULVAMANCY
Dr. Jeremy Weiss

WHAT IS VULVAMANCY?

Vulvamancy is the modern term for a genre of divination that harnesses the unique power of the female vulva as an oracle. The current practice of vulvamancy can be divided into two broad practices of the mantic arts — character readings and divination.

YONI READINGS

Character analysis by female genital reading has a long history, especially in South Asian cultures. Because the vulva is called the yoni in Sanskrit, such vulvamantic readings are also known as yoni readings.

As with other anatomical analyses, like palmistry, Chinese face reading, and the Burr System of Breast Analysis, the typical woman requests a vulvamancy reading to gain deeper insight into herself. She may be seeking self-knowledge to make changes in her life that will lead to greater happiness and satisfaction — or she may wish to clarify her own strengths, weaknesses, proclivities, desires, and dislikes.

Sometimes, the subject of the reading is not the client. In fact, the client may be a current or prospective lover or mate seeking knowledge about his or her partner to gain insight into the couple's compatibility.

Couples may seek out yoni readings as a way to learn about each other, which can make them feel closer. The exercise of the reading itself can be a powerfully rewarding bonding experience.

YONI DIVINATION

Divination is the foretelling or predicting of events. Vulvamancers use one or more of four major methods to do this, namely panty readings, menstrual pad readings, ceromancy pad readings, and fluidic bed sheet readings. Bed sheet readings can make use of menstrual blood, post-coital fluids, amrita (female ejaculate), or a combination of any or all of these.

Divinatory vulvamancy can be done by a person of either gender, but as with other forms of foretelling, reading the future for oneself can be uncertain, so, if possible a professional reader should be consulted.

VULVAMANCY AND NEO-TANTRA

Tantra yoga comprises a loosely-allied set of Hindu and Buddhist rites set forth in texts dating from the 5th century CE to the present in which sexual union, either actual or visualized, may be included along with other practices such as the veneration of female deities and acknowledgement of the sacredness of the female body.

Neo-tantra is a modern term in Europe and the Americas to describe esoteric practices that, rightly or wrongly, claim descent from the sexual aspect of tantra yoga. The term is also broadly applied to non-Asian forms of sexual spirituality like karezza and eulis.

VULVAMANCY AND SEX MAGIC

Sex magic may refer to any magical prayer, spell-casting, or contact work intended to bring about love, romance, or sexual pleasure. It may also include any form of magic in which a sex act is a part of a work which may have as its objective not only sexual aims, but also non-sexual outcomes, such as curative health, psychic contact over distances, or even world peace.

Because the term sex magic is applied to so many forms of magic, there is no one way to integrate vulvamancy (or phallomancy) into magical practice. Therefore, consider these two quite different examples:

A sex magician might be asked to cast a spell on for love-attraction, fertility, or curing. Preparatory to undertaking the spell, the magician might perform a vulvamantic reading on the client to determine what form the work should take and the likelihood of success.

A hoodoo practitioner who wishes to attract or bind a mate might seek out a female-formed root or cowrie shell, dress it with his own sexual fluids, pray over it, and hide it in or under his bed. Employing vulvamancy on the variable vulva-shapes observed in naturally occurring curios such roots or shells would assist him to select the most appropriate curio.

This is a sample from the 96-page book "Vulvamancy" by Dr. Jeremy Weiss, presented as a workshop at the 2017 Festival. The full book is offered for sale through the Lucky Mojo Book Co. Find Dr. Weiss online at Vulvamancy.com.

SETTING UP YOUR MAGICAL WORKING SPACE
Miss Phœnix LeFæ

PRACTICAL TIPS FOR THE ALTAR

FIRE SAFETY

When you work with open flame, do so carefully and safely. Never leave fire unattended. Make sure that you only use fire-safe items as candle holders. This prevents them from breaking, melting, or catching on fire as the wax melts. If there is anything you value and don't want to see burned, covered in wax, or ruined, don't use it or store it where you will be working with fire.

Check to be certain that the smoke alarms in your home are operating properly and keep the batteries fresh. Also make sure that you have the recommended number of smoke alarms. Invest in a fire extinguisher just in case there are any emergencies or accidents. And keep it near your candle-burning area.

WAX SPILLS

Wax will melt and it has a tendency to get all over everything. Be cautious when you remove wax from your altars. Peeling or chipping wax off of a wooden surface can chip off varnish or paint.

If wax gets on carpet or fabric let it dry first, then cover the area with a paper bag. Use an iron on the coolest setting you can and place that warmed up iron on top of the paper bag. The spilled wax will heat up and transfer from your fabric or carpet onto the bag. This will remove that wax from your carpet or fabric without ruining it. Then you can determine if you will just toss that wax out or if you need to ritually dispose of it.

STORAGE SPACE

No matter how often you work at the altar or what kind of work you do, you need tools. You should have a range of bowls, plates, and trays; holders for candles; jars for herbs; and containers for incenses, oils, or powders. If yours is a devotional altar, you will need a way to hold offerings of water, food, drink, perfumes, cigars, coins, or flowers. If you will be burning candles, you will need a set of candle tools. All of these tools require storage space. Plan the storage space into your altar, if you can. The best place is under your altar, using drawers, pull outs, or shelves.

CLEANING AND MAINTAINING ALTARS

Just as we would clean a house before moving into it, so do we clean our altars before first using them. It doesn't matter if your new altar will be on a shelf, an end table, an entire room, the backyard, or a temple; altar creation begins with cleaning.

Cleaning can be thought of in two steps. The first step is to clear away any residue in the space that you will be using. You are neutralizing the area, wiping away anything unintentional or messy. The second step is to create a clean space that matches the intent of the conjure work you will be performing on your altar.

How you carry out the first type of cleaning, the neutralizing part, will depend on the physical surface of your altar. This isn't magical, but totally mundane and practical. No matter what cleaning agent you decide to use, you must make sure that it is safe for the surface you are washing. One of the best cleaners is Chinese Wash, as it is safe on almost all surfaces, and you can also wash altar cloths in it. You might also try an herbal tea mixture that you create as a special wash for your new altar. Making a tea, wash, or scrub water is simple, and many recipes are available. If you have a different favourite cleansing agent, start with that.

If you aren't sure about a product's safety, don't risk it. You don't want to ruin a lovely piece of furniture by choosing poorly. For example, Florida Water Cologne will take the varnish off a 19th century cabinet, but will not harm one that has a polyurethane-coated finish. If you have a wooden surface, you would not want to use harsh Buffalo Ammonia, which will damage it. If your altar's fireproof surface is a marble stone, you must not wash it down with vinegar or lemon juice, because acidic liquids will literally dissolve it.

If you are worried about making a mistake, consider censing the altar with incense smoke; it is generally harmless for most surfaces. Censing and whisking are also favoured ways to perform the second stage of cleaning, laying down a magical intention on your altar.

This is a brief sample from the 96-page book "Hoodoo Shrines and Altars" by Miss Phœnix LeFæ, which was presented as a workshop at the 2015 Festival. The full book is offered for sale through the Lucky Mojo Book Co.

HOW TO MAKE MAGICAL TEAS AND TISANES
Madame Pamita

DRINKING MAGICAL SPELLS

Most rootworkers are comfortable with putting a pinch of an herb in a mojo bag, but what they may not know is that there is a long history of conjure practitioners prescribing these same herbs as teas for clients. Not all herbs are edible or drinkable, of course (and you should always research an herb before ingesting it), but many of the traditional rootwork herbs can be made into magical potions that can be profoundly powerful in bringing about improved conditions for yourself or your clients, or for laying a "sneaky trick" on an unsuspecting target. The difference between your regular cup of tea and a tea spell is in the intention. Praying over your tea can make it into a magically transforming potion.

TEAS, TOOLS, ACCOUTREMENTS

Teas and Tisanes: Tea is a beverage made with the leaves of the Tea plant and tisanes are herbal infusions, but most folks call both drinks "teas."

Heat Source: To boil water, you can use a gas or electric stove or a dedicated electric tea kettle.

Tea Kettle: A metal or enamel tea kettle goes on your heat source; it is not a place for infusing.

Tea Pot: This is a ceramic container into which you can pour hot water. It's one of the two places where infusion may take place; the other is in the tea cup.

Infuser: This is a container that holds the tea as it steeps. It can be a tea ball, tea bag, infusing spoon or muslin bag. If your tea pot has a built-in strainer, the pot itself is an infuser. You can even use the cup as an infuser and drink the leaves.

Infuser Rest: Unless you use the pot or cup as an infuser, you will need a small dish to hold the infuser after you remove it from the water. Do not use the saucer; that would be ugly and messy.

Tea Cup and Saucer: The shape of a tea cup differs from that of a coffee mug; the wide mouth cools the tea quickly and enables tea leaf reading, if you wish to make a divination.

MAKING A MAGICAL CUP

Here's how to make a truly magical potion:

Start with fresh water. Spring or natural rain water is best, if you can get it, but it is not necessary.

While waiting for the water to boil, concentrate on the intention of your spell and put the appropriate herbs into your tea pot or infuser.

Pour the hot water into the tea pot or into the cup with the infuser. As you do, ask the herbs to do their work and say these words with loving conviction. For example, with a Mint tea I would say something like, "Mint, clear away my blocks to prosperity and protect my money."

Hold your hands in the steam over the cup or tea pot, focus your intention, and pray over your spell. Tisanes can be steeped longer than teas. For an extra boost, let the herbs steep for a magical number of minutes: 3, 7, or 9.

Pour the infusion from pot to cup or pull the infuser out of your cup. As the liquid cools, I often talk to my herbal allies, having a little "conversation" out loud, telling the story of what the brew will do. For example, I might say, "Mint, when you work for me, you will help me to find the money to pay for my bills and have some extra money for fun. You will help open my flow of prosperity and bring good opportunities to me so that I can be more abundant. You'll protect what I have so that I don't lose money to broken equipment or unexpected expenses." I will let this monologue go on for a few minutes, telling the herb all the ways that it will help me.

By the time you've finished the conversation, the tea will have cooled to the point that you can drink it. It has been imbued with all your words of intention, all your thoughts, prayers, and will. This is truly a magic potion. Add sugar, honey, milk, cream, or Lemon to taste.

At this point, the infusion is ready. Close your eyes and, sip by sip, drink it all in and feel the power of the magic permeating your body and spirit.

HERBS FOR YOUR INTENTIONS

- **Bergamot** (in Earl Grey Tea): For empowerment, cleansing, and health.
- **Catnip:** Used both to calm the mind and for enticing sexuality.
- **Chamomile:** For gambling luck and money drawing, it is also soothing to the stomach.
- **Cinnamon:** To draw good luck, and to heat up luck in money or love.
- **Cloves:** Used in pairs for sustaining friendship or for money-luck.
- **Cubeb Berry:** Spicy and peppery, it incites sexual heat and passion.
- **Damiana:** A reputed aphrodisiac, used ito draw love and sexuality.
- **Dandelion Root:** For enhancement of intuition and psychic powers.
- **Dill Leaf:** For love uncrossing; to remove a love jinx or curse.
- **Ginger:** For fiery protection an also for heating up love or luck.
- **Hibiscus:** Its petals turn pale tisanes pink or red, the perfect colour to symbolize love and romance.
- **Hyssop:** Drink it and recite Psalms 51 for atonement and purification.
- **Lemongrass:** To remove negativity and bring in good luck.
- **Licorice:** For the exercise of power and control over others.
- **Life Everlasting:** For increasing longevity and good health.
- **Mint:** For spiritual purification, protection, and to protect prosperity.
- **Nettle:** To remove jinxes and crossed conditions; to cleanse.
- **Red Clover:** For happily committed romance, love, and marriage.
- **Rosemary:** For protection, peace, beauty, and feminine power.
- **Sarsaparilla:** For healing, increased prosperity, and sexual love.
- **Sassafras:** For increased health, wealth, and abundance.
- **Self-Heal:** To aid and support the body's natural healing powers.
- **Tea:** An energizer; added to herbal tisanes for more "oomph."
- **Wintergreen:** For good luck in both money and sexual matters.
- **Yarrow Blossom:** For an increased courage and determination.

CUSTOM BLENDS

As with any form of rootwork, you can blend more than one herb for a truly customized potion. For example, you could blend Red Clover, Sarsaparilla, and Licorice to make a dominating love potion, or you could mix Hibiscus, Catnip, Cloves, Damiana, and candied Ginger for a hot, sweet, spicy call to passion.

When blending herbs, also take into consideration fragrance and flavour. Some herbs taste amazing and some … not so much. Some have fabulous fragrances, others smell like nothing special until they hit your taste buds.

If a tea is bitter, you can always add a sweetener. Both honey and sugar have their own magical sweetening qualities — but also consider adding a pleasant herb or using a slice of candied Ginger as a sweet addition to a bitter tea. And don't be afraid to drink something a little bitter. After all, a truly magical potion might require you to have courage!

SNEAKY TEA POTIONS

Of course, you may want to serve a tea potion to someone as a sneaky trick, for example to get someone to have more loving feelings for you. If that's the case, then pray over the herb or herbal blend before you sit down to tea with the other person. Ask the herbs to do your intention and then just prepare the beverage as if you are making a plain cup of tea. Your target will be none the wiser.

RESOURCES

Teas and tisanes are a wonderful and delicious way to bring magic into your life. If you'd like to learn more about their use in rootwork, healing, and other folk magical traditions, I recommend these books:

Hoodoo Herb and Root Magic: Catherine Yronwode
Hoodoo Spiritual Baths: Aura Laforest
Encyclopedia of Magical Herbs: Scott Cunningham
The Herbalist: Joseph E. Meyer
Prescription for Herbal Healing: Phyllis A. Balch
This Amazing Book: Herb Medicine: Cat Yronwode
Herbal Teas: 101 Recipes: Kathleen Brown

Madame Pamita prepared this hand-out — and some delicious herbal teas — for the 2016 Hoodoo Heritage Festival. She can be reached for readings and rootwork at her in-person shop in Los Angeles, and online at HoodooPsychics.com, via ReadersAndRootworkers.com, and through her own web site, ParlourOfWonders.com.

HOODOO HERB AND ROOT MEDICINE
catherine yronwode

TRADITIONAL HERBAL REMEDIES

These simple recipes may serve to get you started in the field of Herbal medicine. Be sure to check all herbs for side effects before mixing them into your recipes.

ANTHELMINTIC TEA

Caution is requested of those who take vermifuge or anthelmintic teas, as a too-strong dose may carry side effects. Combine any of these: Arbor Vitæ, Wafer Ash, Butternut Bark, Horehound, Lamb's Quarters, Male Fern, Pomegranate, Pumpkin Seed, Southernwood. Wormseed, Wormwood.

BLOOD PURIFIER TEA

A mixture of Bilberry, Red Clover, Thyme, and Strawberry Leaves makes an excellent blood purifier.

COUGH SYRUP

Simmer 1 oz. each of Boneset, Coltsfoot, Slippery Elm, Horehound, Flax seed, and Licorice root in 1 quart of water until the volume is reduced to 1/3, then strain off the extract. Add to it 1 pint of blackstrap molasses and ½ lb. sugar. Simmer until the sugar is dissolved and seal in bottles for future use. This may be taken freely for cases of cough and bronchitis.

COUGH AND COLD TEA

Mix two parts Mint, plus one part each Horehound, Hyssop, Lemon Balm, Linden Flowers, and Marshmallow, plus half a part each Sage, Borage, and Thyme. Store in a sealed jar. Use 1 spoonful per cup of hot water to make tea. Sweeten with honey; add a squeeze of Lemon juice and a capful of brandy.

DIURETIC TEA

Diuretics work well in combination. You do not need them all to make an effective tea, but blending a few makes their action more sure: Althæa Leaf, White Ash, Broom Tops, Button Snake Root, Canada Snake Root, Caraway, Chicory Root, Cleavers, Slippery Elm Bark, Figwort, Gravel Root, Horsetail Grass, Juniper Berries, Marshmallow Root, Saxifrage, and Uva-Ursi.

ALTHÆA'S ANTI-CATARRH CHICKEN SOUP

This soup relieves throat troubles and catarrh. To a cup of water, add ¼ teaspoon Chicken Soup Base and ¼ teaspoon Miso Soybean Paste. Heat on the stove at high. Add ¼ teaspoon Aji Amarillo Powder (Yellow Hot Pepper Powder), remove from heat, and add the juice and pulp of ½ Lemon. Allow the patient to dilute this with warm water to taste and temperature. For variety, add orzo pasta or leftover cooked rice while the liquids are heating, remove from heat, and add crumbled Tuna, the Lemon juice, and fresh Basil. Or make it like a combination of Stracciatella alla Romana and Avgolemono, beating one egg with Parmesan cheese, stirring it in, and adding the Lemon and Basil at the end.

FIRST AID POULTICE

All of these herbs are vulneraries or antiseptics: Knotweed, Golden Rod, Plantain, Thyme, Fenugreek, Lady's Mantle, Calendula, Fleabane, Gobernadora, and Yarrow. Combine equal parts of as many as you can obtain. You do not need them all. Mix them and place a nice "pillow" amount in as many small muslin tea bags as the mixture will fill. Store the bags in a sealed glass jar in a dark place. Always carry one bag of this mixture with you in your first aid kit or purse. If you or your family members suffer a scape, bruise, or cut, put the bag into a cup and just cover it with boiling water. Let it steep three minutes, allow the tea-liquid to cool, use it to wash the wound, and pack the herb bag on the wound as a poultice. Hold it in place with plastic wrap, a cloth bandage, or duct tape. If you can add fresh-cut garlic to the herb bag at the time of use, do so; it too is antiseptic.

WOMEN'S TONIC

Add ½ oz. Chamomile, ½ oz. Sweet Balm, ¼ oz. Cramp Bark, and ¼ oz. Spikenard to 1 quart Port wine. Let sit 24 hours, shake it, and strain. A cordial glass may be taken as needed for female regulation. Alternatively, extract the herbs in 1 pint of Brandy; the dosage is then 1 Tablespoon only.

"This Amazing Book: Hoodoo Herb and Root Medicine" by Sunræ and me is an illustrated book given away at the 2017 workshops, It is a medical companion to my 2002 book "Hoodoo Herb and Root Magic." This is a sample; the full book is available from LuckyMojo.com.

HOW TO STORE HERBS, ROOTS, AND CURIOS
Professor Charles Porterfield

THE ENEMIES OF PRESERVATION

Organic spoilage and deterioration is not a matter of happenstance or accident. It occurs by a set of natural and predictable processes. To maintain organic materials and prevent spoilage, we first need to know what causes it. The factors that affect organic spoilage and deterioration include:

- **Microorganisms**
- **Enzymes**
- **Air**
- **Light**
- **Insects, Rodents, and Parasites**
- **Physical Damage**
- **Temperature**
- **Time**

MICROORGANISMS

Various kinds of microorganisms cause spoilage. The microbes that can cause food-borne illness are called pathogenic microorganisms. These grow at room temperatures of 60° to 90°F, but don't thrive at refrigerator or freezer temperatures. They can grow in organic material without a noticeable change in odour, appearance, or taste. Spoilage microorganisms, which include various bacteria, yeasts, and moulds, grow well at temperatures as low as 40°F. When spoilage microorganisms are present, the organic material will often appear and smell bad.

ENZYMES

Enzymes are responsible for the ripening of fruits and vegetables. They cause texture, colour, and flavour changes. For example, as a Banana ripens from green to yellow to brown, not only does its colour change, but also there is a change in its texture.

AIR

Oxidation is a chemical process that produces changes in colour, flavour, and nutrient content. It results when air reacts with organic material — for example, when fats in foods become rancid, oxidation is responsible. Vapour-proof packaging keeps air out and thus helps reduce oxidation problems.

LIGHT

Organic material undergoes a chemical change when exposed to light. This can change colour, nutrients, flavour, and scent. Light affects different organic materials in different ways, depending on the kind of material and the kind of light in question. Light can also aid in the oxidation of fats. Three kinds of light can affect the rate of organic spoilage:

- **Natural sunlight**
- **Incandescent lights**
- **Fluorescent lights**

INSECTS, RODENTS, AND PARASITES

These beings require organic material to survive and damage it by eating it, laying eggs on or in it, and using it for housing or nesting materials. In these ways they make the organic material more vulnerable to further deterioration and damage.

PHYSICAL DAMAGE

Bruises or cracks on material leave areas where microorganisms can easily grow. Improperly packed materials may provide places for microorganisms, air, light, and creatures to enter.

TEMPERATURE

Organic materials deteriorate faster at higher temperatures. To slow microbial growth, enzymatic, and oxidation processes, store materials at lower temperatures. Recommended temperatures for storage areas are:

- **Cupboard or Pantry: 50-70°F**
- **Refrigerator: 34-40°F**
- **Freezer: 0°F or below**

TIME

Microorganisms need time to grow and multiply. Other reactions, such as oxidation and enzymatic action, also require time to develop. Purchase reasonable quantities that will be used in a timely fashion, especially of perishable material, to help avoid degradation arising from long-term storage.

HOW TO PRESERVE YOUR HERBS

When we purchase herbal, mineral, or zoological supplies and curios, we need to make sure that they will be stored in a way that decreases spoilage risks. However, when we harvest our own garden-grown herbs or wildcraft them from nature, we also need to know how to directly and immediately preserve the materials before we store them. The various methods of drying and preserving herbal and zoological materials include:

- **Indoor Air Drying**
- **Solar Drying**
- **Dehydrating with a Machine**
- **Oven Drying**
- **Freezing and Freezer Drying**

INDOOR AIR DRYING

Tie stems in bundles and hang the herbs upside down. Use twist-ties so you can easily tighten the bundles when stems shrink as they dry. A warm, dry spot is best; avoid the kitchen or near heaters. Wrap muslin, a mesh produce bag or a paper bag with several holes around the bundle, and tie it at the neck. A drying screen helps dry leaves or flower petals. Make your own from old window screens stapled to scrap wood or an old picture frame. Put cheesecloth over the screen, and place herbs on the cloth. Place drying screens on radiators, over floor registers, or above a cookstove — anywhere there's heat.

SOLAR DRYING

Solar drying can be as simple as placing drying screens outside until your herbs are brittle. Remember to bring the screens in at night. You can also dry herbs under the windshield or rear window of your car on a hot day. A do-it-yourself solar food dryer with stackable drying screens, a glass top to trap radiation, an absorber plate to transmit heat, and a vent for air circulation is useful, too.

DEHYDRATING WITH A MACHINE

Machine dehydrators have heating elements and a fan to circulate air. Round models with stacking trays are the most energy-efficient. Box models that allow you to remove the trays are useful for drying large items and large batches. Dehydrators range in price from $30.00 to $400.00. High-end models should feature timers and adjustable temperature controls.

OVEN DRYING

Herbs dry best at 100°F, but most ovens don't go that low, so set the oven to 250°F and open the door. Place a metal baking pan on the door, balance a cookie tray on it, and set the herbs on the tray, near the oven. The room may get hot, but the herbs will dry.

FREEZING AND FREEZER DRYING

Spread dry, clean materials on a cookie sheet, freeze overnight, and put the frozen material into sealed containers in the freezer for later use. Materials prepared this way can last for months.

LONG-TERM STORAGE

Your herbs are fully dry when you can crumble them easily, but keeping them whole retains scent longer. Zoological curios are dry when they are devoid of moisture and have shrunken slightly.

VACUUM PACKING

Vacuum sealed materials last longer than those exposed to air. Even if you use an airtight container, the oxygen left inside of the container can be enough to support mould or bacterial life. However, when you vacuum seal the material, you are removing the air from the container, and once the air is gone, moulds, and some bacteria, are unable to live or grow.

PLASTIC OR GLASS?

You can use plastic bags for storage, but plastic is not an oxygen barrier. Mylar and foil are superior, but glass is still the best. Brown and blue glass offer little protection from direct sunlight, so it is best to store dried herbs and curios in airtight jars out of direct light and away from high heat. Label your jars with the date and contents. Check new jars for droplets of moisture or mould. Throw out anything mouldy, and re-dry anything that creates moisture in the jar.

USING DRIED MATERIALS

Use about half the amount of dried herbs in a recipe calling for fresh herbs, and about a quarter as much if the dried herb has been finely ground.

This was a hand-out at the 2014 workshops. Professor Porterfield is a professional reader and root doctor; he can be reached at ProfessorPorterfield.com.

WILDCRAFTING HERBS AROUND HOME
catherine yronwode

WHAT IS WILDCRAFTING?

The term wildcrafting became popular during the 1970s to describe the harvesting and preparation of non-domestic or wild herbs, food-plants, roots, and nuts for personal use or resale.

To some people, a wildcrafter is someone who lives way out in the mountains and earns a living by digging wild Sang Root for the drug trade or harvesting Black Walnuts for sale to the shelling companies. A wildcrafter of this sort knows what is in demand and throughout the course of each season will harvest and dehydrate everything that can reasonably be expected to sell, offering the collected materials to buyers or their brokers.

To other folks, a wildcrafter is someone who harvests and dehydrates wild herbs on contract for specific buyers. When wildcrafters of this type are approached by buyers, they generally contract to gather and dehydrate from ten to fifty pounds of any given plant that is requested, allowing time for the proper season to come around. Contracted wildcrafting of this sort is an ongoing process, as it may take up to a year for a buyer's requested plants to come into season.

Among those outside the herbal drug trade, the word wildcrafter can also apply to a hobby herbalist or picker — someone who knows how to get mistletoe out of the trees and sell it door-to-door during the Winter holiday season or a person who may simply have a few secret places to collect *Boletus edulis* mushrooms to cook as a side dish for supper.

For my purposes, a wildcrafter is all of the above and more. My intention is to empower both rural and urban rootwork practitioners to become wildcrafters for themselves — to be able to identify, gather, dehydrate, and store the leaves and flowers of "wild" plants, no matter where they are found. For my purposes, any herb you pick that you did not grow yourself is wildcrafted, even if you only gather a few fallen Rose petals from a curb side planting and dry them on the dashboard of your car or take home a sprig of Acacia from a tree at the back of a grocery store parking lot and dry it on your radiator.

THE RULES OF WILDCRAFTING

There is definitely a romantic side to wildcrafting — especially if you read old novels about professional wildcrafters, such as *The Harvester* by Gene Stratton Porter, which, although it was published in 1911, is still valid today in terms of the techniques it describes and the lifestyle that it advocates. However, behind the romance, there are some hard and fast rules to be followed, no matter whether you are gathering a handful of Rosemary or fifty pounds of Fennel.

THE "DO" LIST

- **Purchase and carry a field guide:** You can also use the internet to aid in plant identification if you are wildcrafting among non-native species.
- **Take only what you need**: Pick only what you will use in one year. Plant material loses scent and potency over time; you can get more next year.
- **Allow the stand to make seeds or runners:** If you do, it will last for decades.
- **Carry collection materials everywhere you go:** A pair of clippers or shears, a drying tray or screen, a muslin bag, tags for names and dates, and a pen for marking the tags is all you'll need.
- **Invest in or develop a drying system:** Anything from a heater to a cheap plastic dehydrator will do.
- **Invest in a simple storage system:** Keep your herbs dry, cool, and in the dark.
- **Be polite:** If you want to harvest on new territory, start by offering payment or barter.

THE "DO NOT" LIST

- **Do not commit trespass.** No, you may not walk up that old lady's driveway to pick her Roses.
- **Do not harvest without explicit permission:** You need permission for each harvest. What was allowed one year may not be allowed the next. Land owned by one person may have been sold to another person and the new owner may be unfamiliar with you or your activities.
- **Do not take endangered or threatened species:** Don't break seasonal harvesting laws either.
- **Never take more than 25% of the plants:** Leave the stand of plants as intact as possible; never take the outlying or adventitious plants.

HERB GATHERING AT LUCKY MOJO

Even in the most domesticated landscape, you will find plants with magical, medical, and spiritual attributes, if you know what you are looking for. Taking my own property as a sample, i can easily locate 40 plants used in conjure. Some are California natives and some are long-lived domestics or naturalized species that originated in Europe, Asia, or Africa. There is nothing particularly unusual about where i live, beyond the fact that it has a mild climate and i do not employ aggressive weeding, pesticide use, or brush-hogging. Here's an inventory of what grows on my land and within a quarter-mile radius of my home:

- **Acacia Leaf:** Symbolizes the afterlife; the leaves are burned to develop personal power.
- **Althæa Leaf and Root:** To attract kindly spirits, increase psychic ability, heal and soothe.
- **Barberry:** Sprinkled in the paths of your enemies to bar their way and stop them following you.
- **Blackberry Leaf:** To remove evil spirits and to return evil to a person doing you harm.
- **Cherry Bark:** Efficacious in love, romance, sexual attraction, and conjugal relations.
- **Clover Flowers, White:** Used for personal purification and to drive away evil influences.
- **Comfrey Leaf:** Helps you hold onto the money you have or the money you win in gambling.
- **Comfrey Root:** Carried for safety and good health while travelling or when away from home.
- **Dandelion Root:** Drunk as tea or carried to enhance psychic dreams and second sight.
- **Eucalyptus:** To drive away pestiferous people and for personal cleansing after contact with evil.
- **Fennel Seeds:** For protection, to keep the law away, for a woman's courage, to prevent curses.
- **Fern:** Used to prevent jinxes, to remove evil spirits from the home, to help ward off burglars.
- **Feverfew:** Carried by clumsy or accident-prone people to protect them from harm.
- **Hawthorn Berries:** To keep another from trying to become your spouse's lover.
- **Holly Leaves:** For protection of the home, to invite helpful spirits into the household.
- **Honeysuckle Flowers:** A twining vine with sweet flowers, it will entangle and tie a lover to you.
- **Jezebel Root:** Attracts men with money; used in the curse of Jezebel against enemies.
- **Lavender Flowers:** For passion, romance, harmony, friendship, and cooperative love.
- **Lemon Leaves:** To cut and clear or remove old conditions and open the way to new love.

- **Lemon Verbena:** To magically break up or cause discord and strife between two people.
- **Magnolia Leaves:** Placed under the mattress for marital happiness, fidelity, and sexual attraction.
- **Mint:** To break hoodoo spells and jinxes and to gain mental strength during times of difficulty.
- **Mistletoe:** Sacred herb of the Druids; one of the three ingredients in Medieval True Love Powder.
- **Mugwort (Artemisia):** For psychic abilities, made into tea to wash amulets and crystals.
- **Mullein:** Used in dark arts and conjurations; burned with incense when raising spirits.
- **Oregano:** Said to keep the law away; also used to keep troublesome in-laws away.
- **Pennyroyal:** For peace in the home, to end family troubles and solve marital problems.
- **Periwinkle:** Placed under the mattress for love; carried to draw money and to dispel the evil eye.
- **Pine Needles:** A spiritual cleanser, draws money, drives out spirits, removes mental negativity.
- **Plantain Leaf:** An herb that is said to protect one against snakes and also against thieves.
- **Queen Elizabeth Root (Orris Root):** Used to attract men and to cause them to love you.
- **Raspberry Leaves:** Used in an herbal bath by women so that their men will not want to wander.
- **Rose Buds:** For conjugal love; combined with Lavender and Red Clover tops for love-drawing.
- **Rose Petals:** For good luck in love; to remove any love-jinxing someone has done to you.
- **Rosemary:** Protects against evil, ensures fidelity; gives a woman domination in the home.
- **Sage:** For wisdom, discernment, and decision-making; keeps off the evil eye; reverses spells.
- **Thyme:** To make money grow and stay with you; to promote good health; to stop nightmares.
- **Violet Leaf:** Worn in the shoe to attract new love, bring back a lost love, or heal a broken heart.
- **Walnut Leaf:** An herb that is used in hexing, jinxing, crossing, and break up spells.
- **Walnut Whole in Husks:** Used to rid oneself of ties to the past, to remove obsessive love.
- **Willow Leaf:** Brewed into a tea-bath for purification, jinx-removal, and cleansing.
- **Yarrow Flower:** Breaks curses, increases psychism, gives courage in dangerous situations.
- **Yellow Dock Root:** Native Americans use this root for the creation of effigy dolls for love.

This was a hand-out at the 2014 Hoodoo Heritage Festival, at which i led a wildcrafting tour of my 2-acre homestead at the Lucky Mojo Curio Co. The descriptions of the uses of these plants in conjure is supplied courtesy of my HerbMagic.com web site.

HOW TO PREPARE PETITIONS AND PRAYER PAPERS
catherine yronwode

WHAT WHAT TO WRITE UPON

ORDINARY PAPERS AND SPECIAL PAPERS

In hoodoo, the most common writing surface is paper. We do not write on lead sheets like the ancient Greeks (not available) or on wooden staves like the Scandinavians (we never got into runes). We rarely use animal skin or vellum (too expensive), but we often use parchment paper (reasonably priced). We may use gilded Asian spirit money (if we live near Asian people). We may think a 3" square Post-It note is cool (if we work the stickiness in our favour). But we most likely will use lined composition paper, unlined copy paper, fine-grain shopping bag paper, or coarse-grain grocery sack paper, neatly torn on all four sides to make a square or a triangle.

WORDS ON WAX

In addition to writing on paper, we can inscribe free-standing candles. I use a pin, a needle, a nail, or a small pen-knife for this task. Some call it "carving" the candle, but to me "carving" means using a sharp-ended, wood-handled tool to craft an image out of a cylindrical candle. That is "carving." But when we write in wax, we are inscribing, so let's call it that. No, the candle is not paper, but the writing on it sure is writing. Remember that just as we bathe upward to draw or downward to clean, we can apply directionality to candle inscription. The best way is to spiral the petition up or down the candle, like stripes on a barber pole.

HAVE YOU EVER WRITTEN ON A PLATE?

When i was young, i used to watch the Spiritual Church ladies write on white plates. Why? Well, to wash them off, of course. Water that washes off words contains those words. It is imbued with those words, and you can use it in cooking, cleaning, or baths.

WRITING ON MONEY

We prepare currency with written names, wishes, scripture, glyphs, or sigils. This includes signing a name under the Treasurer's name, adding the $$¢¢$$ sigil for trained hunting money, or marking bills with RTM for "Return To Me." We may also inscribe coins.

HANDWRITING SAMPLES

A paper that someone wrote on is a combination writing surface and personal concern. Put your command on it! If you can't get a person's handwriting, why not? Proximity makes for effective magic.

CHECKS, BUSINESS CARDS, AND LOGOS

If your spells concern businesses or bosses, if you face a court case, are seeking a job, or are trying to get a loan, write on paper connected to the enterprise. Ask for or take business cards, print corporate logos off the internet, save notes handed to you at work. These are personal concerns as well as papers.

PLAYING CARDS

Professor Porterfield advises us on playing cards as papers: "The names of clients or targets are easily written onto the heads or feet of the appropriate royal cards with a Sharpie. Add in a birth date and a simple command, and these cards quickly become effective and stylistic name papers. If the card was touched by the target, so much the better, as it becomes a personal concern as well as a symbolic proxy of the person."

ALUMINUM FOIL AND POPSICLE STICKS

Bet you never thought Greco-Roman defixiones and Swedish runkafles would be so modern and up-to-date, did you? Two words, folks: *Aluminum Foil*. Before you wrap a freezer spell in foil, use a soft pencil to impress commands all over the foil. And you know those disposable aluminum pie plates? You probably already use them for burning candles, so now you know to write on them before you set the lights. And don't forget the popsicle stick that someone licked: Write the person's name and your command on it!

PHOTOGRAPHS

Photographs have been around since the mid-19th century. My oldest ancestor who lived long enough to have his photo taken was born in 1794. But people still sometimes balk at using a photo as a name paper. They think it's not "authentic." Oh, yes it is, and with digital technology, you never have to ruin a relic. Just scan the photo and print another later.

WHAT TO WRITE WITH

STYLUS

A stylus is a writing tool that leaves marks but does not emit ink or graphite. We use pins, needles, nails, and knife-points to inscribe candles or wax, or to mark on aluminum foil, pie plates, or the cups that tea-lights come in. A worn-out soft-lead pencil can also be used as a stylus on aluminum foil or pie-plates.

QUILL, DIP-PEN, AND FOUNTAIN PEN

Bird feather quill-pens, metal-nibbed dip pens, and fountain pens still continue in use because they allow one to work with specially prepared and colour-coded inks. Dyed quills are also colour-coded: white for writing petitions of healing, blessing, and protection; red for love and sex; green for money and luck; and black for reversing, revenge, and crossing.

PENCIL

Pencils come in two types, those with erasers and those that were made without erasers. A wise old woman once told me to write petitions with pencils that were made without erasers, "so you can't go back on your word." That resonated with me, and i have been using church pew pencils ever since. It's not a "rule." I just happen to like the way they look and feel.

BALLPOINT, ROLLERBALL, AND MARKER

Moderns pens can be used to write a petition. You can select them by colour (red for love is a common choice) or by base (water-based to wash into water, a permanent marker for use out-of-doors or on a metal or glass surface) or just go with what you've got. If you are writing on laminated playing cards, try a Sharpie.

MAGICAL INKS

The three old-school European magical inks — Dove's Blood Ink, Bat's Blood Ink, and Dragon's Blood Ink — are still manufactured, for those who use feather quills. Of course they are not made with blood, but they are nicely scented, Some old spells ask for petitions written in blood, but frankly, you will see that sort of stuff more often in the movies than in real rootwork.

OTHER STATIONERY SUPPLIES

Have scissors, tape, and glue. You'll need them.

IS REPETITION NECESSARY?

How many times should you write out a name?

My firm belief is that there is no one answer to this question. It depends on what you wish to accomplish, the kind and size of paper you have, where you will be putting that paper, and whether anything will be written on the paper in addition to the name. Sure, some folks who have been in this work for a long time do have favourite numbers — three, seven, and nine are often cited — and they instruct those whom they teach to repeat a name their favourite number of times, almost every time they teach:

"Write his name nine times on a sheet of virgin parchment."

"Write the boss's name three times on the back of his business card."

"Write his name seven times, then turn the paper 90 degrees clockwise and write your name seven times to cross and cover his."

"Write his name twice, diagonally from corner to corner on the back of the business card, like an X."

Those are indeed common instructions, but just as common, and not counted, are these instructions:

"Write his name over and over and over on both sides of the paper, down one side and up the other, very neatly, in rows."

"Write his name as many times as he is years old."

"Write out the entire Psalm with his initials in place of each verse number in the Psalm."

Not only do certain practitioners have favourite numbers, there are also certain ways of working that more or less lead the practitioner to prescribe a certain number of repetitions. For instance, if a worker likes square rather than rectangular papers, repeating the name an odd number of times to form a block will become habit. On the other hand, if the worker makes tiny little tobies, the notion of writing the name only one time will assert itself, because you can't write a name seven times on a paper small enough to seal into a silver locket. In a case like that, you may hear the worker say:

"I want you to write your name one time, really small, on a slip of paper no larger than the kind of paper that comes in a Chinese fortune cookie."

The truth is, some spells will be told with specific numbers cited, and others will not. Sometimes the choice is yours. Get used to it!

"Paper In My Shoe" is a 96-page book i wrote and published in 2015 for my workshop of the same name. These sample pages are adapted from the book, and the entire volume is available from LuckyMojo.com.

HOW TO USE CHARMS AND AMULETS
Ms. Robin

HISTORY OF AMULETS AND CHARMS

Amulets, talismans, and charms are small curios or ornaments that people wear for protection or to bring good luck. Some of us use them in casting spells or work with them at our altars; some keep them in our homes, at our jobs, or in our vehicles. Many of us wear charms on our persons as jewelry, hang them on keychains, or carry them in our pockets, and some people even tattoo charm symbols on their bodies.

Despite the fact that scoffers say that charms are superstitious, they actually have a lot of power. People of all cultures have carried and worn charms in everyday life, for luck, happiness, gambling, protection, and health. Going back as far as the ancient Egyptians, you will see their use of amulets, such as the ankh, which looks like a cross with a loop at the top. The ankh was worn for protection and was also known as the key of life, but before you call that superstitious, remember that we in modern days use a cross to symbolize Jesus' resurrection and wear it both as a religious symbol and as a protective charm.

Conditions: We can look at charms by the conditions they are used for. To give an example, a lot of times you will see an amulet like an eye-bead in a baby's crib or a car; these are generally for protection. Other charms are used for gambling, such as the well-known Rabbit foot or Alligator foot. For general luck, some people hang horseshoes over the door or carry Buckeye nuts or Mojo Beans. To draw or keep love, they may wear jewelry in the form of a heart.

Materials: Another way to look at charms is by what they are made from. Some are natural curio objects, like lucky rocks. Some are man-made, but their power is associated with their everyday use, such as coin charms to draw money. Some are man-made designs that represent items from nature, like a wishbone made of silver. Some are cultural symbols such as numbers, colours, letters, words, or graphic emblems that represent people's beliefs and wishes.

Working with Charms: Finally, we can examine how people use perfumes, powders, oils, incense, or prayers to enhance, prepare, dress, or consecrate their amulets and talismans.

NATURAL CURIOS AS CHARMS

Alligator Tooth: This is a most powerful charm, used for hundreds of years, mostly for gambling. People put herbs inside the hollow and seal it, after which it is called a loaded Alligator tooth.

Alligator Foot: The Alligator's paws grab, so this charm symbolizes grabbing the money. Place a silver dime in its palm, wrap it with green thread, and place it in a green flannel bag to get and protect money.

Alligator Head: This is used as protection by placing it at the front door to send away intruders an unwelcome guests.

Badger Tooth: This is believed to be very powerful in gambling and games of chance like cards, slot machines, or the racetrack. Put Blessing Oil on it and say Psalms 23 to bring you luck.

Black Cat Bone: These are used to cross or hex people; they are also used to reunite old lovers.

Raccoon Penis Bone: This is used for gambling and for personal or sexual power. You can wear it as a necklace or keep it in a pocket or by the bed.

Rabbit's Foot: People use this for good luck or to clear off evil; it is one of the most popular luck charms.

Pyrite: This powerful mineral brings good fortune. People use it on altars, put it in oils, place it in mojo bags, and carry it in a pocket when gambling.

Lodestone Grit: This draws power. Add Magnetic Sand and Pyrite to make it stronger. It is used in many hoodoo practices as a mineral.

Cat's Eye Shell: This shell is used to ward off the evil eye or any misfortune caused by envy.

Cowrie Shell: This draws money, casts off evil and promotes fertility because it is in the shape of a vulva.

Herbs: These herbs are lucky and can be placed in a bag with a charm: Alfalfa, Allspice berries, Cinnamon, Five-Finger Grass, and Bayberry root.

SYMBOLIC LUCK CHARMS

Horseshoe: Hang a real horseshoe over a door to stop evil from entering or to bring in luck. Carry a small one in the pocket or purse for gambling or love luck.

Money Bags: The money bag is to help you with financial prosperity. This charm can be carried on a keychain or necklace or you may put it on your altar.

Four-Leaf Clover: The four leaves stand for faith, hope, love, and luck. It is used to cast off evil, for protection, for luck, and for love. They are popular as jewelry, on a keychain, or in a pocket.

Crown Charm: This charm means wisdom, divine power, great strength, rulership, and success.

Heart with Arrow Charm: This is a classic love charm. It is a heart smitten by Cupid's arrow.

Seals of Solomon and Moses: These Jewish charms go back before Christ. They are talismans that you need to use with a pure body and spirit, and a focus on what you're trying to get. There are many types, for safety, treasures, protection, health, and power. Draw one on a piece of paper and anoint it with oil. Send it up with a prayer, use it as a petition paper, or wear it in your shoe or wallet.

Norse Rune Talismans: Some of these look like Seals of Solomon, but they are from Scandinavia. They are carved on bone and come in many styles, for love, luck, health, court cases, war, and protection.

Lucky 7 Charm Bracelet: This bracelet holds seven rings or seven small keys: 1 is for long life, 2 is for good friends, 3 is for health, 4 is for love, 5 is for wealth, 6 is for peace, and 7 is for happiness.

Wear these charms upon your wrist
And let the luck they hold exist.
By turning one from left to right
Your luck will last from morn till night
All seven complete the lucky week;
Each day provides the wish you seek.

Dice Charm: Dice is a game of chance. People feel they are lucky by hanging dice in their car. You can also anoint them with oils and carry them on you.

Praying Hands Charm: This represents belief in God, and a prayer for blessings, health, or grace.

Money Tree: A small representation can be worn as a charm, but the larger Money Trees are placed on an altar or by the front door of a business.

Glass Eye Bead: This blue anti-evil-eye, called a nazar, is carried or worn for protection against jealousy.

LUCKY MONEY AS A CHARM

British West Africa Half-Penny: This has the protective Star of David on it to protect your money.

Silver Mercury Dime: It is for gambling luck, to warn of evil, and to protect those who wear it at the ankle or neck. It is thought that if black magic is put upon it the colour will change to dark grey or black.

Buffalo Head Nickel: This has been used for a long time as for gambling and for protection.

Shiny Brand New Cent: This symbolizes new beginnings and good luck in money-getting.

Silver Note: This is a rare old one dollar bill and if you have one you're already lucky. People put this in their mojo bags or keep one on their money altar.

Two Dollar Bill: This is the most popular bill used in hoodoo. Place it on your altar and cover it with Pyrite and Lodestone to bring you money, or dress it with Money Drawing Oil and put it in your wallet.

DRESSING YOUR AMULETS

These dressings can enhance your lucky charms:

- **Van Van Oil or Incense**
- **Blessing Oil or Incense**
- **Money Drawing Oil or Incense**
- **Lucky 13 Oil or Incense**
- **Lucky Number Oil or Incense**
- **Love Me Oil or Incense**
- **Stay With Me Oil or Incense**
- **Essence of Bend-Over Oil or Incense**
- **Protection Oil or Incense**
- **Special Dice Oil**
- **Hoyt's Cologne**
- **Whiskey**

Ms. Robin York wrote this flyer for her 2016 HHF workshop on amulets. A member of AIRR, she can also be contacted via her own RobinsMojo.com web site.

SEW MUCH HOODOO: TEXTILES IN CONJURE
Gabrielle Swain

UNDERGROUND RAILROAD QUILTS

In 1829 transportation by rail became possible throughout the United States. In the South, slavery was the lot of most Black people, but in the Northern states and in Canada, freedom and liberty were possible. The term "Underground Railroad" was coined to reflect the new mode of transportation; it referred to the organizations and individuals who helped slaves escape from the South by passing them from "station" to "station" until they were free.

Oral history is varied and often romanticized, and one persistent idea concerns the use of hand-pieced quilts as signals for escape routes along the Underground Railroad. Quilt patterns have names, and many stories tell of coded messages hidden in the designs and pattern-names of quilts that were hung out on clothes lines along particular paths to freedom. As a textile historian with an interest in hoodoo, I am asked if there is any substantiation of these treasured tales.

Unfortunately, historical studies have not uncovered any evidence that the "Underground Railroad Quilts" are more than beautiful folktales carried down through many generations. Still, these family stories hold deep meaning for those who carry them on, as they should for all folklorists.

Academic and textile historians feel that more study on the work of Harriet Tubman and Levi Coffin is crucial to the true migration stories. Concentration on their efforts and risks gives insight that myth and folklore may overlook — yet myth and folklore are the archetypes of our lives. To close with a favourite quote from the excellent book, *Bound for Canaan: The Underground Railroad and the War for the Soul of the South* by Fergus M. Bardevich:

"In an age when self-interest has been elevated in our culture to a political view, the Underground Railroad has something to teach: that every individual, no matter how humble, can make a difference in the world, and that the importance of one's life lies not in money or celebrity, but in doing the right thing, even in silence or secrecy, and without reward. This truth doesn't need to be encoded in fiction in order to be heard."

GEE'S BEND QUILTS

As with other old quilting traditions, the style that developed in Gee's Bend, Alabama, began during the 19th century when enslaved Black women, perhaps influenced in part by patterned African textiles, pieced together strips of cloth to make bedcovers for their families. Their work continued after Emancipation, through the Great Depression, and to the present day.

Gee's Bend quilts can best be described as jazz in cloth. Their innovative designs are unlike the common patchwork patterns seen elsewhere. Folk art collectors, historians, and curators understand the importance of this legacy, not only because Gee's Bend traditions arose from slavery, but also because this art style was original to the circumstances of the women's lives. They were singing the songs of not only oppression, but also of joy.

Gee's Bend quilting is active and vibrant to this day, through the Gee's Bend Collective, a self-owned and operated organization of more than 50 women. Every quilt is unique and is individually made. Gee's Bend quilts have been exhibited at the Whitney Museum, the Philadelphia Museum of Art, and the Museum of Fine Arts in Houston, Texas. Michæl Kimmelman, a noted art reviewer from *The New Yorker,* stated, "Some the most miraculous works of modern American art have been produced by these women."

BASIC SEWING SUPPLIES

The crafting of drawstring bags for mojo hands; the fabrication of stuffed dolls for love or cursing; and the insertion of charms, packets, and petitions into clothes and bedding are all accomplished by means of the domestic art of sewing. These are the basic sewing supplies every conjure worker needs:

- Needles
- Straight pins
- Needle threader
- Thread to match fabric to be sewn
- Thimble
- Scissors — sharp point; only used for fabric
- Permanent black cloth marker — fine-tipped
- Fabric glue
- Polyester or cotton stuffing

HEART SACHETS

Wearing or carrying sachet packets has a long tradition in hoodoo. Since heart sachets imply a message of love and affection, they will convey particular requests. Heart sachets can be strung together in a garland for a baby's room, over a bed, or in a dressing room. Individual heart sachets are perfect for dresser drawers or to carry on you. A heart garland strung on ribbons can be sewn or glued together. Heart bracelets or necklaces are made using the same technique. A heart necklace properly dressed and blessed will be especially potent in conveying your words or wishes to influence others.

Copy the heart pattern from this page and use it as a guide to cut two hearts from your fabric. Thread a needle using a matching thread. Sew around the heart, leaving 1/4" of fabric outside the stitching. Leave a 2" space open — un-stitched — on the left side of the heart. Next clip into the "V" of the heart, but do not cut the stitching. Leaving 1/8" of fabric before the stitching is sufficient. Turn the heart inside out, so the stitching is hidden.

Using the 2" opening, fill the heart with love herbs. You could also add a petition paper or blessing folded into a small square in the middle of the stuffing. When the heart is stuffed, fold the open edges in by 1/4". Apply a light line of fabric glue to one of the folded edges. Press the other folded edge to the glued edge and hold in place until dry. The heart is now ready for use.

This pattern may be enlarged to suit your needs.

A PILLOWCASE FOR DREAMS OF YOU

To make sure your man or woman dreams of you, returns only to you, and follows your desires or commands, choose a pillowcase of the appropriate colour for the work. Write your petition with a fine line permanent pen on one side of a narrow ribbon. Turn the pillowcase inside out and stitch the ribbon near the hem at the bottom. Be sure to use a thread that matches the colour of the fabric. Turn the pillowcase right side out and dust it lightly with an appropriate sachet powder as you place the pillow in the case.

KEEP THEM UNDER FOOT

Using a permanent marker, write the name of the person you want to keep under your foot on the cloth or leather insoles of your shoes. Dust the insides of your shoes with an appropriate sachet powder just as you would with foot powder, then bless or petition the work for your desired results.

KNITTERS AND HOOKERS

Relax, hookers are crocheters — just a loving term knitters use. An easy way to work your will is to make a simple scarf. Use hair collected from your brush or that of another person, according to your intent. Comb it with an anointed pocket comb. Use natural fibers for your scarf. Lay the hair next to a strand of yarn and knit or crochet it into the scarf. As you work repeat your desires, blessings, or protections for the receiver of the gift.

SOMETHING FOR THE LADIES

Use a permanent marker to write the name of the one you desire inside the crotch of your panties. Not at the waist band, but close to your private area. Lightly dust the panties with a sachet powder, such as Come To Me or Love Me. Be sure to state your intent or say a prayer as you do this work.

A SIMPLE KNOT SPELL

To bind your man, wet a piece of soft cord with his semen. Begin, but don't close, a knot in the cord. Call his name, and when he answers, pull the cord tight, sealing the knot and catching him.

The award-winning quilt designer Gabrielle Swain gave this talk at the 2016 HHF workshops. A professional tarot reader, she is online at Facebook.com/mgabrielle.swain.5.

MAKING MAGIC WITH TAROT CARDS
Valentina Burton

USING THE TAROT IN SPELLWORK

I think we have all read about using tarot cards for magic using a strategy in which the worker selects and lays cards out flat and makes them act out the desired outcome. Instead of reading the cards to see what will occur, they place the cards to create the result they wish. To be clear, these instructions are great; they just aren't how I prefer to work.

What I have noticed, in doing magic myself and in teaching it to others, is that the most effective magic takes into account what are called "learning styles" in education. Some folks learn and retain information best by hearing the information, some by reading or seeing it, and some by physically interacting with it. I have noticed that some of my students will have spectacular results simply by creating a visual representation of the desired result. With others, this will have no effect. Some will have great results from either speaking the desired result or hearing it spoken, and many will have the best results from a physical representation and interaction with objects that clearly represent the successful outcome of the magic.

I believe that effective magic must contain some elements of the kinesthetic, as most people display a mix of learning styles, and the physical is so basic. Just looking at an arrangement of cards will not be effective for anyone who is not primarily visual.

The cards of the Rider-Waite-Smith (RWS) deck are extremely useful for my way of working magic with the tarot. Because the illustrator Pamela Colman Smith was actually a set and costume designer, many of the figures she drew seem to be on a stage. They have a theatrical feel, as if they were ready to enact a play. Additionally, RWS decks come in several sizes, which suggests the idea of a small character moving through a larger scene. (If you don't have multiple decks, size the images up or down on your printer.)

Here is an example of how I work with the cards:

First, I select a significator card for my client and add personal concerns to it. I may choose two cards; one is the client at the beginning of the journey, and the other is the client at the end. I glue them together with a bit of hair in between them.

I then select cards to represent the scenery: where the client is now, a path to the goal, and the goal. I manipulate the cards physically to move from "now" to where the client will be, like playing with paper dolls. Let's say my client is a Scorpio, so he is a King of Cups. He desires to be in a King of Coins situation — financial stability. He also has no idea how that could happen. Since he has no pre-conceived plan, his "journey" cards need to reflect that. So, for his "scenes" I choose The Fool, The Wheel of Fortune, and the Ten of Pentacles.

I get a giant RWS deck or blow up the size of the cards on a printer and print out a really large Fool, Wheel, and Ten of Pentacles. I cut the Fool out of his scene and discard him, and mount the three scenic cards on foam core or cardboard. I use small easels to prop them up. I then print out copies of the King of Coins and the King of Cups from a small or miniature RWS deck, and glue them back-to-back with the client's hair and foam core in between. I have a double-sided King card and three "scenes."

Ready to do the spell, I dress a candle and light appropriate incense. I speak in first person and present tense as I move the King through the scenes, using the client's full name as I narrate what is happening to him. First he is propelled into the Fool's world, then he goes around the Wheel, but only from the bottom to the top, then into the prosperous Ten of Pentacles, where I stick him with some tape.

One tip: trimming down the goal of the magic to the *feeling wanted* works better. Everything boils down to feelings anyway! For example, you think you want that job, but what you actually want is the feeling you imagine having that job will give you. You don't actually want that lover, you want the feeling you believe you will have of being adored and in love. That particular person or job is not the only thing that could give you those feelings! If you focus only on the thing you think will give you the feeling you desire, you are placing a layer of requirement between you and the result. The magic will take longer and the result will be more difficult to achieve.

AIRR member Valentina Burton is a Palm, Tarot, and Astrology reader in Dallas, Texas. This flyer was part of her presentation at the 2018 Festival.

OLD-TIME SACHETS, BATHS, and INCENSES
Lewis de Claremont

SACHET POWDERS

THE COMPOSITION OF SACHET POWDERS

Sachet powders are mixtures in the form of moderately fine powder, which are to be inclosed in the little sacks of cloth and placed with linen or wearing apparel or stationery, etc. Sachets are preferred by some to "extracts," because there is no fear of using too much and thus making the user appear "loud" or vulgar.

The objection to sachet powders is the want of permanency; they are liable to lose their odour even if carefully preserved, and the purchaser may therefore receive a sachet powder which can not be compared, in strength or delicacy, with a good extract. For this reason sachets are "freshened" by the addition of the corresponding extract, viz., Violet Sachet by Violet Extract. The best ingredients are required to make good sachet powders; indifferent ingredients cannot but produce poor products.

Sachet powders are composed of two kinds of ingredients, viz., the "body," or vehicle, and the odorous agents. Fine sachets almost invariably contains Orris Root as a scent; this may be combined with Rose Petals, Orange Peel, Lavender Flowers, or other scented herbs. Occult Sachet Powders are made by adding 10% of the consecrated oil that the devotee desires to the basic mixture. When the quality of volatile oil is very small, it may be advantageous first to dissolve in a small amount of alcohol.

In preparing sachet powders, scented herbal ingredients such as Orris Root, Rose Petals, or Lavender Flowers should be ground in a mill. Musk, Civet, Ambergris, Vanilla, and Tonka should be triturated to an intimate mixture. Solid or gum resins, like Benzoin, should be contused in a mortar until reduced to moderately fine powder. After preparation, these ingredients should now be mixed, placed in a large mortar, the oils, tinctures, and other liquids added, and the whole mixed intimately by trituration.

Sachet powders should be preserved in rather small, well-stoppered bottles in a location of moderate temperature and be protected from light.

FORMULA FOR MAKING A SACHET POWDER

• Orris Root	8 parts
• Lavender Flowers	4 parts
• Patchouli Leaves	2 parts
• Cloves	1 part
• Musk	1 part
• Pimento (Allspice)	1 part
• Sandalwood	6 parts
• Scented Oil as desired	10%

BATHS AND WASHES

BAUME TRANQUILLE
FROM THE FRENCH CODEX

This preparation of *The French Codex* consists essentially of fixed oil holding in solution the active matters of certain narcotic and aromatic plants. According to the *Codex,* the fresh narcotic plants, such as Belladonna, Henbane, Black Nightshade, Poppy, and Stramonium, are boiled with Poppy seed in a copper kettle until all their water is driven off; then a gentle heat is maintained until the oil is expressed and the Essential Oils of Rosemary, Lavender, Peppermint, and Thyme are added.

MODERN FORMULA
FOR BAUME TRANQUILLE

• Oil of Lavender	2 c.c.
• Oil of Peppermint	2 c.c.
• Oil of Rosemary	2 c.c.
• Oil of Thyme	2.c.c.
• Infused Oil of Hyoscyamus (Henbane), sufficient to make 1000 c.c.	

CHINESE WASH

• Chinese Oil	1 dram
• Liquid Oil Soap, prepared, if desired	
• Distilled Water, @ 30 degrees centigrade, enough to make 4 oz.	

Pour entire amount of oil into distilled water and shake thoroughly. Mixture should become cloudy and resemble milk. Keep well covered. If made with liquid soap, dilute with water when using.

7 HOLY SPIRIT BATHS

In my many years of contact among the true Chelas, students of the occult practices, I have found that a great percentage of them, before starting on something new for themselves or for anyone coming to them for guidance and advice, would recommend them to take a series of Holy Baths.

The series would usually be seven and they would suggest that they be taken either seven days in succession, or on seven alternate days, that is; take one, skip a day, and so on, for 14 days. Each bath would be of a different oil, each of a different strength, so as to gradually induce, as they would call it, the protective covering over all the body, keeping all evil away and permitting them to start removing whatsoever condition existed and driving away all Crossed Influences or Spells. My procedures would be as follows:

A person would take Bath Oil Number 1, retire into the bathroom and undress, filling the tub with water and, while the tub was being filled, repeat the Apostolic Constitution for the sanctification of objects; and note that with a few changes, this can be used as well for incense or talismans: *"Do thou now sanctify this (oil), through Christ, in the name of (N.N.), and give to it the power of producing health and of driving away disease, of putting to flight Demons, of dispersing every snare through Christ our Hope. Amen."*

After consecrating the oil, one would say, *"Oh God, who art the Creator of all things, strengthen, I beseech thee, thy poor servant, that (s)he may stand fast, without fear through this dealing and work. Enlighten, I beseech thee, Oh Lord, the dark understanding of thy creation, so that (his or her) work may be of avail to help (his or her) fellow servant through these troublesome times."* Then, putting one hand into the water, say, *"And thou, Oh inanimate creature of God, be sanctified and consecrated and blessed to this purpose (of washing all evil off of him or her who bathes) in thy everlasting holiness. Lord, thy will be done on earth as it is in Heaven; make clean our hearts within us and take not thy holy spirit from us. Amen."*

The next bath would follow the same procedure with Bath Oil Number 2, the third with Bath Oil Number 3, etc., for a total of 7 Holy Spirit Baths.

WHITE LAVENDER WASH

- Oil of Lavender Flowers   50 c.c.
- Alcohol, sufficient to make 1000 c.c.

RED LAVENDER WASH

• Oil of Lavender	8 c.c.
• Oil of Rosemary	2 c.c.
• Cloves Powder	5 grms
• Red Saunders Powder	10 grms
• Myristica Powder	10 grms
• Saigon Cinnamon Powder	5 grms
• Alcohol, sufficient to make	1000 c.c.

BUSH BATH, HERB BATH, CONDITION BATH

• Male Lavender	1 lb.
• Blue Bottle Flowers	3 oz.
• Rose Buds, siftings	1 lb.
• Thyme Leaves	2 oz.
• Rosemary Leaves	1 lb.
• Mentha Piperita Leaves	2 oz.
• Lemon Verbena Leaves	8 oz.
• Salvia Officinalis Leaves	2 oz.
• Issue Peas	4 oz.
(pea-sized pieces of peeled Orris Root)	

Take 4 oz. of the mixture and put into a large jar, to which add 2 ounces of cooking salt. For the Bath, take out a handful of this mixture, put into a muslin bag and put this into the tub, letting the hot water run over it and squeezing it, to get out all its fragrance.

FORMULA ONE FOR MAKING INCENSE

• Powdered Sandalwood	30%
• Powdered Frankincense	40%
• Powdered Myrrh	10%
• Powdered Cinnamon	10%
• Powdered Orris Root	4%
• Powdered Patchouli	3%
• Powdered Saltpeter	3%

FORMULA TWO FOR MAKING INCENSE

• Powdered Vetiver Root	15%
• Powdered Sandalwood	50%
• Powdered Myrrh	15%
• Powdered Frankincense	10%
• Powdered Yara Yara	5%
• Powdered Winters Bark	5%

"Legends of Incense, Herb, and Oil Magic" by Lewis de Claremont was first published in 1936. This extract is from the restored and revised 96-page edition that i produced for the Lucky Mojo Curio Co. in 2016 and gave away at my workshop on the Library of Occult Classics project. The entire book is available from LuckyMojo.com.

HOW TO MAKE YOUR OWN SACHET POWDERS
Papa Michæl Bautista

A BLENDED HISTORY

Magical powders entered hoodoo through Congo sorcery's use of foot-track tricks, blowing powders, and drawing powder designs. Scented body powders in envelopes, or sachets, especially when worn for love, have a European origin. In hoodoo we call both African and European style powders "sachets."

TOOLS FOR MAKING POWDERS

MORTARS AND PESTLES

A mortar and pestle set provides a quick way to grind herbs into fine powder. The pestle is the wand with a rounded end; the mortar is the bowl. The substance is ground by rubbing, pounding, or twisting it between the pestle and the wall or floor of the mortar.

FOOD PROCESSORS AND GRINDERS

Food processors and coffee grinders quickly rip large particles into small pieces. They are noisy and they do not always produce uniformly-sized particles, so use a sieve after grinding or finish by finely hand-grinding the materials in your mortar and pestle.

FILES AND RASPS

Files and rasps reduce tough or fibrous materials like wood or metal to powder. They come in many shapes and are rated by the fineness of their cut. Single-cut files have one set of parallel teeth; cross-cut files have two, creating diamond-shaped teeth. Single-cut mill files are very effective in creating particles. A rasp is similar to a file, but it has bigger teeth and provides larger particles of material.

CLASSIFIERS AND SIEVES

A flour sifter excludes chunks, but better results are had with a stack of classifier sieves that sort particles by size. Sieves are rated by space between the wires of the screen, using the ASTM E11:01 Commercial Sieve Mesh Dimension Standard Mesh numbering system. A number 10 sieve, 2000 microns, will sort out large stems, root balls, and rocks. A number 60 sieve, 250 microns, is a good size for powders.

SELECTING MORTARS AND PESTLES

You may wish to keep multiple mortar and pestle sets, each dedicated for work with certain materials. These are factors that go into their selection:

Size: Palm-sized hand-mortars are an ideal size for grinding small batches of powder for home use; large table-top mortars are better when making products for sale. You may find it handy to have two different sizes.

Weight: The heavier the pestle, the more force applied when crushing or grinding. Cast iron and brass are the professional druggists' standards, but a heavy pestle will put some strain on your wrist and arm.

Absorption: If a mortar and pestle set is porous or absorbent, the oily and gummy residues of what you ground in it will transfer to the next substance that you grind. Metal, stone, and ceramic absorb the least, wood absorbs the most. Lava stone provides crevices to which gummy residues may adhere.

Durability: Some materials will break under heavy use sooner than others. Marble gives long use if you do not expose it to lemon juice or vinegar. Acacia and oak can take regular use for a long time, but may develop cracks. Cast iron or brass can last a hundred years, but the equipment is heavy and not portable.

- **Wood:** Wood is a good surface for grinding soft herbs, but not hard roots or minerals. It is porous and thus subject to the absorption of oils.
- **Ceramic:** Ceramic mortars and pestles are capable of grinding substances very finely. They are fragile, but they make good hand-mortars.
- **Stone:** Stone is beautiful, but if not conditioned properly, fine particles of stone can get ground into the spices. Don't grind metals in stone.
- **Metal:** Cast iron, brass, and stainless steel are durable but require a sturdy work surface. Brass is softer than iron; don't grind pyrite in brass.

Toxicity: A mortar and pestle used to grind toxic substances must never be reused to grind herbs that will be employed in making magical or mundane teas or foods. Do not keep it in the kitchen; place it with your magical tools and label it clearly.

USING A MORTAR AND PESTLE

Warning: Use caution when pounding; tools can break if they are struck too hard. Fragments of items being ground may fly up.

Procedure: Place the material in the mortar, filling it no more than ⅓ full. Process your materials in small batches. Use the pestle to work your material to the desired consistency. Hold the mortar in place with one hand and use the pestle in your opposite hand. Pound or use a twisting motion to grind against the ingredients and the mortar so they are worked against its bottom and sides. Continue to work the material until the powder is as fine as you want.

Focus on the Work: Most people think that all you need is a good mortar and pestle to grind herbs into powder and =(BAM)= you have a magical powder. Is that all there is to it? No, not exactly. What makes the difference between a bowl full of powdered herbs and a sachet powder? The answer: Spiritually connecting to the work while grinding your ingredients. Your willed intent and physical effort energize the mixture. Some herbs come in convenient pre-ground form, but they may not be fresh and "alive." Likewise, if you use an electric grinder, it will be difficult to concentrate as the machine whirs. It's okay to use these conveniences, but after mixing in pre-ground herbs or turning the electric grinder off, hold the powder container in your hands and focus on it; mix the powder with a stirring stick or your bare hands to add in the spiritual energy lacking in pre-ground or machine-ground ingredients.

Prayer: Enhance the power of your powder by praying a Psalm or prayer over it. You can pray while you grind ingredients or place the finished powder on a candle altar for a specified period of time. Recite Psalms 37 for protection, Psalms 23 for abundance and good luck, and the Song of Songs 1:2-3 for love.

Clean-Up: Always clean your mortar and pestle between materials and after use by simply brushing out the mortar and wiping the pestle with a clean cloth or paper towel. Wooden sets can be cleaned with warm water if dried completely before storing. Don't use soap; it can leave a residue that will be mixed in with your materials. Oils and gums can foul tools so that they cannot be cleaned; to remove stubborn resins, grind dry white rice in the mortar. The rice will take on the colour and smell of the last substance you worked. Discard the rice and repeat the process until the rice remains white after grinding.

RECIPES FOR MAKING POWDER

Carriers: Sachets may include a base or carrier powder like Arrow Root, Rice powder, Corn starch, talcum, kaolin, cascarilla, sulphur, ash, or dirt. The base should suit the use; for instance, Arrow Root, is better than dirt for a dream powder to dust on bedding.

Colouring: Add food colouring or paint powder if you like powders colour-coordinated with their intent.

Weight versus Volume: A teaspoon of Pyrite and a teaspoon of Basil do not weigh the same. When using recipes, be aware that "parts" generally refers to volume and "ounces" always refers to weight.

Adapting incense Recipes: Any incense recipe can be adapted for use as a sachet if, after grinding, you add an equal amount of carrier powder. Try these:

PROTECTION SACHET

• **Oregano**	1 part
• **Cloves**	½ part
• **Caraway**	½ part

LOVE SACHET

• **Catnip**	1 part
• **Cloves**	½ part
• **Rosemary**	½ part
• **Dill Weed**	½ part

DEPLOYING SACHET POWDERS

Dressing: Use powders to dress candles, papers, shoes, or persons; draw sigils on altars or in dirt; hide them in room corners or under rugs, or add to mojos.

Sprinkling: Sprinkling distributes powders through the earth. Sprinkle in a seed-casting gesture while walking backward and praying or cursing your target. You could walk backward an odd number of steps.

Blowing: Blowing distributes powders through the air. To clear a space of evil, blow a blessing powder and say a prayer to the four directions. To draw money to a room, blow a prosperity powder to all four corners. You may also blow a powder on or toward a person.

This was a hand-out at the 2015 Hoodoo Heritage Festival. Papa Michæl Bautista is the proprietor of Torch and Key at TorchAndKeySpiritualSupply.com.

DIRTS, DUSTS, AND POWDERS IN FOLK MAGIC
Papa Gee

THE MAGIC OF DIRTS AND POWDERS

Graveyard dirt is probably the most well-known magical dirt in African-American rootwork. In using it, you are calling upon the spirits of the deceased to bring about magical change. You may tap into their ancestral love for you, ask for the use of their talents or professional skills, or you may seek to use their aptitude for deceit and criminal activity.

Beyond the graveyard, there is magic to be found in the soil of specific places that correspond to the situation you are dealing with, such as using dirt from a bank to help get a loan.

Sprinkling powders, also known as sachet powders, have also been a part of hoodoo for many years. A large portion of their ingredients have traditionally come from the earth, including powdered minerals, herbs, roots, and sometimes graveyard dirt.

And finally, not all dusts are mineral-based. Culinary powders also play a part in folk magic.

COLLECTING GRAVEYARD DIRT

There are a number of methods for collecting graveyard dirt, but it is largely agreed upon that it should be paid for in some way. Coins are a widely-accepted method of payment but some choose to leave flowers, alcohol, or lighted candles on the grave.

I pay my way into the graveyard by asking the spirits inside if I may enter. I quiet my mind and listen to hear the answer. If it is "Yes," I drop nine pennies on the ground outside the entrance.

Take with you an inconspicuous hand shovel or a large spoon and a plastic bag. If you don't have a specific person in mind, stand in the graveyard and ask who wants to help you and let your intuition guide you. Loosen the earth with your spoon, pull back the sod, dig the dirt from beneath, drop a silver dime (or three) into the hole and replace the sod.

I remove dirt from the head of the grave for positive work, from the heart for matters of love, and from the feet for baneful magic.

THE SOIL OF SPECIFIC PLACES

I mentioned how dirt from a bank can be used the purposes of getting a loan, but it would be especially useful if you were filling out a loan application at the bank the dirt was collected. This type of sample could also be used for all types of prosperity work.

Another source for abundance work is dirt from a mine. Using the flame from a green candle, burn a two-dollar bill and collect its ashes. Mix thoroughly in the mine dirt along with a little Cinnamon powder, and store in a paper bag. Use to sprinkle over your glass-encased money candles and inside your wallet.

Dirt from a church can be used in spiritual matters, prayers, and petitions. Some consider this a good place to collect dirt for love work. For matters of marriage collect dirt from the church you were actually married in to use as an ingredient in work that strengthens your bond.

For protection, gather dirt from seven different churches and mix with dirt from your own property. Pray over for seven days using Psalms 54 then redistribute the dirt onto the four corners of your own property line.

Dirt from a family home or homeland may be used to help connect with the spirits of your ancestors or strengthen your connection to the past. You can incorporate the dirt with that of your own property or in plantings to bring that ancestral connection to your property. Take this soil and place it in a fire-safe bowl and use it to hold offertory candles on your ancestor altar.

Dirt from the property of an enemy could be hard to obtain and may require a midnight stroll to pull it off. The edge of their yard works just as well as the center so be cautious in your collecting. To get a neighbour to move away, mix their yard dirt with Catnip and Magnetic Sand and divide into three parts. For three nights in a row, drive across town and dispose of each part in another neighbourhood. To encourage them to move even further away, dispose of it onto railroad tracks.

BASIC GOOFER DUST RECIPE

Goofer dust is a traditional mixture used in African-American hoodoo to bring grief, trouble, bad luck, illness, and even death to an enemy. Graveyard dirt is generally an ingredient. Some choose dirt from the grave of a criminal, but this can be difficult to find since so many criminals are cremated in prison. I use the mounded dirt from newly dug graves, calling in all the spirits who wish to help me. Recipes vary; this is mine:

- **Graveyard Dirt**
- **Sulphur Powder**
- **Black Pepper Powder**
- **Cayenne Pepper Powder**
- **Salt**
- **Mullein Leaf Powder**
- **Sage Powder**
- **Powdered Insects or Verminous Animals**

The exact amounts used are less significant than the intentionality you use in making it. After mixing it, spread out a thin layer and write into it your petition or words that signify your intention to bring hate, despair, illness, confusion, trouble, pain, or loss. Three common ways to deploy Goofer Dust are to sprinkle it where your enemy walks, sew it into a doll of the enemy, or tie it into a bag placed under their house.

SACHET POWDERS

Sachet powders could be considered "manufactured dirts." Sometimes called "blowing powders," they have traditionally been compounded with natural ingredients such as Arrow Root powder, Corn starch, and Orris Root powder, with talc or bentonite clay. Depending on their use, other powdered herbs, flowers, spices, and even zoological ingredients are added. Their scent comes from the same essential oils found in anointing oils, tapping into the magical power of those plants.

The most famous sachet is Hot Foot Powder, spread where an enemy will walk to "poison them through the feet" and force them to leave your life.

A love sachet powder can be sprinkled where someone walks, but can also be dusted onto love letters, bed sheets, and cards.

Sachet powders can be worn on the body or dusted onto objects someone will touch. I usually blow them onto my candles before they are lit.

CULINARY POWDERS

Here we reach beyond dirt, dust, and powder magic to create edible meals and treats to feed to those whom we wish to affect. If you think dusting the skin with powders is powerful, just consider the impact when culinary powders travel throughout the body.

Most of the time, edible powders are used for work that is positive, sweet, and loving, or to influence another. It is, of course, relatively easy to convince people who are close to us to eat our magical foods, but only use ingredients that you would normally cook with. It is our intention to influence those around us – not to cause bodily harm to someone in a way that might potentially land us in jail. Our "powders" will take the form of sugar, flour, spices, and herbs.

When I was young, my Grandmother started the tradition of making Cinnamon toast for Christmas morning breakfast. She would wake early and spread butter on plain bread then use her fingertips to sprinkle white sugar across the surface of every piece. She would then take a spoon and carefully shake powdered Cinnamon on top of the sugar then bake in the oven until the butter bubbled into the sugar and Cinnamon. This is an excellent recipe for a simple abundance meal. Cinnamon has long been used in hoodoo for money and prosperity. The bread is all the basics in life, the sugar represents all the sweet things coming your way, with the butter binding all these wishes together. Prepare ahead by writing out a petition and placing it into the sugar bowl three days before cooking.

If you are a cook who is creative with magic, the possibilities are endless. Mix flour, salt, pepper, seasonings, and a tiny pinch of sugar together for a fried chicken batter. Before rolling the chicken through it, take a fork and repeatedly write the names of you and your love into the mixture. Pray that with every bite they will think of all the savoury, spicy, and sweet things your relationship provides them. Use this same method of drawing petitions and sigils into the dry ingredients of the cakes you take to neighbours, the muffins or brownies you bring to fellow employees, and the cornbread you bake for gatherings.

Papa Gee wrote this flyer for a workshop he gave at the 2019 Festival. His lives in Nashville, Tennessee, where he runs AromaG's Botanica and the Aromagregory Company. He is a member of HP and AIRR, and the author of several books on soapmaking and spiritual oils.

HOW TO LOAD SOAPS AND BEAUTY PRODUCTS
Co. Meadows

LOADING MORE THAN CANDLES

Those working within the hoodoo, conjure, and rootwork tradition are familiar with the loading of candles for various types of spell-work. With a little research you will discover that loading items did not begin with candles, and that historical examples of this type of work in Afro-cultures and communities is exemplified through the sealing up of hollows within trees, animal horns, gourds, wooden dolls, and more. As the United States moved beyond slavery and we African-Americans were able to keep more personal possessions in our own homes, rootwork tricks of loading items evolved to include additional aspects of life, such as beauty and home products.

A wide variety of everyday products and items in your home can be loaded or fixed for use in your conjure work. Health and beauty products are an excellent way to make direct contact with a desired target on a daily or near daily basis. Traditional hoodoo operates within the framework of contagious magic, and as such, this daily contact will strengthen your work and make it more powerful.

SOAP

Traditionally made from lye and tallow, soap is an incredibly versatile tool. Soap can be fixed with roots, herbs, and oils as it is made, and there are many hoodoo soaps available for a variety of conditions. Commercial soap is also sold in a variety of scents useful in rootwork. Bars of soap can also be carved, anointed, or hollowed and loaded with herbs, roots, and oils in the same way that candles are loaded.

A LOVE DOLL CARVED FROM SOAP

This work comes to us from *Hoodoo Spiritual Baths: Cleansing Conjure with Washes and Waters* by Aura Laforest, and is used to draw a lover to you:

"Carve a love doll from Patchouli or Rose scented soap, name it for your lover, and talk to it every time you bathe, rubbing it on your body, and telling it how much you want love. As the doll shrinks over days of use, tell your lover that his resistance is melting and that he must come to you."

SHAMPOO AND CONDITIONER

Shampoo is a liquid soap. Conditioner is used to aid with tangles and does not rinse completely from one's hair. Both of these products accept the addition of oils well. A pinch of powdered herbs or a sprinkle of sachet powder is also unlikely to be noticed.

PEACEFUL HOME HAIR CONDITIONER

Miss cat of LuckyMojo.com advises us that an excellent way to bring peace to a household of people is to make this simple Peaceful Home recipe with everyday hair conditioner:

"To a bottle of your family's favourite brand of hair conditioner add a pinch each of Rosemary, Basil, and Angelica powder that you have held in your hands and rubbed together. Next add a few drops of Peaceful Home Oil. Stir up the bottle with a Bamboo skewer or a chopstick, then cap it and shake it while praying aloud, *"May all who use this conditioner find love and peace in the home."* Let your family use this dressed conditioner, and as they do they will spread peace throughout your home."

BODY POWDERS

Commercial foot and body powders traditionally used talc as their base. Because breathing talc can damage your lungs, today many of these powders use a corn starch base. Ground herbs, minerals, or pre-packaged sachet powders can be added to foot and body powders to fix them to your needs.

PROTECTIVE FOOT POWDER

This trick was contributed by Christy Porterfield:

"To protect your man without his knowledge, use Dragon's Blood Ink to write out Psalms 23 on a petition paper. Burn the paper to ash as you recite Psalms 23 aloud. Add the ashes to his foot powder, close the container, and pray a heart-felt prayer for his protection and strength as you shake the container to mix it well. Replace it in its usual place, and he will unknowingly dress his own feet daily."

SALVES AND OINTMENTS

A salve is a fatty base that has been used to extract the essences of herbs used to treat various conditions. Any neutral solid fatty substance can be used as a base, or you can start with a pre-prepared ointment like Black and White Ointment or Bag Balm.

BLESSED SALVE

Professor Porterfield shares this old-style recipe:

"Start by emptying a large tin of Watkins Petro-Carbo First Aid Salve into a bowl. Mix in a heaping handful of Blessing Herbs Mixture. Whip the herbs in well. If the mixture is being prepared for a man, pray Jeremiah 30:17 over it. If preparing the salve is for a woman, pray Numbers 12:13 over it. If preparing it for all-purpose use, say Psalms 6:2 over it. Replace the salve into its tin. Apply it to cuts, scrapes, minor burns, and what ails you."

COSMETIC BEAUTY PRODUCTS

You can add spiritual supply oils to beard oil, perfume, cologne, loose face powder, body lotion, and pump-style hair spray. Use your imagination!

BEARD OIL FOR LOVE AND SEX

Beard oil can be loaded on the sly to produce a variety of effects. Choose an oil to match your desired result, such a Love Me Oil, Come To Me Oil, I Dominate My Man Oil, or Nature Oil. While alone in your target's bathroom, add a few drops of the chosen oil to his beard oil. Replace the cap, and as you shake the bottle to mix in the oil, say a quiet prayer expressing your desires. Replace the bottle where you found it, and he will be none the wiser.

DRESSING CHILDREN'S HAIR

This trick can be found in *Women's Work: Home-Style Hoodoo Spells for Marriage, Sex, and Motherhood* by Aura Laforest:

"As you comb, brush, pin up, braid, or fix your children's hair, you have the perfect opportunity to introduce some magic into their lives. Crown of Success Oil is especially appropriate for dressing the head. Add it to conditioners or lightly smooth it in by hand as you fix their hair."

PEACE TO THE HOME SOAP

This working is designed to aid in bringing peace to your home. You will need:

- **2 small "hotel" size bars of soap**
- **Mixed Rosemary, Angelica powder, and Basil**
- **19 1/2" blue and white variegated embroidery floss cut in two, 11" and 8 1/2" long**
- **Peaceful Home Oil**
- **A toothpick or bamboo skewer**
- **A Peaceful Home petition of desires**

Name one bar of soap for you and those like-minded in your home, and name the other bar for the one or ones with whom you desire peace. Use the toothpick or skewer to carve the respective names into each soap. Tie nine knots along the length of each piece of embroidery floss. These two knotted lengths, one longer and one shorter, will be used to create a crossroads to connect and tie the soaps together. Write a petition stating your desire to bring peace between those named on your soaps.

Place the petition, Rosemary, Basil, and Angelica between the two soaps, with the names facing inward. Wrap the soaps longways with one strand of knotted floss while speaking aloud what you desire from your target, then wrap the remaining knotted floss shortways around the soaps while stating what you bring to compliment the target. Once the cross is made and the bar is wrapped, tie the two pieces together to signify a binding peace between you. Using your index finger, dress the longways floss with Peaceful Home Oil while expressing your desire for this blessing to manifest. Then dress the shortways floss while expressing your gratitude and how you will use this blessing to help others. Finally, place a five-spot of Peaceful Home Oil on the outsides or backs of each of the tied soaps.

Place the tied soap on the window sill overnight on the Dark of the Moon, and start using it the next day. By the Full Moon, peace will descend upon your home, understanding will be the power of your breath, and love will be the foundation that gives life to all. *Ase a merci!*

AIRR member Co. Meadows wrote this text for his workshop presentation at the 2017 Festival. He offers readings, rootwork, and his own line of spiritual products through Co. Meadows Conjure, which can be found online at CoMeadows.com.

HOW TO USE FIGURAL CANDLES
Mama E. and Clayton James

MALE AND FEMALE

The male and female candles are used to represent people. These candles may be utilized for a variety of spells like love, reconciliation, break ups, arguments, control, binding, and cursing. In hoodoo, the colour of the candle indicates the purpose of the spell (see the other side of this flyer for guidance). The advantage of these figural candles is that you can find them in every colour and use the appropriate sex of your targets.

HOW TO PLACE THE CANDLES

Candle spells should always be burned on a safe surface. We use metal plates to prevent cracked porcelain dishes. The manner in which the figures are placed depends on the type of spell being performed.

- **Love**: Next to each other, face-to-face.
- **Break ups or arguments**: Back to back.
- **Control, binding, or cursing**: Facing forward.

MOVING CANDLE SPELLS WITH FIGURALS

When working on moving reconciliation or attraction spells, place the figures at a distance, but facing each other. After the figures are carved, and dressed in oil and powders, they are placed at the edge of your working plate and the candles are lit. The appropriate prayers are made and the spell is left to burn. After five minutes, move the candles a little bit closer to each other. Repeat this process until both candles are touching each other, and allow them to finish burning.

When doing a spell to break up, or to distance two people, prepare the spell and place the two figures back-to-back, then light the candles. After five minutes, move them a little bit away from each other. Repeat this process until both candles are at the edge of your plate and let them burn down.

Control, binding, and cursing may be cast on one person or several at the same time. These spells are usually done facing forward, and the candles are prepared according to the spell's aim. In the case of control, cursing, and binding, one can use wire, screws, and nails to control or torment your victim.

CHARGING THE CANDLES

To charge the candles, carve a small hole on the bottom of the figural candle and insert personal concerns, herbs, oils, minerals, or powders. Cover the hole with the wax you carved out. Use a lighter or another candle to melt the wax over the opening so that it forms a seal to keep the material inside.

SKULL CANDLES

Skull candles are mainly used to influence an individual. The colour of the candle symbolizes the intention of the spell, and the oils, herbs, and powders combine to achieve the spell's aim. The best part about skull candles is that they can be charged at the bottom or any other available orifice. Christening the candle in their name and using their personal concerns solidifies the connection between the individual and the candle, and the other spell materials influence the person in a positive or a negative manner as intended.

While skull candles are usually used alone, they can also be used with other candles to refine a spell. For example, if you are trying to influence your target to financially prosper, you can use a skull candle in the center of the spell area and surround it by two green candles (for prosperity) and two yellow candles (for opening the roads). Place the candles at the front and the back (green), and at the left and the right (yellow) of the skull. This symbolizes the crossroads. The candles should be prepared appropriately with oils and herbs for money. The skull should be charged with personal concerns, and a petition paper placed beneath.

This flyer was distributed at the 2018 Festival. Mama E. is a member of the Association of Independent Readers and Rootworkers, a graduate of catherine yronwode's HRCC, and the owner of Dr. E. Products Legacy. She is available for rootwork and personal consultations through ConjureDoctor.com. Clayton James is the founder of Transcendent Candles and an integral part of Dr. E. Products Legacy. As Dr. E.'s life partner, Clayton learned and benefitted from his many years of experience across countless traditions, practices, and spiritual circles. He can be reached at TranscendentCandles.com.

MOVING CANDLE SPELLS
Doctor Beverley Smith

THE MOVING FLAME

Candles are ancient. Originally made of tallow or beeswax, and later of paraffin or mineral wax, they have been burned for millennia, not only for practical lighting purposes, but also as part of religious and spiritual ceremonies. The use of the candle in hoodoo went through a transformation during the industrial revolution, reflecting new methods in the commercial production of candles and their distribution throughout the country by rail. In the early 20th century the invention of aniline dyes came about, and the coloured candle was born.

New Orleans, diverse and rich in cultures, is where the marriage of Roman Catholic candle burning and African-American folk magic took hold, both for use in prayer and in laying tricks. Good things travel fast, and by the late 1940s this new style of candle magic was firmly established throughout the South.

THE OLDEST MOVING CANDLE SPELL

Books like *Legends of Incense, Herb, and Oil Magic* by Lewis de Claremont (1936), *The Guiding Light to Power and Success* by Mikhail Strabo (1941), and *The Master Book of Candle Burning* by Henri Gamache (1942) transmitted the new styles of candle work. Gamache's book was the first to provide detailed instructions for dozens of moving candle spells, but this type of work was already being performed in New Orleans several years earlier.

In February, 1940 the Anglican minister and folklorist Harry Hyatt was wrapping up four years of collecting conjure spells from 1,600 African-American practitioners when he recorded an early example of what we now call a "moving candle spell." In this version, each candle stays in one place, but the series of candles inches its way toward the worker. His informant was a woman living in Algiers, Louisiana:

This spell was set into standard spelling and annotated by cat yronwode from Harry M. Hyatt's 5-volume, 4766-page collection of folkloric material, *Hoodoo - Conjuration - Witchcraft - Rootwork*. She has also created a reference page of the informants at: **LuckyMojo.com/hyattinformants.html**

TO RETURN YOUR LOVER

"*If your loved one is gone, your man or your husband, or whomsoever, and you want him back, you get nine pink altar candles and a sheet of white parchment paper, and write his name nine times on the paper, like a list. I tried this myself. What I am telling you, I did that myself. So I know.*

"*Set the paper on the table with the head of the paper facing you, and set the first candle at the bottom name, farthest from you. And every candle you set, you set it up higher, toward you a little, one name at a time. The first candle you put down at the bottom of the paper on the first name, right there. After you have burned that one, see, you set the next candle at the second name. And each candle is on the next name.*

"*Now, when you go to light each candle, you wash it. You wash your candle first, but you turn it bottom upward so that the wick won't get wet, and you wash it off only at the bottom with clean water and just let the water drip off it. Then you light that candle.*

"*And then you get that Temple Incense. That goes with those candles. [Temple Incense was a popular brand at that time, equivalent to Lucky Spirit Incense.] You burn that incense. You put a little dribble of it, say a dram, in a saucer. Then you put the candle in another saucer and you burn that light on the paper. See, each kind of candle has an incense that makes the smoke that goes with the reason for burning that candle.*

"*Now, sometimes in burning these candles it'll bring your man back before nine days. And he'll come unexpectedly. When he appears at the door, you've got to rush back and pinch it out. Don't blow it out. You'll have to wet your fingers and pinch the light out.*

"*I burn these candles in a zinc wash tub, because, you know, a candle is something that catches fire sometimes if it falls over. So you put both saucers and the paper in a tub and you burn it in your private room where you sleep. That means in your bedroom, not in your front room, but right in your back bedroom; neither in the side rooms nor the hall. You've got to burn it right where you sleep, in your bedroom, to bring back your loved one. It's got to be right there, where you're at.*"

TOPPLING THE TOWER

For this social justice work, carve each knob of a black 7-knob candle with these words, one per knob:

Racism, Homo/transphobia, Capitalism, Misogyny, Police State, Corruption, Classism.

This is the Tower of Injustice. Dress it with Destruction and Damnation Oil and roll it in herbs of commanding and crossing. Insert a pin into each knob of the candle. Set the candle on a heatproof dish in the center of your Justice altar atop a Seven of Spades playing card that has these words written one per edge:

Police Brutality, School-to-Prison Pipeline, Racial Disparities, White Superiority.

Prepare four oil lamps or purple helper candles dressed with Justice Oil and herbs for success, victory, and control. Under each, set a petition paper asking for the qualities written on the paper to be removed and otherwise withheld from the power of the Tower. Surround the Tower with them. As the lamps are moved the petition papers will be moved with them.

Each day burn a new knob as you also burn the lamps of success, resources, cooperation, and determination. Each day move the lamps further from the Tower. At the end of the week the black candle will be completely burned. Take the remains of the wax along with the pins and playing card and discard by burying them in a graveyard or tossing them into a river. I enjoy tossing these remains into the bag I use to clean up after my dog's feces and toss it over my shoulder into the garbage truck on trash days.

After toppling the Tower and disposing of the spell remains, carve each knob of a white 7-knob candle with these words, one per knob:

Equality, Due Process, Accountability, Truth, Justice, Freedom, Liberty.

Dress it with Justice and Success Oil, and roll it in success and blessing herbs. Place it at the center of your altar, with the four lamps still at the farthest points. Each day light the candle and the lamps and and burn one knob, with the lamps representing success and determination moved closer to it. By the end of the week all the knobs are burned and the four lamps have moved into tight formation around it, representing the forces of good replacing the forces of evil and division.

We are now surrounded by the forces of success, determination, and cooperation. The remains from this part of the spell may be buried on-site or carried to the grave of a truth and justice worker for safekeeping.

I perform this spell once a month, beginning seven days before the New Moon, with the Tower completely toppled on the Dark of the Moon, and the seven-day healing beginning immediately on the New Waxing Moon, for a total of 14 days.

TRIPLE TITANS OF PROTECTION

This moving candle spell for protection begins by placing a candle and a photo representing you or your client in the center of your workspace, with the candle on a flameproof dish atop the photo.

Use three candles to represent your pillars of protection, or "Triple Titans." Onto these candles carve three names, one per candle. These names are the powers that you will call upon to be your Triple Titans.

My name suggestions include the Holy Trinity; Maiden, Mother, and Crone; Truth, Righteousness, and Justice; Blessed Mother Mary and Saints; or a trio of archangels or guardians.

Arrange the Triple Titans around your personal candle at a distance. Begin on the New Moon, and each day for seven days, light your candle and pray Psalms 59:1-4, then light the Triple Titans and burn them for 15 minutes. Each day move the Triple Titans closer to your candle before you light them, invoking their protective shield around you. On the last day they will form a tight triangular wall of protection around your personal candle.

This spell can be revised for gambling luck by using three Aces dressed with Hoyt's Cologne and dusted with Lady Luck Sachet Powder attached by a pin to the three Triple Titan candles. Dress each candle with a condition oil for luck, and recite Psalms 41 for prosperity. Repeat this spell monthly over a 7-day period that ends on the Full Moon.

This flyer was prepared for use at the 2017 Hoodoo Heritage Festival workshop by Doctor Beverley Smith. A natural empath with a soft spot for those in "the sporting life," she is a mother, lover, rootworker, and artist who finds her joy exploring the vast fields of Spring wildflowers of the Southern California deserts.

OUR FAVOURITE LODESTONE SPELLS
Susan Barnes, Madame Pamita, Miss Michæle,
Valentina Burton, Marin Graves

THE JACK POT LODESTONE MOJO
BY SUSAN BARNES

The night before you make this mojo, talk to the Lodestone and tell it it's going to take a bath. Treat it like a living, breathing thing with a soul that wants to work for you. Place it in a jar of Hoyt's Cologne or Crown Royal Whiskey. The next day, take it out of the jar, dry it, say nice things to it about money, and name it with a name that reminds you of wealth, such as Jack Pot. Dress it with Lodestone Oil and a sprinkle of Magnetic Sand.

Sew a silver charm representing money to a purple Crown Royal bag. Write a petition like "Money come to me!" Write it five times. Write "[My Name] a winner" five times over the petition. Place a hair or a nail clipping in the center of the paper. Five-spot the paper with Money Drawing Oil. Fold the petition toward you four times and put it in the mojo bag. Always be talking about money and prosperity during the time you are doing this. Thank God for bringing you the money. Praise God. You can also play music while working; either gospel music or songs about money.

In the bag put your Lodestone, your petition with the hair or nail clipping inside it, a pinch of Alfalfa, and a pinch of Cinnamon.

To bring life into the Jack Pot Mojo, open it up and breathe into it while focussing on your intent. Be very focussed on what you want. Tell the mojo to work for you, but in a nice way. Close it up. Tie it three times and knot it up. Using Money Drawing Incense or Lady Luck Incense, pass the mojo back and forth over the smoke. You'll feel it when it's ready; then take Money Drawing Oil or Lady Luck Oil or Crown Royal Whiskey, and five spot that mojo.

When you win any money, take the Lodestone out and say, "Jack Pot, thank you for that money!" or whatever you'd like to say to it. Feed it to reward it. Give it some Lodestone Oil and a little bit of Magnetic Sand. Put the Lodestone back in the mojo.

Do not let anyone — and I mean anyone! — see your Jack Pot Lodestone Mojo. If they do, you're gonna have to remake it from scratch.

FIERY LODESTONE SPELL FOR LOVE
BY MADAME PAMITA

This spell is to attract someone for love.

You'll need these ingredients: 13 small red candles (birthday candles or chime candles will do); a condition oil for passionate love such as Bewitching Oil, Fire of Love Oil, or Kiss Me Now Oil; a finely-cut love herb such as Patchouli, Damiana, or Catnip; a pair of Lodestones anointed with Lodestone Oil and fed with Magnetic Sand (one representing you, one representing your love-target); and a long platter, cookie sheet, or tray.

Dress the candles in the condition oil of your choice and roll them in the herbs. Affix the candles to the tray, platter, or cookie sheet in a single line. Place the two Lodestones in front of the two "outer candles" on the ends of the line. Light the two outer candles only (the ones next to the Lodestones) saying, "My true love, you are drawn to me as irresistibly as these stones feel the pull toward each other," and let these candles burn completely.

The second night, move the Lodestones a step closer so that they are in front of the new "outer candles" and light these candles only as you repeat the intention and speak your petition or prayer.

The third night, move the Lodestones to the new "outer candles" and repeat the ritual as before.

Each night over six nights, you will move your Lodestones in front of a new pair of "outer candles" — moving them closer and closer, until finally, on the seventh night, you will have both Lodestones touching in front of a single candle.

On this night, you will say, "My true love, we are together, and together we will remain in love and passion until I part these Lodestones."

When the single candle has completed burning, you may move your Lodestones together and place them on an altar for love, hide them under your bed, or carry them together in a single bag in your pocket or purse as a powerful love talisman.

TO DRAW UNKNOWN FRIENDS
BY MISS MICHÆLE

Make a set of little paper dolls or buy a set of Guatemalan "worry dolls." Name each doll for a type of friend you would like to have: "Adventurous," "Supportive," "Imaginative," "Loyal," etc. Each doll can have several different qualities. If using paper, write the desired qualities on each doll. For worry dolls, whisper the desired qualities into each doll.

Put a steel pin through each from head to foot; not to harm them but only to make them magnetizable. (For worry dolls, you may need several pins, or you can sew a finishing nail or paperclip to its back.) Prepare and feed a large Lodestone. When it is ready, Recite 1 Corinthians 13:5-8. Pick up the pinned dolls with it and put it in a place of honour in your home. If necessary, you can arrange the dolls by hand so they completely cover the Lodestone. Recite Psalms 133. You can do this spell a few dolls at a time over a period of three, seven or thirteen days, if you wish.

FOR REPEAT READING CLIENTS
BY VALENTINA BURTON

This is to keep my reading calendar always full.

Mix these 13 ingredients in any proportion to create 6 cups of herbs, then grind it to powder: Allspice, Basil, Boldo, Bayberry root, Calamus root, Cinnamon, Deer's Tongue, Dill seed, Fenugreek seed, Five Finger Grass, Licorice root, Gravel root, Irish Moss. Speak into the mix and tell it what to do, then add Lodestone Grit and Magnetic Sand to it (as much as you wish), and talk to it some more.

I have a medium-sized bucket of bottled waters by the door in my working space. Some of this mix goes into the bottom of that bucket. It just looks like sand in the bottom, but it tricks all of those waters, which are consumed by clients in session with me or when I offer a water to them as they go out the door.

I also use the mix in a wooden box that holds the printed-out natal charts of all my clients. I consider the charts their personal concerns. I layer the charts with handfuls of the mix. I rub the wooden box with Money and Attraction Oils. If things ever get slow, I would burn candles on the box to stimulate business, but since I have begun doing these two Lodestone Grit tricks, things have never been slow — in fact, I actually have a hard time getting days off!

LODESTONE FOR SELLING A HOME
BY MARIN GRAVES

Obtain two paired Lodestones, a red flannel mojo bag, 2 oz. of Lodestone Grit, and a wallet-sized photo of the home you wish to sell.

Separate your paired Lodestones and hold one in each hand. Consecrate them by telling them what it is they are being implored to do: One will securely remain at the home, while the other will diligently search for a buyer and draw that individual to the home, ultimately reuniting the Lodestones that so desperately want to be reconnected.

Place the Lodestone that was held in your left hand somewhere on the property near the entrance, perhaps in a potted plant by the door, near the base of a hand rail, or to the side of a stepping stone.

Set the Lodestone that was held in your right hand inside the red mojo bag, along with the Lodestone Grit and the photograph of the home. Place the bag in your purse, car, or place where you will have access to the mojo when you come and go from your home. Every time you have complete your intended tasks away from home, center yourself for a second and visualize your home. Open the bag, take a small pinch of the Lodestone Grit, and sprinkle it in an inconspicuous location, anywhere there is foot traffic and someone will be magnetized. After placing the Grit, see the energy trail from the location of the Lodestone Grit, all the way home, until you reach and walk past the planted Lodestone near your front door. See the enormous energy and attraction to this home, drawing the two Lodestones back together, and drawing the buyer.

Once you have secured the buyer for the home, collect the Lodestone you had placed at your door, reunite it with the Lodestone in the mojo bag, and bury them in the bag on the property at the close of escrow.

"Our Favourite Lodestone Spells" was a hand-out at the 2015 Hoodoo Heritage Festival panel discussion. Susan Barnes is a member of AIRR; she can be reached at SusanBarnesAuthor.com. Madame Pamita is a member of AIRR and is available at ParlourOfWonders.com. Miss Michæle is a member of AIRR; she can be found via HoodooFoundry.com. Valentina Burton is a member of AIRR and she is available at ValentinaBurton.com. Marin Graves is a member of AIRR; she can be contacted via MarinGraves.com.

SPELL PAPERS AND SIGIL MAGIC
Angela Marie Horner

MAGIC AS OLD AS HUMANKIND

Sigils, runes, glyphs, and symbols have been used as magical writing for as long as people have woven spells to send our will into the universe. Pictographic writing came before written systems of recording language.

Magical sigils and seals attributed to the Biblical Moses and King Solomon were first published in English translations in the late 19th century. Since then, generations of Pennsylvania Dutch, African-American, and Jamaican folk magicians have copied or printed them onto parchment paper and employed them in candle magic, as petitions folded into tobies and mojo hands, or by dissolving them into liquids to drink or bathe in. Beginning in the late 20th century, some hoodoo practitioners enlarged their repertoire by adding the sacred veves or glyphs of Haitian Voodoo to the earlier Jewish and Christian emblems.

For a deeper understanding of this history, see *"Paper in my Shoe"* by Catherine Yronwode and Chapter Ten of *"Legends of Incense, Herb, and Oil Magic,"* by Lewis de Claremont.

Working within and expanding this old tradition, I have developed a unique form of hoodoo sigil magic that, in addition to the traditional Jewish versicles and planetary-angelic names, incorporates Norse Futhark runes, Icelandic galdr bind runes, and personal glyphs. The sigils I most often use include the following:

- **Futhark Runes:** Runes used by Scandinavian people as a form of alphabet and a means of magical writing.
- **Solomonic and Mosaic Seals:** Magical angelic, planetary, and Biblical talismanic designs attributed to ancient Hebrew wise men.
- **Glyphs:** Seals composed of artisticly combined words; they may also incorporate symbols that remind us of words or phrases.
- **Galdr Bind Runes:** Phrases or magical spells fashioned into glyphs; the Icelandic ones here employ the Norse Futhark alphabet and were originally carved into bone to create amulets.
- **Astrological Symbols:** Symbols that denote planets and the signs of the zodiac they rule.

YOUR NAME AS PERSONAL SIGIL

To make your name into a sigil you only need to decide what you want it to look like. You can use the Roman alphabet or some other language you are familiar with. Think of J. R. R. Tolkien, who used his initials in an artistic way as his signature.

You can arrange your letters to look like an animal or a design. Take your full name, John Doe Smith, and drop all the letters that repeat, leaving JohnDeSmit. Use runes or other characters to replace these letters and make a bind rune or some other picture out of them.

My preference is to use the Futhark runes :

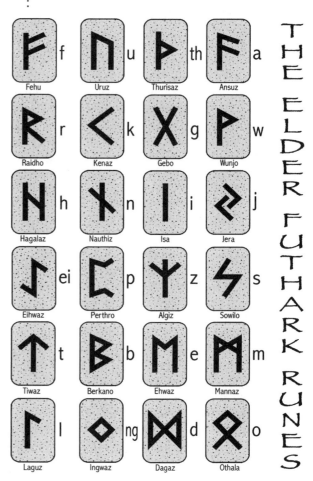

THE ELDER FUTHARK RUNES

SIGIL WORK AS A PERMANENT SPELL

My style of sigil work, which can be called a spell page or spell paper, is a collage of sigils, glyphs, photos, and petitions, that come together to make a powerful spell that cannot easily be broken.

The Spell Star is your base. See the colour insert. Place a symbol, or the client's photo, at the center. You can also use a Solomonic seal, astrological chart, tarot card, or other image as your base.

Use Red Ink if possible. I print out or draw all of my images on parchment paper. Whenever possible, I use red ink to print or write the glyphs and sigils, for red represents the blood power in the work.

Place Seals at the Star's points. Solomonic or Mosaic seals, angelic images, tarot cards, galdrbok bind-runes, astrological symbols, and other icons of power are glued to the circles at each point. Write petitions, names, or dates on the back of each before gluing. It is wise to familiarize yourself with the runes, sigils, and symbols you wish to use in your work.

Write your overall petition in the double circle. The spell, which you may also speak aloud as a chant, is written within the double circle. Futhark, English, or Hebrew letters, or glyphic symbols can be used.

Place Guardians in the four corners. These Guardians can be more sigils, planetary or zodiacal signs, pictures of ancestors, angels, or people, or other watchtower type symbols of your choice.

Correspondences add yet another level. You may make your collage in a certain planetary hour or with the Moon in a particular zodiac sign. Colour magic may also inform your choices.

YOUR SPELL PAPER TELLS A STORY

Your spell paper should read like a story, with the subject or client placed in the middle of the whole. The design depends on the spell you are casting and the intent of the story you are telling. Do not forget to add a name paper and / or a petition on the back of each paper as you glue it to the Spell Star.

Completed spell papers can be affixed to or laid under candles, set on silver trays for use with jar spells, placed under the marriage bed, or hidden from view by being inserted behind a framed photo or art print.

BIRTHING YOUR SPELL INTO BEING

Follow this basic plan, according to your own style:

Birth the spell into being as you place your images in the physical world. When birthing the work, visualize what you are trying to accomplish. Focus on your intention as you choose the pieces for your collage. Now pull this thoughtform into the physical world by placing it on the parchment paper.

Baptize the spell page by flicking or spritzing it with Florida Water, Holy Water, or Life Everlasting tea. Do not soak the page unless it is to be steeped and drunk.

Smoke the papers in a mix of Abramelin Incense and Life Everlasting flowers to bring them to life. You can smoke each piece or the whole page when finished. Then, once a month, smoke the spell in a mix of Frankincense, Life Everlasting, and a condition incense selected to keep the magic working.

Your spell paper is intended to be permanent. It can sit on your altar space so you will always see it first thing when you are ready to do your work. Only by destroying the spell paper do you end the spell.

PUTTING YOUR SPELL TO SLEEP

When done with the work, either set it aside or put it to sleep by smoking it with Vervain, Lavender, and Abramelin Incense, thus putting it to "bed" — using a box dedicated for this purpose and large enough for the page to go in unfolded.

KILLING YOUR SPELL

Finished spells that are "snuffed out" should be ritually killed with respect. The spell is a living, breathing thing, so its death may require a trip to the graveyard to bury it, or you may consecrate a special place in the backyard as a spell garden or spell cemetery. If the intention is to break a curse, burn it to release the subject from the condition and then set up protection to keep the curse from returning. Be prepared, for if you are very sensitive you may experience a spiritual response to killing the spell.

Angela Marie Horner is member of AIRR, a reader at HP and MISC, a Certified Massage Therapist, and a First Aid instructor for the Red Cross. This workshop was presented at the 2018 Hoodoo Heritage Festival.

ASTROLOGICAL SYMBOLS

Astrological symbols distributed at Angela Marie Horner's 2018 workshop on sigil magic. The upper three rows are Planetary. The lower three rows are Zodiacal. They can be copied and cut up for use with the Spell Star layout facing page 65.

GALDR BIND-RUNES

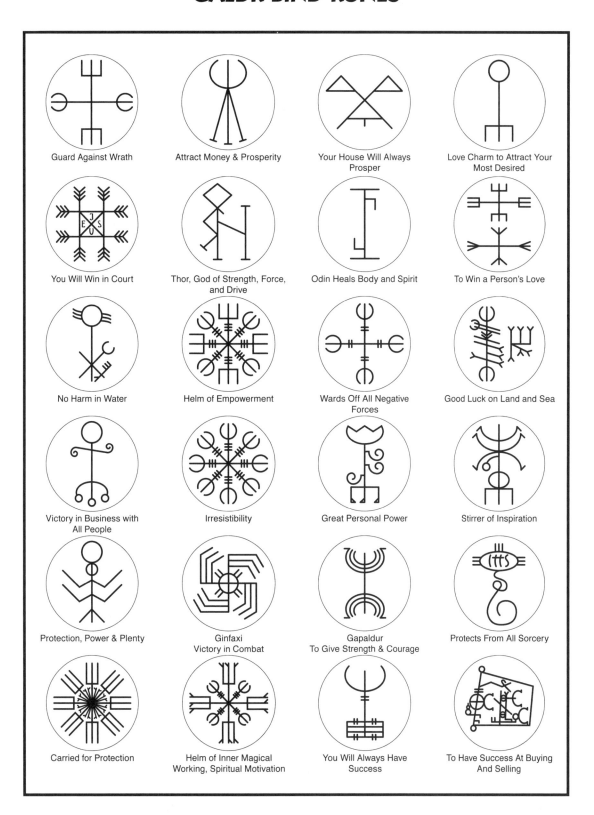

Guard Against Wrath

Attract Money & Prosperity

Your House Will Always Prosper

Love Charm to Attract Your Most Desired

You Will Win in Court

Thor, God of Strength, Force, and Drive

Odin Heals Body and Spirit

To Win a Person's Love

No Harm in Water

Helm of Empowerment

Wards Off All Negative Forces

Good Luck on Land and Sea

Victory in Business with All People

Irresistibility

Great Personal Power

Stirrer of Inspiration

Protection, Power & Plenty

Ginfaxi
Victory in Combat

Gapaldur
To Give Strength & Courage

Protects From All Sorcery

Carried for Protection

Helm of Inner Magical Working, Spiritual Motivation

You Will Always Have Success

To Have Success At Buying And Selling

Galdr bind-runes distributed at Angela Marie Horner's 2018 workshop on sigil magic. These are symbols found in Icelandic, Norwegian, and Swedish grimoires. They can be copied and cut up for use with the Spell Star layout facing page 65.

THE SEALS OF SOLOMON

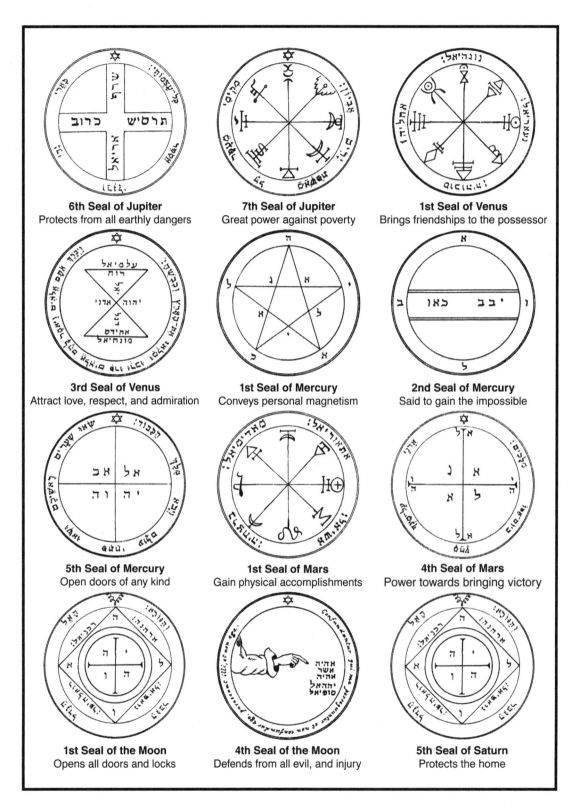

6th Seal of Jupiter
Protects from all earthly dangers

7th Seal of Jupiter
Great power against poverty

1st Seal of Venus
Brings friendships to the possessor

3rd Seal of Venus
Attract love, respect, and admiration

1st Seal of Mercury
Conveys personal magnetism

2nd Seal of Mercury
Said to gain the impossible

5th Seal of Mercury
Open doors of any kind

1st Seal of Mars
Gain physical accomplishments

4th Seal of Mars
Power towards bringing victory

1st Seal of the Moon
Opens all doors and locks

4th Seal of the Moon
Defends from all evil, and injury

5th Seal of Saturn
Protects the home

Solomonic planetary seals distributed at Angela Marie Horner's 2018 workshop on sigil magic. These are from *The Key of Solomon,* a 14th - 17th century grimoire. They can be copied and cut up for use with the Spell Star layout facing page 65.

THE SEALS OF MOSES

SPECIAL SEAL OF TREASURE

Fig. 2: It is alleged in the Book that if this Seal is buried in the earth where treasures exist, they will come to the surface of themselves.

SEAL OF GOOD FORTUNE

Fig. 3: If a man carries this Seal with him, it will bring him great fortune and blessing; it is the truest and highest Seal of Good Fortune.

SEAL OF LOVE

Fig. 4: The Book states that if you carry this Seal it will cause you to be very agreeable and much beloved, and it will also defeat all your enemies.

SEAL OF LONG LIFE

Fig. 5: The Book states that to carry this Seal on the body will save a person from misery and give the greatest fortune and long life.

SEAL OF POWER

Fig. 6: This Seal, it says in the Book, is for health. If it be laid upon the sick in full, true faith, it will restore anyone who has not lived the full number of his days.

SEAL OF DREAMS AND VISIONS

Fig. 7: The Book states that to wear this Seal in bed while sleeping will help one learn what he desires to know through dreams and visions.

Page 91 of *Legends of Incense, Herb, and Oil Magic* by Lewis de Claremont, originally published in 1936. The art and text are adapted from *The Sixth and Seventh Books of Moses*, a grimoire in wide distribution from the 18th century to the present. This colour flyer was first released at the 2016 Hoodoo Heritage Festival workshop at which cat yronwode presented her edited, revised, and restored re-publication of *Legends*, and introduced the new Lucky Mojo Library of Occult Classics. The flyer was also given away at the 2018 Festival as part of Angela Marie Horner's "Spell Papers and Sigil Magic" workshop.

Plate I

SPELL STAR FOR SIGIL MAGIC

Spell Star and representational symbols to use at its center, prepared for Angela Marie Horner's 2018 workshop on "Spell Papers and Sigil Magic." See pages 60 - 61 for instructions. You may draw or print out copies of the Star and the various sigils, seals, runes, and galdrbok images needed in your work. Art by Grey Townsend and Deacon Millett.

Plate II

INTRODUCTION TO ANGELS AND ARCHANGELS
Miss Elvyra Curcuruto-Love

WHAT ARE ARCHANGELS?

The word Archangel comes from the Greek "Archi," meaning first or chief, and "Angelos," meaning winged messenger. Known in Hebrew as Malakhi Adonai ("Agents of the Lord") they are formed of pure light, force, and energy, described in ancient texts as the spirits before the Throne of God. They act as a prism to refract the brilliance of Deity and as agents who execute the creative Will. Each Archangel has a specialty, similar to a facet on a gemstone.

As we know them, the Archangels all bear Hebrew names. Although they seem to have originated as Canaanite deities called Elohim (gods), they are found in the earliest forms of Judaism. They also exist as the Amesha Spenta ("Bounteous Immortals") in Zoroastrianism. Similar entities, such as the Shining Ones or the Thunder Beings, are found in other cultures. With names borrowed from Jewish usage, Archangels also feature in Christianity and Islam.

These Archangels are linked to days of the week

- **Michæl:** "Like Unto God."
- **Gabriel:** "Strength of God."
- **Sammæl / Chamuel:** "Wrath / Seer of God."
- **Raphæl:** "Healer of God."
- **Tzadkiel / Sachiel:** "Righteousness of God."
- **Anæl / Haniel:** "Grace / Joy of God."
- **Cassiel:** "Speed of God."

The Amesha Spenta, once gods and goddesses of prehistoric Iran, became angelic helpers to Ahura Mazda (Ohrmazd), the Zoroastrian creator god. For example, Spenta Armaiti (also called Spandermat), an Earth-Mother goddess whose sacred herb was Espand, became the Archangel of the Earth.

The heptad of Zoroastrian Amesha Spenta are:

* **Spenta Mainyu:** "Holy Spirit" (Emanation).
- **Vohu Mano:** "Good Mind" (Guardian of Cattle).
- **Asha Vahishta:** "Truth, Righteousness" (Fire).
- **Khshathra Vairya:** "Desirable Dominion" (Metal).
- **Spenta Armaiti:** "Holy Devotion" (Earth).
- **Haurvatat:** "Perfection, Health" (Water).
- **Ameretat:** "Immortality" (Tthe Hereafter).

WHAT ARE ANGELS?

Angels, called malakhi in Hebrew, are spirits of light who help with the vast functions of the created world. Created as beings of pure consciousness, Angels are deathless entities, unlimited by time and space. They are a focus of power, wisdom, and love as well as an emanation of God/dess. They channel without distortion the divine light, carrying messages between humankind and God/dess. Many serve humankind as guardians, counsellors, guides, interpreters, comforters, and matchmakers. Within structured theology, there exist hierarchies of angels:

- **Seraphs:** As described in Isaiah 6:1-8, these are six-winged fiery angels who fly around the Throne of God crying, "Holy, holy, holy."
- **Cherubs:** They attend on the Deity; in ancient Middle-Eastern art they are Lions or Bulls with Eagle wings and human faces; in Christianity they may be portrayed as child-angels.
- **Yazads or Yezidi:** These Zoroastrian angels include the well-known Mithra and Ahriman.
- **Guardian Angels:** They are assigned to help individual beings on Earth. The Zoroastrians call them Fravashis or Frohars.

TABLE OF CORRESPONDENCES

The accompanying table shows correspondences between magical, psychological, physical, and occult subjects, and well-known Archangels. Such tables have existed for millennia and, despite the fact that not all of them agree, you may find such lists useful in your work. These are not the only Archangels; post-Biblical Judaism identifies dozens more among the heavenly host, and Christians, too, have added to angelic lore.

In seeking the aid of heavenly beings, you may understand that although Archangels and Angels have been associated with the genders of the deities from whom they derive, they can also be seen as pure spirit energy and thus sexless. Additionally, Archangels are the overseers of Angels. Angels associate closely with people on a daily basis; Archangels, on the other hand, help find solutions to human problems, but they do not engage with humans unless they are petitioned or invoked, as humankind has free will.

Archangel	Michael	Gabriel	Samael / Chamuel	Raphael	Sachiel	Anael / Haniel	Cassiel / Kaziel	Uriel	Jophiel / Zophiel	Metatron	Sandalphon
Name "of El"	Like Unto	Strength	Wrath / Seer	Healer	Righteousness	Grace / Joy	Speed	Light	Beauty / Rock	Watchman	Co-Brother
Week Day	Sunday	Monday	Tuesday	Wednesday	Thursday	Friday	Saturday				
Planet	Sun	Moon	Mars	Mercury	Jupiter	Venus	Saturn	Uranus	Zodiac	Earth	Earth
Colours	Red, Orange / Pink, Purple	Blue, Aqua / Silver, Teal	Red / Magenta	Yellow, White / Blue, Violet	Blue, Violet / Purple	Pink / Dark Green	Black / Indigo	Black, Green / Olive, Tan	Yellow / White, Clear	Turquoise	
Animals	Lion, Wolf / Sparrow Hawk	Sea Bird, Seal / Shellfish	Ram, Horse / Bear, Wolf	Monkey / Ibis	Stag, Fish / Dolphin	Dove, Rabbit / Sparrow	Crow / Crocodile	Cattle / Goats	Tortoise	Unicorn	Elephant / Eagle, Snake
Trees	Almond / Cedar, Beech	Willow, Bay / Hazel, Palm	Rowan, Holly / Hawthorn	Aspen / Mulberry	Pine, Spruce / Chestnut	Eucalyptus / Elder, Quince	Yew / Cypress	Oak	Lemon	Fir	All Trees
Plants	Garlic, Onion / Red Pepper / Mustard / Marigold / Heliotrope	Lotus, Iris / Seaweed / Motherwort / Rush, Melon / Cucumber	Cardamom / Rose, Thyme / Nettle, Rue / Pomegranate / Thistle	Vervain, Pansy / Primrose / Frankincense / Lavender / Cinquefoil	Marjoram / Sage / Liverwort / Betony / Flax	Hyacinth / Lily, Willow / Maidenhair / Damiana / Carnation	Houseleek / Aconite / Henbane / Hellebore / Tomato	Ivy, Grass / Grains / Apples / Comfrey / Pokeweed	Nightshade / Wolfsbane / Coltsfoot / Belladonna / Mistletoe	Buttercup / Olive	All Plants
Stones	Ruby, Garnet / Fire Opal / Fire Agate / Tiger's Eye	Pearl / Moonstone / River Pebbles / Fluorite	Bloodstone / Diamond / Jasper, Fluorite / Ruby, Garnet	Topaz, Citrine / Serpentine / Agate / Chalcedony	Lapis Lazuli / Amethyst / Sapphire / Sugilite / Beryl	Emerald / Rose Quartz / Turquoise / Beryl	Jet, Salt / Onyx / Lodestone / Jet	Malachite / Hematite / Granite, Jade / Picture Jasper	Citrine / Rubelite	Quartz Crystal / Smokey Quartz / Diamond / Turquoise	
Metals	Gold	Silver	Iron, Bronze	Mercury	Tin, Zinc	Copper	Lead	Platinum	Meteorite	Iron	
Incense	Frankincense / Copal Oro	Camphor / Sandalwood	Dragon's Blood / Benzoin	Cinnamon	Saffron / Cloves	Ambergris / Musk	Myrrh	Jasmine	Bergamot	Frankincense	Sandalwood / Vetiver
Consciousness Will	Will	Wisdom	Wrath	Intelligence	Righteousness	Independence	Philanthropy	Memory	Illumination	Enlightenment	Transcendence
Quality	Protection	Vision	Courage	Healing	Diplomacy	Harmony	Responsibility	Teaching	Gratitude	Empathy	Spirituality
Viewpoint	Future	Inward	Outward					Past		Holistic	Centered
Finger	Little Finger	Ring Finger	Index Finger					Middle Finger		Thumb	
Time of Day	Noon	Sunset	Dawn					Midnight		Now	Any time
Elementals	Salamanders	Undines	Sylphs					Gnomes			Angels
Season	Summer	Fall	Spring					Winter			
Cardinal Sign	Aries	Cancer	Libra					Capricorn			
Fixed Sign	Leo	Scorpio	Aquarius					Taurus			
Mutable Sign	Sagittarius	Pisces	Gemini					Virgo			
Tarot Courts	Knight	Queen	King					Page			
Tarot Suits	Wands	Cups	Swords					Pentacles			
Card Suits	Clubs	Hearts	Spades					Diamonds			

This hand-out was distributed at the 2015 Festival. Miss Elvyra is a member of AIRR and HP; you can also find her at Elvyra.com.

WORKING WITH PATRON SAINTS
Papa Newt

WHAT ARE SAINTS AND PATRONAGE?

Saints in the Catholic tradition are the honoured dead who, in life, held such a strong faith that many were martyred. Though dead, they help the living by intercession, lifting up their prayers to the divine. Saints are by no means deities, but their believers have developed folkways to help empower their lives, overcoming times of opposition.

Starting to pray to a saint or develop a working relationship can feel overwhelming to those not familiar with these types of spirits, but with an understanding, anyone can start working with them.

Many saints have been associated with or assigned a specific focus on the spectrum of life that is known to be their patronage. A patronage can cover matters of illness, occupation, nation, church, or condition of human life. These details come from stories of their lives, the intercessions associated with the saint, and widely-accepted folklore that may or may not be church doctrine.

Those who are of the Catholic faith may be asked to select a saint's name in preparation for one of the sacraments such as confirmation. There is even a belief that being born on their feast day or sharing the same name as a saint automatically aligns you to that specific saint.

THE SAINTS GO MARCHING IN

Many saints have crossed over into conjure, particularly in New Orleans, Maryland, and other areas originally populated by Catholics. Sometimes a component of syncretism was at play, as a "safe" saint came to take on the attributes of a "forbidden" figure or deity. The Spiritualist Church may also have played a role in spreading the idea of candles and saints in the hoodoo community.

Honouring a saint on their feast day is a longstanding tradition. You may say novenas (a nine-day prayer), light a candle, offer incense, create a special altar, do charitable acts in the saint's name, take a pilgrimage, or any combination thereof.

SOME FAVOURITE SAINTS, AND TRICKS TO BRING THEIR AID

Here are some favourite tips and tricks, from both traditional Catholicism and folk magic:

SAINT JOSEPH HELPS GAIN EMPLOYMENT

Saint Joseph is one of the few Saints that we find referenced in the Holy Bible itself. The would-be husband to the Blessed Virgin Mary and the earthly father to Jesus Christ, Joseph was a simple working man who followed the traditions of Judaism as it was practiced in his day. His kindness to his pregnant fiancé shows his gentle and faithful heart.

To gain employment, get the logo or dirt from the place you are applying, and keep an image of Saint Joseph on top of it before going for the interview. Pray your heartfelt petition to Saint Joseph, who was always a steadfast workman throughout his life.

SAINT DYMPHNA CLEARS THE MIND

When Dymphna was 13 years old, her father (a pagan king) made incestuous advances. She escaped, but her father followed, chopping off her head. Saint Dymphna is the patron saint of those with mental afflictions, anxiety disorders, PTSD, and victims of incest.

Burn Bay leaves to Saint Dymphna while praying for her aid in clearing the mind, whether for a loved one or for yourself.

SAINT RAYMOND BRINGS YOU MONEY

Patron of childbirth, midwives and pregnant women, Saint Raymond Nonnatus (literally "not born") was delivered by cæsarean section after his mother's death. He also aids hostage negotiators, bail bondsmen, and those who have been falsely accused or imprisoned.

Burning green candles every Tuesday, Thursday, and Saturday for nine days is said to gain Saint Raymond's aid to help draw you money. When he comes through, offer him flowers or green Parsley.

SAINT MICHÆL PROTECTS THOSE IN NEED

Saint Michæl is recognized as an archangel in Jewish, Christian, and Islamic traditions and is one of only a few Jewish archangels who has been made a saint in the Catholic church. Mentioned by name in the Books of Daniel, Jude, and Revelation in the Bible, he is usually pictured as the Field Commander of the Army of God.

For protection, get a wallet-size prayer card and dust it with Saint Michæl Sachet Powder. Offer a red candle and pray to the angel for protection. Keep the card behind your driver's license.

SAINT CYPRIAN REVERSES BAD MAGIC

A pagan sorcerer who lived in Antioch in the 4th century, Cyprian used his power to command demons and sexually harass women. Defeated in both by the sign of the cross, he converted to Christianity and was eventually martyred.

Since he is the patron saint of rootworkers, bringing the influence of Saint Cyprian into reversal jobs is a powerful aid. Anoint your hands with Saint Cyprian Oil and pray for his help before starting.

SAINT MARY BRINGS PEACE AND HEALING

The Virgin Mother has appeared as an apparition or vision many times. The icon known as the Mother of Perpetual Help is but one, a painting stolen by a merchant sailing to Rome from Crete. In rough waters, the sailors prayed for help to the icon and reached Rome safely.

In her role as Mother of Perpetual Help, Saint Mary is believed to help bring a job, keep peace in the home, and heal when you are sick. Offer a pink candle when praying for her intercession.

SAINT ANTHONY FINDS THE RIGHT WORDS

Saint Anthony of Padua is well-known for finding lost items (and even lost love). Because he travelled widely, he is appealed to for safe travel. In Portugal, France, Italy, and Spain, he is beloved by those who work on the sea, and sailors may keep a statue of him on the mast of their ships.

Saint Anthony can help in times when you need to speak elegantly or find the right words. Anoint your throat with Saint Anthony Oil while praying to him.

SAINT MARTIN DE PORRES KEEPS PETS WELL

Saint Martin may have been the first Black man to officially wear the habit of a monastic order, taking vows in 1603 as a Dominican brother. He worked as a barber, pharmacist, doctor, and veterinarian and was believed to be able to levitate and communicate with animals. His patronage includes African-Americans, barbers, hairdressers, race relations, social justice, those with mixed race heritage, the poor, the nation of Peru, and the city of Biloxi, Mississippi.

Dissolve Saint Martin de Porres Bath Crystals into a spray bottle and spray the bedding or space your pet enjoys sleeping. It is said to help keep your pet healthy.

SAINT RITA PACIFIES A TROUBLED HOME

Saint Rita was married to a rage-filled husband. For 18 years, she endured his tirades, cheating, and violence, giving him two sons just like him. When the sons wanted revenge on their father's killers, Saint Rita prayed to God for Him to take away their lives. They died of illness a year later.

Saint Rita can aid in controlling a husband and to help bring peace to a troubled home. Placing her image above the door of your house will help keep those within quiet and make them behave.

SAINT EXPEDITE SPEEDS THINGS ALONG

Saint Expedite (a.k.a. Saint Expeditus or Saint Espedee) is the patron saint of those who need help in a hurry, whether for love, money, or even court case work. A Roman centurion martyred in the 4th century, Expedite wears a soldier's uniform, holds the cross, and steps upon a black Crow. In recent times, he has become revered as the saint of computer programmers and procrastinators.

To help get Saint Expedite moving on an issue, give him a cup of strong black coffee at the time you request his aid. This is not a payment for what you are asking for, but to help him wake up and get on the case. Once Saint Expedite comes through for you, pound cake and flowers are the favoured offering.

This flyer accompanied Papa Newt's workshop in 2018. Raised within the Catholic religion and a long time student of magical traditions and sorcery, he uses Christian magic and other occult techniques to help clients. Find him at AIRR, HP, or PapaNewt.com.

CATHOLIC FOLK MAGIC
Papa Newt

A RELIGIOUS FORM OF MAGIC

Roman Catholicism has spread around the world to become one of the largest religions on Earth. Carried far from its native home in Europe through the twin agencies of colonialism and faith, it is now found in diverse cultures that have blended into the clerical religious traditions local magical practices that may not be fully endorsed by the church. These popular Catholic beliefs continue to thrive, generation after generation, as practitioners proclaim the help and miracles that they have wrought.

The diversity of Catholic folk magic around the world goes well beyond what can be written here, but as with any form of religious magic, the practitioner works by faith. In Catholic folk magic that faith is founded on a belief in God, his son Jesus, the Blessed Virgin Mary, the Bible, and the canonized Saints and Angels who intercede or assist the believer. In addition, objects blessed in the name of Jesus and his church, which are called sacramentals, find employment in folk magic, and those objects that have been blessed by a priest are believed to have the greatest efficacy.

THE HOLY BIBLE

One of the best selling books published, the Bible is a vital tool. Believed to be the word of God, it holds many stories and powerful phrases that spiritual workers use. Practitioners keep petition papers, pressed flowers, money, and prayers among the pages that correspond to the work at hand. The Bible is filled with Psalms and other scriptural passages that are read to help empower the work.

BIBLE PASSAGE TO REMOVE BLOCKAGES

Reading Joshua 6:1-27 while burning a vigil candle dressed with Block Buster Oil for seven days is said to help remove blockages in your way.

BIBLE PASSAGE TO REKINDLE PASSION

The reading of Proverbs 5:18-19 while burning a red candle (a penis candle would be fantastic!) to rekindle a man's passion.

THE ROSARY

This is a set of beads that the Virgin Mary is said to have given to Saint Dominic in 1214. Essentially a form of folk magic until approved by Pope Pius V in 1569, it is typically prayed in a pattern, such as this: On the crucifix, the Apostles' Creed; on the single beads, the Our Father; on the lengths of chain, the Glory Be (and optional O My Jesus). At each decade of ten beads, meditate on the selected Mystery (a focus on the life and death of Jesus), pray the Our Father, then say a Hail Mary on each bead. Repeat to finish all five decades; conclude with the Hail Holy Queen.

PRAYING INTO THE ROSARY OF OTHERS

The Rosary can be prayed alone or with a group of people. Generally, a Mystery is chosen before the group begins its practice of meditation or pleading for intercession. People in the know attend group Rosary sessions and secretly say their own petitions and prayers into each Hail Mary to empower their work.

THE SCAPULAR

Scapulars are holy necklaces. Originally made from squares of rough brown wool cloth worn by monks, they hang around the neck, one piece in front, near the heart, and the other in back, at the shoulder blades.

IT IS GOOD TO DIE WITH A SCAPULAR ON

It is said that a person who dies while wearing a scapular blessed by a priest will be delivered from Purgatory on the Saturday following his or her death.

HOLY WATER

Water that has been blessed by a member of the clergy, commonly used in the church for baptisms and spiritual cleansing, is believed to protect against evil, and to bring peace to all that it touches.

PROTECT YOUR SLEEP WITH HOLY WATER

Anoint yourself with holy water in the sign of the cross and sprinkle the water upon your bed. Say three Hail Marys before going to sleep and you will be safe.

HOLY IMAGES

Biblical imagery intended for use in contemplative prayer or devotion was originally found only in church, but 19th century mass production made statuary, medals, and art prints readily available to the public.

WORKING WITH IMAGES IN THE CHURCH

In the old days, the women of Turkey would go to church on the Feast of Saint Anthony, remove the baby Jesus from the saint's arms and pray that he would find them a husband. In Mexico, folks lit two candles, holding one in the right hand while saying good prayers to distract the saint, while with the left hand they crossed and cursed their enemies.

HOLY STATUES IN THE HOME

Common practices with statues and statuettes in the home include burying the statue of Saint Joseph to sell a home, taking the baby away from Saint Anthony for the return of a missing object or person, removing the hands from the Infant of Prague to get a wish granted, and covering or turning a statue of Mary or a saint to the wall when doing negative work.

HOLY CARDS TO CARRY AND USE

Small, colourful holy cards bearing images of popular saints, Jesus, and the Blessed Virgin Mary, often with a prayer on the reverse, are carried in the wallet or purse, of used as bookmarks in the Bible.

A CHROMO DRAWS ATTENTION

Chromolithographs, called chromos, are described in early hoodoo spell-books, such as the *Genuine Black and White Magic of Marie Laveau*. In 1940, the folklorist Harry M. Hyatt met a professional female root doctor in Algiers, Louisiana, whom he called "Informant 1580," and she told him how to use one:

"Now, if you want to draw the attention of anyone that you cares for, you get nine teaspoonsful of sugar and draw a glass of water, and you put the sugar in the water and you offer it up to the [print] of the Sacred Heart of Jesus. You offer that glass of sweetened water to the Sacred Heart of Jesus and I'll guarantee you it'll bring their mind to you and they'll come to you. No names [need be written]. Put the glass under the picture and just offer it to the Sacred Heart of Jesus, and I'll guarantee you."

BLESSED PALM LEAVES

In my family, I recall my mother placing a blessed Palm leaf from Palm Sunday above the door. Because this item is a sacramental, a blessed item, it will protect those living within the home and keep the Devil out.

PALMS FOR PROTECTION DURING A STORM

A lady whose hair my mother would fix every week said that burning a blessed Palm leaf during a storm and praying the Our Father and the Hail Mary would aid in protecting the home. It is advisable that you use a Palm leaf that has been thoroughly dried. My mother grabbed one not quite dry in the commotion of tornado sirens, and it was a challenge to keep it lit!

THE THREE NAILS

The three nails are a powerful symbol of the nails used to pierce the body of Christ. It is a common practice in Sicily to use three horseshoe nails for this sort of work; others use square-cut house nails.

HELPING THE SICK WITH THREE NAILS

Take three nails and anoint them with Jesus Christ the King Oil and then hammer the nails into the bed post saying, *"Three nails pierced the body of Christ to free us from sin. Three nails pierce the sick bed of _____ to relieve and heal them of their ailments. Amen."*

REMOVING ADDICTION WITH THREE NAILS

Write the name of the troubling addiction on a red piece of paper. Rub the paper into the substance of addiction; if it is an alcohol then place a couple drops onto the paper. If the substance is not present, brush the paper down upon the one inflicted with the addiction. Take the paper to the edge of town and nail it to a tree with three nails while saying, *"I nail you, spirit of addiction, to deny you as the thief who mocked Jesus on the cross was denied entry into heaven. In name of God the Father, God the Son, and God the Holy Spirit, and so it is done. Amen."*

"Catholic Folk Magic" was prepared for Papa Newt's 2019 workshop at the 2019 Hoodoo Heritage Festival. A member of AIRR and HP, he can be reached at his web site, PapaNewt.com.

A DOMINICAN MESA BLANCA
Candelo Kimbisa and Mama E.

WHAT IS A MESA?

A mesa blanca is a table (mesa) covered with a white (blanca) cloth that is used as an ancestor altar. Glasses of water on the table signify our ancestors, with the main glass in the middle, and other glasses placed around it to show our spiritual chords. The purpose of the mesa is to communicate with our ancestors, which allows us to find out things seen and unseen. Through these Spiritist reunions we learn to speak to our ancestors, both known and unknown.

ALLAN KARDEC AND SPIRITISM

Hippolyte Leon Denizard Rivail (1804-1869) was a French author, translator, and educator who used the pen name Allan Kardec. He is credited as the founder of the denomination of Spiritualism known as Spiritism, and he wrote five books which codified Spiritist practice, collectively known as *The Five Fundamental Works of Spiritism*. The prayers by Allan Kardec we will employ here are taken from *The New Devotionary Spiritist: A Collection of Selected Prayers* and are to be used during the mesa blanca for those present and the mediums overseeing.

ELEVATING AN ANCESTOR

When creating a mesa in your home, it is important to elevate the spirit that you will bring to your altar in the main glass placed in the center of your mesa. My method for elevation is related to Catholicism and Holy Mass because of my background, but non-Catholics can also use this method to elevate their ancestors. I am not aware of any Protestant prayers for the departed, but the Jewish Kaddish could be used in place of the Mass.

CATHOLIC SUFFRAGES

In Catholicism it is believed that when people die they are no longer able to do anything to reach Heaven, but by good works and prayer, their loved ones can help them obtain forgiveness from sins to shorten their time in Purgatory and allow their ascent to Heaven. These prayers for the dead, or *fieles difuntos*, are called suffrages and the highest suffrage is to offer a Holy Mass for the deceased.

STEALING A MASS

The first step in this method of ancestor elevation is to steal a Mass. To do this, first go to a Catholic church for Mass, usually on a Wednesday, but November 2nd is also an excellent day, as it is the day Catholics devote to prayer for the faithful departed. Sit down and listen to the Mass, and when the priest reaches the point where he recites the names of those who have passed on, then you will sneak in the name of your dearly departed. Remain seated until just before the collection plate is passed, and then get up, leave the church, and go straight home. You have now stolen a Mass.

THE NOVENA

Once you arrive home with your stolen Mass, fill a glass with water. Christen the glass of water in the name of the ancestor you are trying to elevate — *"I name you in the name of John Doe."*

Begin by placing the glass somewhere relatively low in your home. Recite Psalms 23 and say an Our Father, also known as the Lord's Prayer, over the glass. Repeat these prayers each day for nine days, and on each day elevate the glass to a higher place. You can do this either by moving the glass from place to place on furniture, such as tables and bookcases, or by stacking books, bricks, or other items to achieve additional height. On the ninth day the glass should reach the highest point in your home.

Once the glass has reached the highest point in your home and you have given that spirit a novena (nine days of prayer), then the glass is emptied out the front or back door. The glass is refilled, and that is the first glass you place upon the altar, after which you say the prayer, *The Heading of the Reunion*, from *The New Devotionary Spiritist* by Allan Kardec.

After the main glass is placed on the altar, you can add other glasses for the ancestors who will represent your spiritual chord or spiritual court. The main glass can also be used to add new spirits to your altar, but you would only want to use it for spirits who have recently passed away or who have not yet gone through the proper steps to fully realize that they have passed on and are now spirits.

OUR FATHER (THE LORD'S PRAYER)

"Our Father,
Who art in heaven,
hallowed be Thy name;
Thy kingdom come;
Thy will be done on earth as it is in heaven.
Give us this day our daily bread;
and forgive us our trespasses
as we forgive those who trespass against us;
and lead us not into temptation,
but deliver us from evil. Amen."

THE HEADING OF THE REUNION

AT THE BEGINNING OF THE REUNION

"We pray to the Lord God Omnipotent to send us good spirits to assist us, to keep away those spirits who may mislead us, and to give us the necessary light to distinguish the truth from the imposture. We pray that you also separate from us the evil spirits, either incarnate or disincarnate, who might try to establish discord between us and in doing so to divert us from the expression of charity and love to our neighbours. If any of these bad spirits intends to enter here, please do not permit them, Lord, to find access through one of us.

"Good spirits that deign to come here to instruct us, lead us to yield to your advice and follow your instructions, and divert from us all selfishness, pride, envy, and jealousy. Inspire us with indulgence and benevolence toward our fellow beings, present and absent, living and deceased, friends and enemies. Magnify our feelings of charity, humility, and self-denial, so that in the end we will feel encouraged to recognize and acknowledge your healthy influence.

"Give the mediums, whom you entrust to transmit your teachings, an awareness of the sanctity of the mandate entrusted to them and of the seriousness of the activities they are to fulfill, so that they may have the necessary fervour and recollection.

"If in this reunion there are people who were attracted by a feeling other than that of good, open their eyes to the light, and may God forgive them if they came with bad intentions. We pray very particularly to the spirit of [name your ancestor whom you have elevated], our spiritual guide, to assist us and watch over us."

AT THE END OF THE REUNION

"We give thanks to the good spirits who have wanted to come and communicate with us. We ask you to help us put into practice the instructions that have been given to us, and as we go forth from this Reunion, to fortify and strengthen each one of us in the practice of goodness and love toward our neighbours. We also wish these instructions to be helpful to any suffering, ignorant, or vicious spirits who have attended this meeting, and upon them we implore the Mercy of God."

FOR THE MEDIUMS

"It will come to pass in the last days," God says, "that I will pour out a portion of my spirit upon all flesh. Your sons and your daughters shall prophesy, your young men shall see visions, your old men shall dream dreams. Indeed, upon my servants and my handmaids I will pour out a portion of my spirit in those days, and they shall prophesy."
— Acts 2: 17-18.

FURTHER RESOURCES

Those who wish to learn more about the Spiritualist tradition, Kardecian Spiritism, mediumship, and working with one's ancestors or the dead can find many web pages filled with additional helpful information at the web site of the Association of Independent Readers and Rootworkers, located at:
ReadersAndRootworkers.org

For other ways that ancestors may be venerated or elevated, you may read more in this book:
"Deliverance!" by Khi Armand

Detailed instructions on how to make and use altars in the hoodoo tradition can be found in this book:
"Hoodoo Shrines and Altars" by Phœnix LeFæ

This handout was prepared for the Sunday Opening Ceremony at the 2017 Hoodoo Heritage Festival, led by Mama E. and Candelo Kimbisa. Mama E. is a member of AIRR, the Association of Independent Readers and Rootworkers. She is the proprietor of ConjureDoctor.com, the home of Dr. E. Products. An initiated priestess of Oshun in the Lukumi faith, she is also scratched in Palo Kimbisa. Candelo Kimbisa hosts a radio show, Candelo's Corner, and offers his line of spiritual products at Kimbisa.org. He is trained in the Palo Mayombe tradition and is an initiate in Santeria.

NORTH ASIAN SERJIM: A TRADITIONAL SHAMANIC RITE
David Borji Shi

THE SERJIM SACRIFICE

The Mongolian or Manchurian serjim resembles an offering in that materials are presented and sacrificed to spirits. However, an offering is generally done to honour spirits and gain favour and blessings, while serjim is a sacrifice where one offers the essence of materials in exchange for a spirit's aid and empowerment. Offerings are typically given to a host of spirits, but the serjim is directed toward specific spirits with stated intentions. Those who wish to perform serjim are recommended to have some level of experience with trance-like states. However, a serjim need not be performed by a shaman, as it does not require journeying or merging with spirits. The serjim is a preferred practice of shamans when granting simple client requests without spending much time or exhaustive effort, and it may make up half of a shaman's everyday work.

The most common form of serjim is with liquor. Vodka is preferred, but any clear liquor will do; avoid coloured liquor, such as whiskey. Clear liquors are considered pure, and coloured liquor will insult the spirits. Before the serjim, perform a divination. Quickly stuff from one to three lit matches into a bottle of vodka and close it. The smoke from the sputtering matches at the bottle's neck will reveal the spiritual situation of the person requesting the serjim. At this point, ask the spirits if the serjim needs to be "hot" or "cold."

THE COLD LIQUOR SERJIM

The cold serjim is easy to perform. It requires two ceremonial cups made of silver, copper, or bronze, or they can be Chinese teacups. After the divination has been done, pour the vodka into one cup. Then spoon the vodka from the first cup to the second while invoking the spirits and stating the intentions. When the intentions are sufficiently stated and speaking with the spirits is done, any remaining vodka in the first cup is poured into the second cup. This vodka is then thrown out the window or a door that leads outside.

To determine the effectiveness of the serjim, part of the vodka may be thrown against a wall, ceiling, or window glass while yelling the word of power "Tooreg!" which tells the spirits to reveal information. The splash patterns and drips can be read and interpreted.

THE HOT LIQUOR SERJIM

A hot serjim involves the use of fire. After the divination, pour a little vodka into a small shallow bowl or metal tray — just enough to cover the bottom — and pour more vodka into a ceremonial cup, until the bottle is half empty. Then, while gesturing and calling the sky spirits and the earth spirits, light three matches, and carefully touch them to the vodka in the tray so that a brilliant blue flame erupts. This flame is the direct manifestation of primal fire and energy, the gol. Invoke the spirits while using a metal spoon to feed the fire with vodka from the cup. After invoking the spirits, state the spell's intentions to the fire, so that it enters the flame. Feed more vodka while stating intentions as necessary to keep the fire alive but not so much that it overflows. The intentions may be restated multiple times to give the serjim energy.

After the intentions are stated, watch the fire prayerfully as the alcohol is depleted and it goes out. Remaining liquid in the tray may be thrown out a window or door to the outside. Make sure the fire is completely out before it's thrown! Remaining liquid in the cup may be partially thrown out and partially poured back into the bottle. Save the bottle of vodka, as it has been energized with the intentions of the serjim, and may be used as a ceremonial drink or for offerings. It is customary for those involved in the serjim to take a drink as well, and to offer the vodka until the intention comes true or the vodka runs out, according to the inclination of the participants.

OTHER FORMS OF SERJIM

Liquor serjim can be used for any purpose. Other forms of serjim are associated with specific intentions. For example, tea serjim is used for healing and protection from illness. A three-liquid serjim of vodka, tea, and milk is used for cleansing. Serjim with salt can provide protection, and a serjim of salt, sand, and rice transmutes negative energy into positive. Juniper serjim can enhance power, while food and money serjim are used for gaining spiritual favours.

David Borji Shi is the author of "North Asian Magic," a ground-breaking book that accompanied his presentation on the topic at the 2016 Festival. The full 96-page book is available from YIPPIE, through LMCCo. Distributing.

WORKING WITH ASIAN DEITIES
Devi Spring

EAST MEETS WEST

Asian spirituality was widely introduced to the USA at the World's Congress of Religions, held in Chicago in 1893. Adherents of Theosophy and New Thought embraced these teachings, and makers of occult supplies, such as L. W. DeLaurence, Lewis de Claremont, and Dr. E. P. Read, introduced products like Chinese Wash, Hin-Doo Devil-Chaser Incense, Lucky Buddha Oil, Chi Chi sticks, and other goods derived from Buddhist, Hindu, and Taoist traditions. Meanwhile, during the era of racial segregation, African-American conjurers and performers like Rajah Rabo (Carl Z. Talbot), Rhadolph Marcelliee (Marcellus Clark), and Korla Pandit (John Roland Redd) regularly presented themselves as turban-wearing Indians. During the 1960s, American interest in martial arts and yoga saw Hindu deities like Ganesha and Kali further integrated into urban hoodoo. See:

LuckyMojo.com/hinduismandhoodoo.html
LuckyMojo.com/hoodoohistory.html#admixtures2

Hinduism and Buddhism are living religions with over 1.6 billion followers. Their spiritual protocols should be respected; start by developing a devotional relationship prior to petitioning for your needs.

PUJA: RITUALS OF DEVOTION

Puja (POO-jah) are rituals of devotion performed for Hindu and Buddhist spirits. Presenting offerings before petitioning is a traditional practice. In Hinduism, protocol is to always acknowledge Ganesha first, as he acts as a gatekeeper for the pantheon. Some Buddhist traditions also utilize a gatekeeper. There are many traditional offerings prescribed in sacred texts, but they can be simplified to offering each of the five elements:

- **Earth:** Food, flowers.
- **Air:** Incense.
- **Fire:** Oil lamps or candles.
- **Water:** Fresh, cool water.
- **Æther (Spirit):** Prayers, hymns, mantras.

Each item is circled in front of of the deity at least three times clockwise, and then left on an offering tray. At the conclusion, food and water are imbibed by the devotee as a form of blessing called *prasad* ("grace").

HINDU MANTRAS IN CONJURE

Mantras are magical prayer-chants that originated in the Indian Vedic tradition. Designed to have dramatic transformative effects when chanted, mantras are key elements in Hindu Indian folk magic, as well as among Buddhists. Mantras help cultivate resonance between the devotee and a deity. In addition to mantras, each deity is also represented by a *yantra* or symbolic geometric design.

Obtain a *japa mala* (prayer bead string) to count recitations. Most have 108 beads, a sacred number. 108 recitations equals "one round." Daily recitation of one or more rounds is important until you've attained your goal. Traditionally, mantras are chanted for 40 days to manifest a specific result. Proper pronunciation and cadence are said to yield better results. It's easy to find recordings of native Hindus and Buddhists chanting online. The stronger and clearer your intent while chanting, the better.

Prepare the appropriate condition items (oils, candles, incense, etc.) so they are ready for use. Perform a puja before launching into the conjure work of dressing and setting candles, crafting mojos, or bottles. The conjure will remain the same, but with mantras in place of prayers from other traditions.

Ganesha (Road Opening, Obstacle Removal)
OM GAM Ganapataye namaha

Lakshmi (Abundance, Wealth, Success)
OM SHRIM Mahalakshmiyei swaha

Saraswati (Academics, Arts, Knowledge)
OM AIM Saraswatiyei namaha

Durga (Protection, Empowerment)
OM DUM Durgayei namaha

Kali (Transformative Destruction, Dissolution)
OM KRIM Kalikayei namaha

Shiva (Transformation, Spirituality, Gnosis)
OM namah Shivaya

Krishna (Selfless Service, Love, Joy)
OM Krishnaya namaha

LAUGHING WITH LUCKY BUDDHA

Lucky Buddha condition formulas found in conjure shops generally use label images of the Buddha of Happiness, known as Hotei (Japanese) or Budai (Chinese), and often called the "fat" or "laughing" Buddha. Lucky Buddha formulas usually contain Asian perfume ingredients as well as this "exotic" image.

Buddhist folk priest Zac Lui explains that the Buddhist perspective of "good fortune" is inextricably linked to generosity. If practitioners are generous, they'll be blessed with well-being. Those who want gambling luck or more money would likely go to more worldly Taoist or Shinto spirits. Hotei can be petitioned for luck experienced as inner contentment with one's current situation, or for aid with growing wealth through right livelihood and action. Making regular offerings, concurrent with mindful engagement in generosity, are traditional ways to work with Hotei. Note also that Hotei is traditionally suited to long-term prosperity work, moreso than to quick gains.

Hotei Buddha Prosperity mantra (Mandarin): *Namo Xiao Fo* (nah-moh shee-oww foh)

GANESHA OBSTACLE REMOVAL

- **White Wo/Man Candle**
- **Three 4" Orange Candles**
- **Road Opener, Block Buster, or Ganesha Oil and Incense, plus condition oil for your goal**
- **Block Buster Herb Mix**
- **Ganesha altar image**
- **Tray with offerings**
- **Japa mala**
- **Petition Paper and Personal Concerns**

1) Wash hands and mouth. Prepare offerings on the tray. Perform Ganesha puja and leave offerings.
2) Load and dress the figural candle. Use personal concerns and condition oil. Roll in herbs.
3) Draw a 6-pointed star with herbs. Place the petition paper at center with the figural candle on top.
4) Dress orange candles in Road Opener Oil. Place in a triangle around the star, point upwards, creating the central figure of Ganesha's yantra.
5) Light the candles and chant. Recite one to ten rounds of *OM GAM Ganapataye namaha*, holding your intentions firm.
6) Consume the offerings. Then clean the tray.
7) Repeat for three to seven days. Continue chanting the mantra for 40 days.

WHY MANTRAS?

Mantras were received by ancient Indian *rishis* (mystic seers) in states of deep meditation. They believed everything in existence vibrates in varying frequencies. Mantras are those frequencies experienced as sound. Abstract elements within existence have abstract, one syllable sounds, called *bija* (seed) mantras. As the concepts represented become more concrete, they start being able to translate into words. Sanskrit is the language that was built out of these mystic sounds.

To illustrate: OM is taught by the rishis as a sound of Universal existence. When OM is chanted, the chanters increase their resonance with the whole of existence — both infinite potentiality and physical manifestation. There is no translation for OM, an auditory representation of a large abstract concept.

Mantras can be difficult to translate even when the words have concrete linguistic meaning. This breakdown of a mantra for Ganesha, **OM GAM Ganapataye namaha**, translated as "Salutations to Ganesha, remover of obstacles; I bow to you" demonstrates this disparity:

- **OM**: Taps into the infinite Universal tapestry.
- **GAM**: Bija of the abstract idea of "obstacles." From the infinite tapestry of existence, the cord of yarn that deals with obstacles is plucked.
- **Ganapataye**: The named personification of the concrete control inherent in obstacle removal in manifest reality. The ending "yei" catalyzes the Shakti (energy), shifting it from potentiality into an active force. The single thread from that cord of GAM which pertains to actively removing obstacles is chosen.
- **Namaha**: shows gratitude to those forces.

Most common mantras have the OM, a bija, and a divine name, making them easy to work with. When chanting a mantra, the specific vibrational frequencies that you're trying to manifest are intoned. By immersing yourself and your area in this vibration, you work to co-create reality, shaping it in the way you desire.

Devi Spring is an initiate of the Sri Chaitanya Saraswat Math lineage of Hinduism and has taken lay Buddhist vows at Tengye Ling Tibetan Buddhist Temple. She has a Religious Studies BA and has practiced folk magic since 1997. She presented this workshop at the 2018 Festival.

WITCHCRAFT AND THE FÆRY TRADITION
Storm Færywolf

THE HIDDEN COMPANY

Due to its nebulous nature, the term "Færy" is often misunderstood. Related to the Latin "fata," meaning "fate," it referred to things of magic and enchantment before being attached to a race of beings and the realm in which they live. If something was "fæ" it was enchanted, magical, or otherworldly.

Folklore from several different cultures describes a variety of magical beings said to engage our world, at times in strikingly similar terms. Germanic Elves, Irish Færies, and Hawaiian Menehune are each unique beings, and yet they all exist under the same umbrella, that of preternatural life forms who inhabit the natural world and yet most often prefer to remain hidden, revealing themselves to humanity only in certain places, or under certain conditions.

Popular culture speaks of færies as creatures of delight and whimsy, but folklore reveals a different story. Far from the Victorian era's harmless pixies, folk beliefs describe the Fæ as magically powerful, morally confusing, potentially helpful, but extremely dangerous. In fact, most folkloric magic concerning the Fæ focuses on magic to protect against them.

WITCHCRAFT AND FÆRY

Witchcraft cannot be divorced from Færy. In the American folklorist Charles Godfrey Leland's *Aradia, or the Gospel of the Witches*, the titular figure Aradia is sent to Earth to teach the art of witchcraft to the oppressed. She is the avatar of the supreme deity: the Goddess Diana, who is described in the text as the Queen of the Witches and Færies.

Pre-modern European witchcraft tales provide us with a recurring theme, that of a relationship between a familiar spirit and a magical practitioner. A commonly held belief was that each witch or warlock was in communion with an otherworldly spirit who either granted them powers or provided them magical instruction and assistance. These spirits could take many forms: animals, humans, demons, or imps. Their nature as shape-shifters is one clue to their true nature. They are Færy.

THE ANDERSON FERI TRADITION

Although the initiatory lineage of the Færy tradition is said to have originated with the Færy race, described as the extra-temporal descendants of humans and fallen angels, it was, in fact, popularized and given form by the late Victor Anderson (1917-2001), Grandmaster and "Fairy Chief." His unique initiation as a child in the woods by a stranger, and his subsequent adoption into a witch coven as a teen in 1932, along with his physical blindness, all aided in the development of his etheric sight and formed the basis of his spiritual outlook.

The Færy tradition stresses intimate communion with the spirits of nature within the guidelines of some simple personal practices and observances, and the engagement of art, poetry, and revelry.

Labeled "Feri" by some modern practitioners, this lineage shares similarities with a number of traditional forms of folk magic and spirit-work, like hoodoo, conjure, braucherei, and trolldom, as well as resembling certain ceremonial religions, such as Vodou, Wicca, Druidry, and other Neo-Pagan paths.

Unlike manu in Wicca, arguably the most popular form of witchcraft religion, practitioners of Færy focus not on fertility and agriculture, but on ecstasy: the act of transcending normal consciousness. It is this state of controlled enchantment in which the practitioner communes deeply with the spirits that inhabit the universe, and at times enlists their aid toward the betterment of personal magical goals.

Although their religious lineage is named after these beings of power and transmits a deep lore that speaks of them as the mythological progenitors of this magical path, not all Feri practitioners work with the Færy realm directly. The tradition is sufficiently diverse to give even the most seasoned initiate headaches when trying to decide exactly what material is central to the religion or indeed how privately or secretly that material should be held. Just as in the folkloric descriptions of the tradition's namesake, Færy is a thing of liminality, or being "in between the worlds." The boundaries are blurred and uncertain. Færy, as always, is a mystery.

"ALL GODS ARE FERI GODS"

Another detail that sets the Færy tradition apart from most of its Neo-Pagan cousins is the fact that it has no set pantheon. While it is traditional in Færy to speak of the female and male divine forces in terms such as the Star Goddess or "God Herself," for the divine feminine and of her "son, lover, and other half," for the dualistic and masculine God, the tradition is one of personal connections, and so any and all deities and spirits may be equally honoured in this path. The only determining factor would be the practitioner's own experiences. Because of this, different lineages have developed their own customs as to which particular spirits they may predominantly work with or honour.

WORKING WITH THE FÆ

A Færy ally can be an invaluable asset for the witch, as well as providing a relationship that is deeply personal, intimate, and possibly romantic or erotic, just as with any human one might engage.

To begin a relationship with the Fæ you must first quiet your mind and attune your attention to the natural world. The Fæ comprise the spiritual consciousness of the land, and as such they must be approached with thoughtfulness and respect. One time-honoured method of engaging them is to appease them with offerings of milk and honey, with dancing and song, and by providing spaces for them ornamented with bells and shiny objects.

When engaging the Fæ you may be given certain folkloric keys as well as certain prohibitions by which you can more safely navigate the Færy encounter. In trance, you may seek them in the Underworld, generally by envisioning the visual key of an opening in the earth and journeying below into the Shining Realm.

As a traveller, you are admonished not to bring iron into the Fæ's realm, as it dispels their magic. You are also advised to not eat or drink anything you might find or be offered by them during your stay, lest you become connected to or trapped in the Færy realm forever. Perhaps the strangest admonishment is to never say "Thank you" to the Fæ, an act that speaks of how little our word as humans is valued there. In the land of the Fæ, actions speak louder than words.

THE BLUE GOD

In the Færy tradition it is taught that another name for one's personal God or "God Soul" is Dian y Glas. Dian y Glas is depicted as a youthful effeminate male with blue skin, peacock feathers in his hair, and a green serpent coiled around his neck. He is one's natural divine state of beauty, pride, and sexual exuberance. He is the child of the Mother, as we are all Her children.

Collectively, the individual God Souls of humanity are reflected in another aspect of the Blue God, the Peacock Angel of the Yazidis of Iraq, Melek Ta'us, who filled the earth with flora and fauna. In this form he is the god of free will and redemption, as well as the potential for both light and dark in all humankind. We offer him acts of devotion to cleanse, empower, and elevate him, in order to inspire and guide the evolution of the world.

INVOKING THE BLUE GOD

It is said that the Blue God is the unification of the higher and lower selves, symbolized by the dove and the serpent. These are the Divine Twins, a reminder that we do not honour only the enlightened parts of ourselves; that the primal is equally holy. Call to the Blue God with acts of sensuality and joy. Adorn yourself with beautiful clothing or jewelry. Dance, sing, and shake your tail feathers! Light a blue candle in his honour and anoint yourself with scented oils. Use peacock feathers as his holy symbol. Admire your beauty in a mirror; behold how beautiful you are!

INVOCATION TO THE BLUE GOD

*"Arise! Descend! Thy Twins of flame,
Who flow as one into my heart
We call the Winged Serpent's name:
Dian y Glas, son of the Arte!"*

Behold how beautiful you are!

This flyer was prepared for the opening ceremony of the 2017 Hoodoo Heritage Festival. Storm Færywolf is an author, poet, artist, and teacher of American Traditional Witchcraft. An initiate of the Færy tradition, he holds the Black Wand of a Færy Master and is the founder of his own lineage, Blue Rose. Storm is a co-owner of The Mystic Dream, a spiritual and magical supply store, online at TheMysticDream.com.

NEW THOUGHT AND THE LAW OF ATTRACTION
Madame Nadia and Jaiye Dania

THE LAW OF ATTRACTION

The Law of Attraction is a key principle of the New Thought Movement, whose core precept is an everlasting and infinite intelligence, dwelling in every one of us. By being one with the Divine, we resonate with a universal magnetic force that draws similar energies together. This law suggests that through the power of focussed intention we are capable of manifesting anything we desire. As we become more conscious of our subconscious, we harness greater control over ourselves, our immediate environment, and the world at large.

HISTORY

The Law of Attraction is an expression whose philosophy is rooted in antiquity. It is found in the spiritual and philosophical teachings of ancient Greeks like Hermes Trismegistus and Plato and in Eastern religions such as Taoism and Buddhism. It saw a renaissance in the 19th Century United States, where many began looking beyond the Bible to science in search of enlightenment. During this time the New Thought Movement was born.

THEORY

The Law of Attraction implies that by changing our intentions, thoughts, and frequency, we can change our reality. The results of scientific experiments lend credence to this theory, including those by Dr. Masaru Emoto, whose experiments used microscopic photography to prove that water intentioned with visualization, prayer, and positive words create magnificent crystalline structures, while negative words create ugly, chaotic formations. Our bodies are 70% water, so it follows that our thoughts shape our reality. Furthermore, we each possess an energetic frequency which affects the events and circumstances we attract. Dr. David Hawkins established a scale to measure this frequency. His vibrational scale measures from 0 to 1000. The higher an individual measures on the scale, the more at ease they are with life, with 1000 being the state of an ascended master. The vibration of love starts at 500, while lower frequencies like guilt, shame, and apathy are the densest energies. How do we ascend higher?

PRACTICE

Hypnotherapist Marisa Peer tells us that we hold on to childhood beliefs that no longer serve us; in particular the belief that we aren't enough. Peer teaches that our brain resonates with the familiar and does what it thinks we want. The way we feel about any event and how our minds respond is the result of the pictures we make in our heads and the words we say to ourselves. Therefore, to succeed at anything we must make the unfamiliar familiar, and the familiar unfamiliar. In other words, our mind is wired to recreate situations with which it is familiar, and to change this unhealthy paradigm we must replace our negative mind scripts with positive ones.

One of the best ways to replace negative scripts is through affirmative prayer and intentional and consistent repetition of values we desire to instill into our psyche. This can be done repeating affirmations, such as, "I am enough," alongside pictorial constructs like sigils or vision boards.

Sigils are inscribed, drawn, or painted symbols or seals considered to have magical power. They are found amongst the magical practices of cultures around the world. Some examples are Jewish kabbalistical seals, Norse Galdrabok sigils, Haitian veves, Arabic caligrams, Hindu yantras, and Taoist calligraphic charms.

Read more about sigils in folk magic in this book: **"Paper in My Shoe" by catherine yronwode.**

THE IDEAL PHYSIQUE

There is a skill used for bodybuilding training called the "Mind-Muscle Connection," which is the movement of a muscle from point A to B while visualizing what the body will look like under such continuous intent. Exercising without focussing on the outcome activates fewer muscle fibers. This phenomenon is measured using electromyography (EMG). A 2012 study concluded that training alone cannot create the body you want. Continuous emphasis on manifesting that body is as important as the tedious task of exercising. We put this theory to the test and were amazed by the difference it made. This is an incredible tool for physical transformation.

INTENTION

The connection between man and food is not new, and we aren't here to tell you what to eat or avoid. We want to help you understand your relationship with food. One may remember in childhood praying over food, asking for nourishment from the divine before each meal. To eat with intention and expecting benefit from our meals should be part of our daily routine. Speaking to our food and water is no different than talking to the herbs we use in our work. We can use the food we eat to help manifest changes in our lives.

EXECUTION AND MANIFESTATION

An obstacle to achieving the physique we desire is our perception of food. Food can be rewarding, seductive, and delicious, especially after a long and stressful day, but we must outsmart the instinct that makes us over eat by convincing us to find comfort in food. We must consciously remind ourselves to chew our food, enjoy it, savour it, and will the expected benefit into existence. Change happens as a result of reducing what we consume that is bad for us or has no nutritional benefit to the body or spirit.

Be gentle with your body. Trust the process and be truthful and objective with yourself. If impatience for results equated to how fast we damage our bodies, would we still be so anxious? Healing, repairing, and rebuilding doesn't happen overnight. The ability to manifest and believe in our gifts is one of the most important tools we can utilize without limitation if we understand that being healthy is not just about being happy with our physicality, but also about being better vessels for our work. So dream, believe, and manifest!

FIT AND FOXY FAVOURITES

We like these supplies when working for attraction.

CANDLES

- **A 7-Knob Wishing Candles in green:** To draw monetary success, red to increase glamour and romance, and white for general attraction.
- **A green Eye in Pyramid Candle:** To focus on our vision and to increase wealth.
- **A Glass-Encased Vigil Candle:** Use purple for mastery and orange to open roads or to replace negative scripts with positive ones.
- **A white Skull Candle:** For mastery over your own mind and thoughts.

OILS AND OTHER SPIRITUAL SUPPLIES

Our favourite attraction oils, sachets, and bath crystals include Magnet, Attraction, Lady Luck, Crown of Success, Mastery, and Look Me Over.

ATTRACTION CURIOS

Our favourite drawing curios are Lodestones and Lodestone Grit, Pyrite, Magnets, and Mercury Dimes.

HEALTH, FITNESS, AND MAGIC WITH HERBS

- **Damiana:** Stimulates muscular contractions and delivers oxygen to the genitals, while increasing desire and energy. It has aphrodisiac qualities and is used to attract and fascinate a romantic partner.
- **Ginseng:** Increases circulation, remedies a lack of energy, and improves mood and concentration. It is used for empowering, particularly for men, and for increasing sexual charm.
- **Ginger:** Helps fight inflammation, aids in digestion, and eases stomach discomfort. It is also a strong antioxidant. It heats up your work and is used to attract lovers, romantically enchant, and protect your business enterprises.
- **Hyssop:** Helps expel mucus from the respiratory tract, relieves congestion, fights parasites and infections, and increases circulation. It is a Biblical herb of cleansing, and removes guilt and negative thought patterns from mistakes of the past.
- **Licorice:** Reduces muscle spasms, fights inflammation, and wards off viral, bacterial, and parasitic infections; promotes adrenal function. It aids in establishing control and dominion over opponents and is useful in self-confidence spells.
- **Rosemary:** Boosts immune system function, helps with maintaining blood pressure levels, and is great for circulation, especially to the brain. A great spirit guardian, it gives advantage, esteem, and empowerment to women. It is also said to help with memory, as well as to induce prophetic dreams to help visualize and manifest your goals.

This flyer was prepared for the 2017 Hoodoo Heritage Festival. A member of AIRR, Madame Nadia is a gifted Russian-born rootworker, card reader, fortune teller, Palera, Quimbandera, and an initiate to Shakta Tantra. A glamour activist, she is also a Priestess of The Gloss Fox. Jaiye Dania is a Nigerian-born spiritualist and card reader with expertise in hoodoo and Quimbanda, as well as a professional body builder and nutrition advisor. Together they hosted Fit and Foxy on the LMC Radio Network.

HOW TO TAKE A SPIRITUAL BATH
Aura Laforest

TWELVE STEPS TO CLEANLINESS

1. Start clean: Make sure that you're physically clean already. You do not need to take a pre-bath, but if you're going to be doing a pre-dawn spiritual bath, you should take a regular shower or bath with soap and water the night before, so that you wake up clean.

2. Bathe before dawn: Rise before dawn so that the bath can be completed by the time the Sun rises. This is traditional if you are performing the bath for gain or increase of any kind, for as the Sun rises, so will good things come to you. However, if the bath you are taking has a different timing, respect the timing prescribed.

3. Add optional candles: For a cleansing, jinx removing, or uncrossing bath, you may light a small tea light or white candle on either side of your tub or shower. For other baths, a candle of appropriate colour anointed with suitable condition oil may be used; however, you do not need a candle to take a spiritual bath.

4. Enter the bath: Take two or three long and deep breaths to calm your body and mind. If you are using candles, walk between them to enter the bathing area. If you are taking a pour-over bath, bring your warm bath-tea diluted with water to the area. If you are taking a soaking bath, step into the tub of prepared water.

5. Pour or soak with prayers: If you are taking a poured bath in the shower or tub, pour over your head a cup at a time as you pray. If you are taking a soaking bath, immerse your body. Either way, get your entire body wet as you pray from the Bible or from the heart. If your hairdo is such that you cannot wash your hair, bathe from the neck down and wash your face. If your hair permits, pour over it or dunk your head under it.

6. Bathe with directionality: To rid yourself of a jinx, negative condition, bad habit, unnatural illness, or bad luck, wash downward, head to toe. If you have filled the tub, start by soaking, then open the drain, and stand with your hands crossed, right hand on left shoulder, left hand on right shoulder. Uncross your arms and stroke downward with your hands. To bring in a desire, faithful lover, better job, higher wages, gambling luck, or happiness, wash upward, toe to head. If you are taking a pour-over bath, pour the water on yourself, then stroke upward, and finish by folding your hands in prayer.

7. Keep a representative sample of your bath water: This is the water with your essence in it. In the days before indoor plumbing, baths were taken out of doors and the entire tub was dumped out. Now, after a soaking bath, you may keep a cup by placing it in the tub and letting the water out the drain while it remains in place. If taking a pour-over bath, place a small bowl at your feet as you pour and let the container catch the liquid you'll keep.

8. Come out of your bath or shower and air dry: If you used candles at Step 3, exit the bath between them. You can drink a cup of your herb tea now (or another cup of herbal tea you've brewed) to enhance your spell as you air dry. It's also a great time to pray. Observe the changes you feel in your mind and body as the water evaporates from your skin.

9. After uncrossing, prepare for your blessings: If you've taken an uncrossing or cleansing bath, now is the time to oil or powder your body with a formula for luck, love, protection, or money.

10. Dress in clean clothes and dispose of the sample of water: Pour out the representative sample taken earlier either by casting it into your yard or into a crossroads. Throw the water East, toward the rising Sun, for gain, or toward the West, the direction of the setting Sun, for removal. No specific crossroad is required; choose one that is conveniently located for you. Walk or drive home and don't look back.

11. Use the left-over bath water in other rites: You may also keep some of your wash water to cleanse the home you live in or your place of business if you wish the work to extend to and affect these locations as well.

12. Stay clean as long as possible: Although it is rarely suggested nowadays, it is an old custom to try to avoid touching others or shaking their hands on the day that you have taken a spiritual bath. This is done to keep the work on you and to avoid getting messed up again.

This is an extract from Aura Laforest's 96-page book, "Hoodoo Spiritual Baths," presented as a workshop at the 2014 Hoodoo Heritage festival by Miss Phœnix LeFæ and Lou Florez. The full book is available from the publisher, Lucky Mojo Curio Co. Aura is online at AuraLaforest.com.

CLEANSING, BLESSING, AND PROTECTING THE HOME
Ambrozine LeGare

THE IMPORTANCE OF HOME

"Where thou art — that — is home."
Emily Dickinson

Your home, whether it is a palatial estate, a studio apartment in the city, a room on campus, etc. is the place where you should feel most at ease. In our often very busy lives, we may overlook the one space where we start and end each day.

Spiritual cleansing and blessing of one's home is a practice that can be found on every continent and in every culture. In conjure, the practice of house cleansing and blessing can be done to remove unwanted spirits, renew the space for a new season, aid in changing one's fortunes, etc. There are numerous ways in which a person can cleanse and bless their home. Below are a few ways in which you can make your home your castle.

CLEANSING YOUR HOME

The cleansing and blessing of your space go hand-in-hand. The act of performing a spiritual cleansing to remove negativity should be followed by a "blessing" which will draw in the condition that you desire. Cleansing can include using washes, incense, prayers, candles, or a combination to remove unwanted conditions from your space.

To start your cleansing and blessing work, gather the cleaning tools, herbs, incense, candles, and prayers that you will need. Once all of your items are prepared, you are ready to begin.

Open the windows, in each room light a tea light or small white candle and incense, if desired, and begin your prayers. In conjure, the most common way to cleanse is to start from the back of your residence and work toward the front, and from the top to the bottom. Clean every area of your space, including corners, door frames, windows, and the front steps of your house or outside area of your apartment or room. Once you have cleaned your entire space, end at your front door by sweeping or mopping the remaining wash outward. Any leftover wash can be discarded with thanks at the crossroads if you do not live in a house.

CLEANSING HELPERS

Here are a number of simple, straightforward, mostly three-ingredient washes and incense mixes that you can prepare and use in your home. Try them out and stick with the ones whose feel and scent appeal most to you. After all, the smell of each person's home is a very distinct and personal one.

SCRIPTURES FOR CLEANSING

The power of the Bible and scripture is frequently used not only in cleansing and protection, but also in the whole of hoodoo. Several Psalms from the Bible that are useful while cleansing are Psalms 23, Psalms 51, Psalms 88, and Psalms 91. Recite them as you make your washes or light incense.

FLOOR AND WALL WASH #1

Mix together in a large bucket of water one cup of strong black Coffee, a handful of Salt, and some of your first urine of the day.

FLOOR AND WALL WASH #2

Prepare a strong tea from Rue, Hyssop, and Devil's Shoe Strings. Add this to your cleaning water.

FLOOR AND WALL WASH #3

Mix together in a large bucket of water Chinese Floor Wash and one cap of Ammonia.

INCENSE MIX #1

Combine Frankincense, Camphor, and Bay Leaf together, and burn on charcoal.

INCENSE MIX #2

Combine Frankincense, Sage, and Rue together, and burn on charcoal.

INCENSE MIX #3

Combine Frankincense, Dragon's Blood, and Coffee grounds together, and burn on charcoal.

CLEANSING TIPS

Here are a few helpful tips to make the job of cleansing your entire home a little easier.

REACHING HIGH PLACES

Put some of your wash water into a spray bottle. This will enable you to reach higher places and to spray walls, door frames, and shelves with ease.

CLEANING CARPETED FLOORS

In carpeted areas, substitute cleansing sachets for the wash; vacuum them up just like a carpet freshener.

KEEPING A STOCK OF CLEANSING TEA

Make a large batch of cleansing tea and store it in your refrigerator. It will keep for up to two months.

BLESSING YOUR HOME

After cleansing your home, follow up with work for money drawing, peace, love, or any blessings you desire. To begin, start on the outside of your property and move inward toward your house without talking to anyone. Lay down your blessing work while praying the scriptures or prayers that you have chosen.

BLESSING HELPERS

The importance of having effective and strong blessings on one's home cannot be stressed enough; however, when it comes to self-blessing, often people find themselves at a loss. Here are a number of simple yet effective tips and tricks to not only bring blessings to your home, but also to do so quickly and with ease.

SCRIPTURES FOR BLESSING

A few scriptures to aid in blessing and protection are Psalms 23, Psalms 32, and Isaiah 32:18.

BLESSING WITH INCENSE

Burn a blessing incense for money, peace, or love drawing in each room of your home.

BLESSING YOUR DOORS AND STEPS

Wash down your front door and front steps with Van Van Oil, Peace Water, or other blessing oil or wash.

BLESSING TEA SPRAY

Make a blessing tea from Bay Leaf, Angelica Root, and Basil. Use a spray bottle and spray your home while praying for blessings. Burn a blessing incense with the same herbs or roots you used for the tea.

PROTECTING YOUR HOME

Now that you have cleansed and blessed your home, add a layer of protection. Hanging a talisman such as a hamsa hand or cross and strategically placing mirrors or fixed items to ward off evil, hexes, or misfortune will help keep your home protected.

PROTECTING HELPERS

These tried and true methods bring protection. Give them a try and see which ones work best for you, as the type and degree of protection that one needs varies from home to home.

SCRIPTURES FOR PROTECTION

Psalms 91 is recited for safety and protection.

NAIL DOWN YOUR PROPERTY

Dress railroad spikes or large nails with your urine, and nail down the corners of your property.

SALT AND CAMPHOR FOR PROTECTION

Place Salt or Camphor in the four corners of each room of your home.

FIERY WALL TO PROTECT YOUR PROPERTY

Burn Fiery Wall of Protection Incense Powder and anoint all entry points with Fiery Wall of Protection Oil while praying for protection.

FINISHING THE JOB

Discard any remaining candle wax, incense ash, or wash water at the crossroads with thanks!

Ambrozine LeGare presented "Cleansing, Blessing, and Protection for Your Home" at the 2016 Hoodoo Heritage Festival workshops. An actor, reader, rootworker, and host of the Liquid Libations Radio show, she can be found online at AmbrozineLeGare.com.

HELP FOR ADDICTIONS AND BAD HABITS
Aura Laforest

HEALING BLUE BATH FOR HELP WITH ADDICTIONS

Mix a crushed square of Reckitt's Crown Blue; a cup of Salt, and a splash of Holy Water in a full tub of hot water. Pray 1 Corinthians 6:12 *("All things are lawful unto me, but all things are not expedient: all things are lawful for me, but I will not be brought under the power of any.")* during the bath. Soak for 20 minutes, washing downward from head to toe. Air-dry and dress in clean clothes. Dispose of some of the used bath water in a crossroads toward the setting Sun and return home without looking back.

MOJO TO OVERCOME BAD HABITS

Combine a small John the Conqueror Root, a pinch of Yarrow, a pinch of White Oak bark chips, and a pinch of Blessed Thistle in a red flannel bag. Add your name paper with your hairs in it, folded towards you. Breathe into the hand, then wrap or tie it shut. Feed it weekly with a blend of John the Conqueror and Rose of Crucifixion oils.

WALNUT, EUCALYPTUS, AND LEMON TO BREAK A HABIT

Boil up a bath-tea with one Black or English Walnut, still in its shell, plus a handful of Eucalyptus leaves. Strain the liquid and add the strained juice of one Lemon. Freeze the liquid in cubes, then dissolve and dilute them in your bath or floorwash as needed. Adding a cube to a hot bath once a week helps to drive off wicked companions and put a stop to tobacco, drug, or alcohol dependency.

KNOTWEED TO TIE DOWN TOBACCO OR MARIJUANA CRAVINGS

Mix Knot Weed with soft wax and roll it around a pinch of Marijuana or Tobacco, forming a ball. On a piece of paper, write your desire for Tobacco or Marijuana to die out of your life, wrap the paper around the ball, and tie it with a mop string. Bury the ball in a graveyard, asking the dead to tie down your problem until you return; then walk away.

BATH CRYSTAL BLEND FOR FIGHTING TEMPTATION

Combine equal parts Cast Off Evil Bath Crystals, Eucalyptus Bath Crystals, and Run Devil Run Bath Crystals in a tub of water. Soak for 20 minutes, washing downward from head to toe. During the bath, pray 1 Corinthians 10:13 *("God is faithful, who will not suffer you to be tempted above that ye are able; but will with the temptation also make a way to escape, that ye may be able to bear it.")* Dispose of some of the used bath water in a crossroads toward the setting Sun and walk away.

HERBS FOR HELP WITH ADDICTIONS

- **Angelica Root:** A strong guardian in times of crisis, strength, or weakness.
- **Bay Leaf:** Clears the mind and brings both insight and wisdom.
- **Black Walnut:** Kills off the desire for no-good things, situations, or people.
- **Eucalyptus:** Gives strength to stay away from evil temptations, people, or places; helps one breathe easier when thoughts or sensations within the body are oppressive.
- **Goldenseal:** Improves health and nurtures beauty, strength and wisdom, making it easier to leave old hurtful habits behind; often used in conjunction with Holy Ghost Root (Angelica).
- **John the Conqueror Root:** Fosters the strength, personal mastery, and energy needed to overcome obstacles; it combines well with Master of the Woods for this purpose.
- **Knotweed (Ladies Thumb):** Ties down things to be cast away.
- **Lemon:** Clears away spiritual dirt and dross; refreshes the mind.
- **Master of the Woods:** Increases our energy to overcome obstacles; it combines well with John the Conqueror for this purpose.
- **Sage:** Purifies and gives strength to women, and imparts wisdom to all.
- **Salt:** Sends away evil; protects against its return.

This is an extract from Aura Laforest's 96-page book, "Women's Work," which she presented at the 2016 HHF. The full book is available from the Lucky Mojo Curio Co.

BIBLE SPELLS FOR HELPING, BLESSING, AND HEALING
Miss Michæle and Professor Charles Porterfield

AN OLD TRADITION

We do not present these Bible-based healing spells as a substitute for professional medical consultation, care, or treatment. They are simply traditional in our community and we hold them in high regard, believing as we do that the healing sought and conveyed by them comes from a higher spiritual power.

SAINT LAZARUS FOR SKIN RASHES

Saint Lazarus the Beggar (Luke 16-31) is the patron saint of skin problems. If your dermatologist allows it, wash with a dilute solution of Saint Lazarus Bath Crystals in Holy Water while reciting Luke 17:11-19 and petitioning Saint Lazarus for intercession. Luke 17:11-19 recounts how Jesus cleansed the ten lepers. Be sure to offer thanks afterwards.

TO STOP BLEEDING WITH EZEKIEL

This old tradition to stop bleeding came to America with German immigrants. To accomplish the goal one recites over the wound Ezekiel 16:6: *"And when I passed by thee, and saw thee polluted in thine own blood, I said unto thee when thou wast in thy blood, Live; yea, I said unto thee when thou wast in thy blood, Live."*

ANOTHER BLOOD STOPPING SPELL

This remedy to stop bleeding, is said to cure no matter how far away a person is, so long as their first name is rightly pronounced while using it. Call upon the Lord by saying aloud:

"Jesus Christ dearest blood!
That stoppeth the pain and stoppeth the blood,
In this help you [the person's first name only],
God the Father, God the Son,
God the Holy Ghost. Amen."

BACKACHE MASSAGE WITH PSALMS 3

If you suffer from backache, write a copy of Psalms 3 on a clean sheet of paper and then burn it to ashes. Mix the ashes with Olive Oil or 7-11 Holy Oil and a few drops of Peppermint Oil. Pray Psalms 3 over the mixture as well, then use it to massage your back.

FRUITS OF THE SPIRIT ARTHRITIS SPELL

To help with arthritis, take a box of golden raisins and place them in a shallow lidded container. Cover the raisins with gin as you recite aloud Galatians 5:22-23: *"But the fruit of the Spirit is love, joy, peace, longsuffering, gentleness, goodness, faith, meekness, temperance: against such there is no law."* Put the lid on the container and let the raisins soak for two to three weeks. Each day take nine raisins from the jar, recite Jeremiah 17:14: *"Heal me, O Lord, and I shall be healed; save me, and I shall be saved: for thou art my praise"* over them, and eat them.

SELF-FORGIVENESS RITUAL BATH

For this ritual you will need Hyssop, salt, two small white candles, Blessing Oil, a photo of yourself, and a Bible.

Start just before sunrise. Set the two white candles on either side of your tub so you pass between them as you enter the bath. Draw the bath and add Hyssop to the water, either as an herb-tea or supplies such as Hyssop Bath Crystals or Hyssop Oil. Light the candles and recite the 23rd Psalm as you enter the bath. Soak in the water, and when ready, pour water over your head while reciting Psalms 51:7: *"Purge me with Hyssop, and I shall be clean: wash me, and I shall be whiter than snow."* When you feel ready, stand up and step backwards out of the tub between the two candles and say, *"In Jesus name, Amen."*

Save a cupful of the bath water before draining the tub. Take this water to a crossroads, and throw it backwards over your shoulder, to the East. Walk away without looking back.

MORNING RITE FOR SELF-BLESSING

Recite Psalms 34:8 over a glass of spring water or seltzer: *"O taste and see that the Lord is good: blessed is the man that trusteth in him."* Then drink the water and set about your day's activities.

Miss Michæle and Professor Porterfield presented their 96-page book "Hoodoo Bible Magic" at the 2014 Hoodoo Heritage Festival workshops. The full book is available from the Lucky Mojo Curio Co.

DELIVERANCE AND PROTECTION FROM SPIRITUAL ATTACK
Khi Armand

TO PROTECT A HOME'S INHABITANTS

Take the 10 of Clubs out of the deck of cards and write a list of the home's inhabitants in the center. Touch each club on the card while saying the name of one of Jesus's 12 Apostles along with the phrase "Protect and fortify us." Wrap the card around a whole Angelica Root with white string and keep in a white flannel bag inside of the home near the front door. Feed the bag once per week with whiskey or Fiery Wall of Protection Oil.

PERSONAL PROTECTION MOJO

Combine Bay Leaf, Devil's Shoe Strings, and Rue in a red flannel bag. Breathe it to life, name it, and feed it whiskey, Protection, or Fiery Wall of Protection Oil once a week. Keep it pinned inside your clothing against your skin for a week aside from showering and sleeping during which you can keep it pinned to the inside of your pillow. Afterwards, keep in a safe place.

PROTECTION AND BLESSING OIL

Pray Psalms 23 over Olive Oil and over it, ensuring that your breath touches the oil itself. Keep in a cool, dry place, and if you want it ensure its longevity, add a squirt of Vitamin E or Jojoba oil to it. This is a fantastic oil for protection, blessing, money, and all good works.

PROTECT A SPACE FROM THE EVIL EYE

To ward off the effects of covetous people entering your home or business, hang a nazar evil eye charm outside the door or inside the space directly facing the front door. To empower it, wash it in an infusion of Rue or smoke it in either Rue or Aspand before hanging it.

PROTECTION WHILE YOU SLEEP

To protect against spirit intrusions and spiritual attacks during the night, keep a Bible open to Psalms 91 under your bed with a pair of open metal scissors laid over the pages. You may anoint the scissors with a protection oil. A Bible once owned by a beloved family member is said to hold power and would be appropriate in such a working. To keep it clean, cover it with clear plastic or, more traditionally, a white cloth.

HERBS THAT PROTECT THE HOME

Hang dried Rue stalks or a flannel bag filled with Rue above the door frame inside your home to ward off evil and spiritual attacks.

Basil and Black Snake Root can be sprinkled around the home and prayerfully swept out the door to protect a home against intruders and evil.

A small cloth packet filled with Grains of Paradise, to which an image of Archangel Michæl is glued, may be placed at each door for protection.

Angelica Root, Bay Leaf, and Salt have popularly been placed in the corners of a room or a home to ward against harm. If a center rug is present, The same materials can be placed under it as well to invoke the five-spot, or the transformative power of the crossroads.

PROTECTIVE LEMON FREEZER SPELL

To stop a person from harassing you or to get them off your back, take a sheet of aluminum foil and place a Lemon on top. Make a slit in the Lemon and insert a petition with a statement such as "LEAVE ME ALONE" or "BACK OFF" written across their name along with their photo or personal concerns. Also copy out Psalms 37 if you work with scriptural passages. Add a pinch of Black Pepper, Red Pepper, and Oregano. If the person is a gossiper, add some Alum Powder in the spell to shut them up. Pin the slit together with nine pins or needles. Sprinkle a bit of your urine on the Lemon to dominate the person and wrap it in the foil by rolling it away from you. Throw the mess in the back of your freezer, slamming the door shut.

REVERSING EVIL WITH A MIRROR

If your neighbours are evil, get a 3-inch convex lens "blind spot" car mirror, dress the surface with an X of Reversing Oil, and glue it to the outside of your house, facing in their direction. Renew the X at every full moon.

These spells come from Khi Armand's 96-page book "Deliverance! Hoodoo Spells for Uncrossing, Healing, and Protection," presented at a Festival workshop in 2015. The complete book is available from the Lucky Mojo Curio Co.

A NORSE TROLLKNYTE (TROLL BUNDLE) FOR PROTECTION
Johannes Gårdbäck

CREATING THE TROLLKNYTE

The Scandinavian trollknyte (troll bundle) or trollpåse (troll bag) is the regional equivalent of the hoodoo mojo bag. The troll bundle consists of magical ingredients wrapped in cloth and tied shut, while the trollpåse ingredients are contained within a sewn bag made of cloth or chamois skin.

If the purpose of the bag or bundle is benevolent, such as for protection or luck, it is worn on a cord, either around the neck or under the arm pit. If the purpose of the bag or bundle is malevolent, it is typically buried close to the enemy, hidden in the house of the enemy, or hidden in the place to be förgjord or magically destroyed.

To make a trollknyte for personal protection from malevolent magic, disease, and evil influences, you will start by taking a piece of cloth and a string and choosing any nine out of thirteen listed ingredients. The number nine is dominant when it comes to trolldom due to the ancient Teutonic belief that all evil had nine varieties and thus should best be prevented by nine protective things.

INGREDIENTS TO CHOOSE FROM

Ett Kronans Mynt (A Coin of the Crown): When steel and iron are used as protection, they are commonly given the tyda that "As hard as the coin is, as hard shall the wearer be against all evil." A "coin of the crown" refers to coins that had been issued by the monarchy, which in older days indicated that the content was legitimate and hard.

Mossa Från Kyrkogårdshörn (Moss from the Four Corners of a Cemetery): Corners indicate ownership, so Moss from the four corners of a cemetery gives you the power over anything evil coming from the dead.

Dyvelsträck (Asafœtida, Devil's Dung): Dyvelis an old Swedish word that originates from Teufel, the German word for Devil. Träck is an old word for dung or shit, so Dyvelsträck accurately translates into English as Devil's Dung. In trolldom it is one of the most-used materials against evil of all kinds.

Kamfer (Camphor): This has long been used to keep evil and diseases away.

Vitlök (Garlic): A very common ingredient in protective trolldom. It is thought to remove the power from all evil.

Bävergäll (Castoreum): This is a tincture made from the scent glands of the Eurasian Beaver. Long used in folk medicine, partly due to its high content of salicylic acid, and partly due to its scent, it occurs in recipes and remedies that restore destroyed conditions, remove evil, and protect from evil.

Tibast (Spurge Laurel, Paradise Tree, Daphne mezereum): A common ingredient in protective troll bundles. All parts of the plant are used for magical protection. This plant is poisonous; do not eat it.

Vänderot (Vandal Root, Valerian Root): In Swedish it is called Vänderot or Turning Root due to an old belief that the plant turned once a year so that what was the top end one year would be the roots the next year; it is used in many restoration recipes and also worn for magical protection.

Johannesört, Fans Flykt (Saint John's Wort, Devil's Flight, Hypericum perforatum): The famous Swedish botanist Linnæus called this plant Fuga Demonum (Devil's Scourge); it can be found in many medieval medical dictionaries and is used to protect from evil and to restore destroyed conditions.

Flygrönn (Flying Rowan): This is wood from a Rowan tree that has grown in another tree or on a cliff and has never touched ground. It is mainly used for protection.

Älvanäver, Tuschlav (Elven Bark, Rock Tripe, Lasallia pustulata): The term Elven Bark is actually used for several different lichen species. This plant is most commonly used as incense against nasty elves and the various skin conditions caused by angry elves.

Pionfrö (Peony Seed, Pæonia): This is found in lots of old recipes for troll bundles and bags. It is used for protection from the evil eye, nasty spirits, elf shots, and malicious trolldom.

Salt och Malt (Salt and Malt): This combination occurs in spells designed to stop something evil from having an effect. It works to make something not "bite" on you. It is also a common offering to give to spirits and elves in order to avoid their "bite."

All these ingredients have the tyda of protection. (For an explanation of tydor, see *Trolldom: Spells and Methods of the Norse Folk Magic Tradition* or TSM).

WRAPPING AND RECITING

Place your nine ingredients, one by one, in the middle of the cloth. Pick up the cloth so as to gather it into a conical wrap containing the herbs. Hold it in your right hand and place your mouth close to the opening. Take a deep breath and speak the troll formula below. (For more on troll formulas, see TSM).

As you speak, keep your teeth clenched and speak "inside your mouth" without breathing out. When you complete the recitation, breathe out into the bag. Follow this with another deep breath and repeat the formula twice more, for a total of three times. You need only recite the English version. When you see a + in the text, make the sign of an equal armed cross with your left hand over the opening of the bundle.

SPOKEN TROLL FORMULA: ENGLISH

I stand up today. I dress myself in God's power and might. I stand up today. I sign myself as hard and sturdy as the Virgin Mary blessed her beloved son Jesus Christ. She followed him to the shore. She pushed him out from land. The shield of Heaven she put on him and the girdle of Earth she shot on him. As hard and sturdy I sign and enchant myself today, in this day and in this year and as long as the world shall stand. Against swords and knives. Against guns and bullets. Against cuts and sticks. Against strikes and shots. Against cuffs and bonds. Against fire and weather and winds. Against all damaging weapons. Against all evil. I sign and enchant myself against storm and bad weather. Against robbers and enemies, visible and invisible, secret or obvious, present and absent, with the same words that the Virgin Mary blessed and enchanted her blessed son Jesus Christ. In this moment and in this year and as long as this world stands. God's word. Amen.

Michæl + Gabriel + Raphæl + In the name of God the Father + Son + and Holy Spirit + Amen.

SPOKEN TROLL FORMULA: DANISH

Jeg oppstaær i Dag, jeg klæder mig i Guds Kraft og Magt; jeg opstaær i Dag, jeg signer mig ligesaa art of fast, som Jomfru Maria signet sin kjære Sön Jesum Christ. Hun fulde hannem til Strande, hun skød hannem ud fra Lande; Himmeriges Skjold hun paa hanem sædt, og Jorderiges Skjød hun paa hannem skjød. Lige saa hardt og fast signer og galdrer jeg mig i denne Dag og i dette Aaroog alt saa længe verden staar. Imod Sverd og Knive, emod Bøsser og Lodt, imod Hug og Sting, imod Slag og Skud, imod Fængsel og Baand, imod Ild og Veyr og Vand, imod alle skadelige Vaaben og emod alt det onde, som er til. Jeg signer og galdrer mig imod Storm og Uvejr, imod Røvere og Fjender, synlige og usynlige, hemmelige og aabenbære, nærværende og fraværende, med de samme Ord, som Jomfru Maria signet og galdret sin signede Sön Jesum Christum, i denne Stund og i denne Dagog i dette Aar og alt saa lenge Verden staær. Guds Ord. Amen.

Michæl † Gabriel † Raphæl † I Navn Gud Faders † Söns † og hellig Aands † Amen.

(Denmark, 19th century)

FINISHING THE BUNDLE

When the reading is done, pinch the bundled wrap closed and tie it up closely with the string. The trollknyte is now complete and can be worn around the neck or in the arm pit, or it can he hung by the door to protect a building.

Do not reveal to anyone the words of the formula you have spoken, in order to keep the power intact. (See more about why one does not share a spoken troll formula or trollformel in TSM).

If needed, you can refresh the bundle once every third month, preferably on a Thursday following the New Moon, by loosening the knots and speaking your troll formula anew three times into the bundle as described.

This was a hand-out at the 2014 Hoodoo Heritage Festival workshops. Johannes Gårdbäck is a member of the Association of Independent Readers and Rootworkers and the author of "Trolldom: Spells and Methods of the Norse Folk Magic Tradition." He can be reached at his web site, TheRootDoctor.se.

AFRO-CARIBBEAN PROTECTION MAGIC
Candelo Kimbisa

PROTECTION MACUTO

A macuto is a contained charm, somewhat akin to a mojo hand, conjure bag, or bundle used in the hoodoo and rootwork tradition. It is, however, more closely related to the ouanga or nkisi of West and Central Africa than to the American mojo, although one of the possible derivations of the mojo bag is also from the nkisi. More distant analogues from other lands are the trollknyte of Scandinavia and the medicine bundles of Native America.

A typical macuto is used as either a container or beacon for a spirit or ancestor, or for a specific purpose, similar to a mojo. There are several distinct styles of macuto, including Santeria and Palo Mayombe styles made in the Caribbean and a South Western beaded-style made by people of mixed African, Native American, and Hispanic ancestry.

This macuto for protection is contained inside a small Cowrie shell. The shell is filled with the following ingredients:

- **Devil's Shoe Strings**
- **Graveyard dirt**
- **Raw Cotton**
- **Crossroads dirt**
- **Hyssop**

First the Cowrie Shell is cleaned and made ready to receive the dirts and herbs. After this is done, a small amount of the graveyard and crossroads dirt is added into the shell and carefully pushed into its opening. Next a small piece of Devil's Shoe Strings is added, followed by Hyssop, and topped off with a small bit of raw cotton. Once the materials are inside the Cowrie Shell its opening is sealed over with wax and allowed to cool and set.

After the herbs, dirts, and wax are set, it is time to wake up the macuto to do its work of keeping its bearer protected. To accomplish this we breathe onto the macuto, activating it with our *ndoki*, which is our own personal power or spirit. Once this is finished and the macuto has been activated, it is ready to be carried or kept by the person who is in need of protection and aid.

PROTECTION CARD LAMP

This is a method of lamp making that I learned from my father. By selecting any card from a deck of playing cards the work can be changed to fit your needs. Here we will use the Ace of Hearts to protect your home or business.

Get a green Coconut, find how it will sit level, and when you know that, take a machete, chop off the top of the Coconut, and empty the milk out. Fill the Coconut with Olive or Canola Oil, then add seven crumbled Bay leaves and seven pieces of Devil's Shoe Strings.

Take out the Ace of Hearts from a new deck of cards and cut a small cross in the center of the card with a very sharp knife. Thread a loose natural fiber wick through this opening, and carefully float the card on the surface of the oil. Say the Lord's Prayer over the lamp as you light it, and place it near your front door where people coming into your house will have to pass by it, or in a window where it can be seen from the street. When the oil burns away, replace it and pray over it again.

JINX KILLER PIN WORK

For this work you will need a small bottle with a lid, such as a baby food jar, 121 pins, Ammonia, urine, and Jinx Killer Oil. Place everything into the bottle along with the name of the person throwing on you. If the name is not known, write out a petition asking for the jinx to go back to whoever sent it 121 times over. Breathe on the jar three times hard to put your *ndoki* into it to give it life and strength, and then close it up tightly.

I recommend using a covered barbecue grill for this part. Start a fire, place the bottle on top of it, and run! As the liquid boils, the bottle will explode and send the pins in all directions, returning the jinx, curse, or whatever was thrown on you back on the sender 121 times over. Then pick up each and every pin; a magnet makes this easier. Tie the 121 pins up in a black handkerchief with three knots. Go to the nearest cemetery and place it on an unkept grave, leaving all of the troubles, jinxes, and foolishness behind.

OKRA PROTECTION BATH

Okra is a common cooking ingredient in Africa, the Caribbean, and the United States, but few know that it can be used as a powerful protection against evil spirits, curses, and spiritual attacks. It also aids in stopping gossip and people speaking ill of you or slandering you. Whatever others try to put on you or throw at you, the Okra's slimy nature causes it to slide right off you. Bathing with Okra is one of the best ways to protect yourself.

An Okra bath of this kind can be done once a month, bi-weekly, or even weekly. Those who are allergic to Okra should not engage in this type of bath, but you can easily find out if you are allergic to Okra by cutting an Okra pod in half and putting some of the juice onto the back of your hand. Wait at least fifteen minutes to half an hour to make sure you have no allergic reaction.

Cut Okra emits a juice, which when added to water creates a mucilage. This slimy juice is used to help protect you and drive off evil. For this bath you will need about one pound — or at least twenty-one — fresh Okra pods, a large basin or pot, clean water, a strainer or colander, and two white candles.

First cut or tear open the Okra pods into small pieces, squeezing them into the basin to get all the juice out that you can before adding the pieces to the basin as well. Add enough clean water to the basin to cover the Okra, at least two cups. Allow the Okra to sit in the water for half an hour or more, and then strain out the Okra pieces, saving the liquid.

Take the basin with you to the bathroom and place two white candles, one on each end of the side of your bathtub. Light the candles, saying the 23rd Psalm over them as you do. Disrobe, take the basin into the tub with you, and pray the 91st Psalm aloud as you pour the mucilage over yourself from head to feet. Make sure to completely cover yourself with the liquid over your entire body.

After you are fully covered, wash the slime off by taking a shower or regular bath. Once you have it all off, leave the bathtub, stepping between the two candles as you do. Do not save any of the used water or let any Okra slime dry on your skin. Let it all go down the drain. After you are finished and dried off, you should then dress yourself in clean, light-coloured clothes.

PROTECTING MOTHERS-TO-BE

To help keep expectant mothers safe from harm so that they can carry their babies to term, a protective cord can be made. This protective cord is made from coloured ribbons, and you will need ribbon of seven different colours. Any colours may be used, but black should never be used for protective work of this nature.

Take seven long ribbons, each at least five feet long, of different colours and braid them together to form a long cord. As you braid the ribbons together pray quietly over them for the protection of both the mother and the unborn child. Once the cord is complete it is tied around the belly of the expectant mother and worn at all times.

FOR WOMEN AND MOTHERS

Women, and mothers with children should have extra protection when visiting a hospital, funeral home, cemetery, or any place of sickness or death. A simple and effective way to gain this protection is for a woman to place a tuft of raw, unprocessed cotton into her belly button while visiting such places. After she leaves, the cotton should be disposed of, and a new bit can be used on the next visit.

FOUR GUARDIANS FOR A HOME

To guard your house from harm you can call upon the spirits of the land. In America these spirits are those of the deceased Native American ancestors.

You will need four railroad spikes, smoked Corn, smoked Fish, cigar Tobacco, and rum or whiskey. Some workers also add Jutia Humada, a smoked, dried rodent that can be bought at botanicas. Because some Native American spirits do not like to be paid with alcohol, always divine first to make sure that rum or whiskey can be used.

Dig a hole at each corner of your property. Into each hole place a railroad spike point down, smoked Fish and smoked Corn, and Jutia Humada if you are using it, then cover the hole. As you do this greet the spirits and call on them to help protect not only your home but also theirs. Feed each of these once a week with rum or whiskey and Tobacco.

This was a hand-out at the 2015 Festival. Candelo Kimbisa can be reached at his web site Kimbisa.com.

DEFENDING YOURSELF AGAINST THE DARK ARTS
ConjureMan Ali

KNOWING THE SIGNS OF ATTACK

We live in a world of light and dark. Just as there are a myriad ways that magic can be used to our benefit, so too are there a variety of ways it can be used as a weapon and tool of aggression. If you are involved in the world of magic and spirit, knowing how to defend yourself against these dark forces is of paramount importance.

Every time you light a candle, every time you whisper a prayer, you attract the attention of an angel, or pique the curiosity of a demon. So before all else comes protection. Only from a place of power, where we are safe from the forces we unleash and that are unleashed against us, can we truly work wondrous magic.

There are a variety of ways that one can become the target of dark magic. Knowing their effects will help you discover what is being worked against you and strategize accordingly. Each method of attack will have certain effects which, if you recognize them, will let you know what is being done against you.

Here are some common signs of spiritual attack:

- **Candles:** Fevers, headaches, feeling disoriented, restlessness, objects break, projects fall apart.
- **Powders:** Bodily pain, especially feet; accidents, with automobiles; uncontrollable emotions.
- **Incense:** Light-headed, feeling scatterbrained, respiratory pain and ill-health, unusual smells.
- **Doll-Babies:** Bodily pricks and acute pain, feeling out of sorts, feelings of dread, not being able to breathe, strange thoughts, lethargy.
- **Souring:** Angry and upset for no reason, taste of vinegar or lemon, unshakable sense of negativity, presence of many flies or gnats, cyclical bad luck.
- **Trapping or Restricting:** Feelings of suffocation, helplessness, joint pain, feeling disoriented, projects fall through, physical accidents.
- **Spirits of the Dead:** Feeling watched, having nightmares, chaos in the house, phantom sounds, drained energy, depression.
- **Demonic Spirits:** Uncontrollable rage, night terrors, waking up in pain and feeling like you've been abused, seeing shadows.

CONFIRMING THE SIGNS OF ATTACK

To confirm a magical assault, you can either divine for yourself or consult a professional. Anything from a pendulum to tarot can reveal the presence of a spiritual attack, but be careful that you do not allow yourself to panic. If you have any doubt, consult a professional reader. Here is a simple ceromantic method of divination:

Take a white candle and pass it over your head three times in a circle, or roll it on your body from head to toe, absorbing any influence that is on you. Light the candle and slowly drip the wax into a bowl of water and examine the signs that are revealed. Images of the Devil, horns, crosses, snakes, and skulls are usual indications of a magical attack.

COMBAT AND DEFENSE

Once you've determined that you are under attack, the first thing to do is throw off the assault. This can be done through cleansing and reversal work. You want to remove whatever has been thrown at you before you put up the walls of protection.

Knowing the type of work that has been done against you can help you customize the type of reversal work that you undertake.

One simple reversal method that can be used for almost any type of assault involves an egg and Florida Water. Basically, you rub an egg on yourself from head to toe to absorb whatever negative condition has been placed on you. For more detailed instructions, you can refer to *The Black Folder,* in the article entitled "Hands-on Conjure for Cleansing and Blessing."

Once you have cleansed yourself with the egg, place this in a heat-proof container like a small cauldron. Pour in enough Florida Water to cover it completely. Light it on fire and pray for all evil thrown at you to be sent back to its sender. Let it burn out and dispose of the mess at the crossroads, or if you know where the person lives, toss it on their property. When you are cleansed, put up protection to ensure you cannot be struck again.

TYPES OF PROTECTION

In traditional hoodoo there are four methods of protection.

1. Barriers: These include work that sets boundaries and keeps enemies from crossing a threshold, reaching their target, or entering your space. Methods include the use of powders like Fiery Wall of Protection, sprinkling small seeds on the floor for a hag to count, or setting out a sieve so that the hag must count every hole in it.

2. Alarms: This is work designed to warn you that enemies are afoot. It includes silver dimes, tricked objects meant to fall or break, and dream spells.

3. Apotropaic Charms: These are talismans for warding off evil and are generally kept on the person or in the home. They include mirrors in the home, evil eye charms, or amulets carried on the person, or Salt and Pepper worn in the shoes.

4. Guardians: This work consists of enlisting intelligences and spirits to protect and guard oneself. They can be ancestors called upon for aid, spirits of the dead employed to guard the house, or, for those working from a folk-Catholic perspective, a guardian saint.

These are neat categories into which a folklorist may divide up protection magic, but the boundaries are permeable, and most protection magic — and indeed the best — may touch provide several different styles of protection. A perfect example of this is found in old-time spells for making a guardian.

THE GUARDIAN IN MANY LANDS

Hoodooing a guardian for your protection is old-school work not commonly found in today's era of internet hoodoo. Through magical means, a protector is made that is set to fulfill a specific purpose, in this case to guard a person or a place.

Techniques for making a guardian can be traced back to the folk magic of Europe, to the golem in Jewish magic, and to the West African and Congo magic that is at the core of hoodoo. A guardian has much in common with a mojo bag, but its true African ancestor is the Congo nkisi or nkisi ndoki, a protective statue that may contain herbs, roots, or ancestral ashes, and is called a "fetish" by anthropologists.

CREATING THE GUARDIAN

To make this guardian you will need:

- **Clay or Wax**
- **Bay Leaf**
- **Grains of Paradise**
- **Angelica Root**
- **Devil's Shoe Strings Root**
- **Cat's Eye Shell**
- **Ginger Root**
- **Agrimony**

Additional herbs and curios may be added, as can the graveyard dirt of a powerful, protective ancestor.

Write "Protect" on one side of the Bay Leaf and the name you'll give your guardian on the other. Roll your clay or wax into a ball and add the ingredients one by one, with prayer and intent. Make sure that the Cat's Eye shell is peeking through the clay to act as an eye. The clay may be formed into an image or statue or, if you prefer, it can be loaded into a pre-made statue.

To awaken the guardian, first bathe it in Life Everlasting tea. You can dunk it in the tea like a full-body baptism, or lightly wash it, using your fingertips dipped in the tea. Next, anoint it with Van Van, Fiery Wall of Protection, or Guardian Angel Oil. Finally, pray Genesis 1:26-27 and Psalms 91, and breathe on the guardian to awaken it. As you breathe, call its name three times and state its purpose. Alternatively, recite Psalms 139, for in traditional lore Psalms 139:16 is associated with the golem.

Keep the guardian in your home where it will stand watch over you. Once a month give it a white candle smoked in Dragon's Blood, Frankincense and Myrrh, or Tobacco incense, and dressed with Van Van or Protection Oil to which is added Life Everlasting.

The guardian creates a boundary so that evil cannot cross your threshold. It acts as an alarm by coming to you in a dream or falling over if you are attacked. It turns away the evil eye. Alive, sentient, and intelligent, it can chase out evil spirits, read the intent of visitors, and provide protection against enemies. Build a relationship with your guardian and you will have a mighty ally against the dark arts.

This was a hand-out at the 2014 HHF. ConjureMan Ali is a member of AIRR and co-hosts the Lucky Mojo Hoodoo Rootwork Hour; find him at TheConjureMan.com.

HOW TO MAKE JEWISH SPELL BOWLS FOR PROTECTION
Dr. Jeremy Weiss

WHAT ARE THEY?

Jewish incantation bowls, also called amulet bowls or demon bowls, are protective magical objects. Formed as inscribed clay bowls, they were made from 500 BC to 800 AD by the Jews of Mesopotamia and Syria. The largest cache unearthed to date has been discovered in Nippur. Most are inscribed in Aramaic.

WHAT IS THEIR PURPOSE?

The primary use of amulet bowls is to provide magical protection from malevolent forces for people, their families, and their property. Most of the bowls uncovered so far share these characteristics:

- **Inscriptions:** To protect against evil entities, the inscriptions are written in a spiral inside the bowl.
- **Petitions:** Requests are made of G-d, specific angels, or famous rabbis for aid and assistance.
- **Formal legal language:** The language of ancient Jewish divorce law, called a *get,* literally issues a divorce certificate to evil spirits.
- **Scriptural citations and designs:** These include permutations of the name of G-d, scriptural quotations such as Deuteronomy 6:4 or Zechariah 3:2, magic number squares, or images of demonic figures in shackles or trapped in a box.
- **Made for a specific person or family:** They may also include protective coverage of the home and property.

HOW ARE THEY USED?

It is unknown exactly how the bowls were used. Many have been discovered either buried upside-down or paired lip-to-lip with another bowl under the doorways of homes. Archeologists theorize that this form of burial was intended to create a space in which to catch and trap demons who tried to enter the home.

A separate ritual thought to be associated with the bowls involved writing the name of a demon on the bowl along with a series of binding adjurations and then shattering the bowl, probably against a North-facing wall. A few pre-scored bowls have been found, leading archæologists to speculate that breaking them was an alternate form of deployment.

HOW ARE THEY MADE?

RITUAL PURIFICATION COMES FIRST

In the Jewish folk magic tradition, a period of purification is often required prior to the performance of a spell or creation of an amulet. The requirements for a "purified state" vary, as does the length of time one must remain pure. Purification may include sexual abstinence and avoidance of certain foods and beverages, such as wine. It may also include wearing white robes, praying, and other ascetic practices. Due to the burdensome nature of these purified states, amulet making can be quite difficult. However, ritual purification is not a requirement for one who makes an amulet bowl, as the ancient methods of their creation remain mysterious. I make my bowls according to the times listed in *Sefer Raziel (the Book of Raziel the Angel),* a 13th century text, despite the fact that it was written well after amulet bowls were used, and I also follow the purification rituals it prescribes.

CLAY AND THE CEMETERY CONNECTION

The exact methods by which these bowls were made in the past are no longer known. However, it is suspected that production involved the use of a cemetery, either as the source of pottery clay or as a place where the bowls were formed or fired. Although most have been found under houses, a few were found buried in cemeteries. I do not make my bowls in a cemetery but I do incorporate grave dirt in my clay. Depending on the function of my bowl, I may use the dirt from a particular person. For instance, as I live in Seattle, I might include the grave dirt of Bruce Lee to help fight demons. According to Jewish tradition, music and noise drives away demons, so sometimes I incorporate the grave dirt of Jimi Hendrix.

IMAGES

Images are sometimes found in the center of the bowls. These may include protective symbols, such as a hamsa hand, fish, menorah, angel, and other anti-evil eye imagery; generic demons with claws, matted hair, and wings; or named malevolent entities, such as Lilith, depicted in chains, handcuffs, enclosed in geometric shapes, or in a jail.

WRITTEN SPELLS

Incantations generally are inscribed or written on the inside surface of the bowls, although a few with spells on the outer surface have also been found. The Priestly Blessing from Numbers 6:24-27, selected Psalms, the 72 names of G-d, and the names of angels may be included. Usually, the incantation is written in a spiral. Spirals running from the bowl's center to the rim-edge expel evil; those spiralling from the rim inward may lure in and trap demons or illnesses. A typical spell might read as follows:

"Appointed is this bowl for the sealing and guarding of the house and body of (first name) son / daughter of (mother's first name). Bind and banish all tormentors, evil dreams, glares, curses, spells, devils, demons, ghosts, liliths, satans, encroachments, and terrors. Banned is illness, fire, flood, unhappiness, and disease. Only love, good fortune, and health are welcome here. YHWH, angels, and holy forces of good, I adjure you and appeal to you to make it so."

REDUCTIVE NOTARIKON

Permutations or notarikons of demonic names are used to entrap the evil entity or cause it to disappear. For example, here is a reduction of the name of the demon Shabriri:

Shabriri
Shabrir
Shabri
Shabr
Shab
Sha
Sh
S

NUMEROLOGY AND YOUR PERSONAL PSALM

Numerology may be included in amulet bowls. I use a system that links the person to be protected's birthday and their corresponding Psalm. For example: If the person's birthday is March 27, 1962, it is enumerated as 3 + 27 + 19 + 62 = 111 and thus their mystical number is 111. We then subtract 20 (the number of years in a cycle in which the date on the lunar calendar matches and negates the date on the solar calendar). The result is the number of the Psalm for that particular birthday. In this case, their special Psalm is the mystical number 111 minus 20 = 91, so their Psalm happens to be the 91st Psalm.

SMOKING THE BOWL

As part of their preparation and sanctification, I tend to either besmoke the bowls I make with Incense of Abramelin or anoint them with Oil of Abramelin. This oil and incense blend only became available several millennia after the earliest amulet bowls. It is based on the formula found in Exodus 30:23-24, but was modified during the Middle Ages, in accord with the Biblical instruction to never exactly copy the Holy Oil of the Temple. Over the years, mistranslations of the Abramelin Oil recipe have led to variant forumulations. The brand I use is Lucky Mojo's product, which is correct with respect to the Abramelin recipe and of excellent quality.

SUNLIGHT AND MOONLIGHT

While it is not a Jewish tradition, I have adopted Reverend Jon Saint Germain's method of charging ritual objects with the power of Sunlight baths for healing and the force of Moonlight baths for magical purposes. My personal suggestion is to charge the bowl in Sunlight when banishing an illness-causing demon, such as Shibriri, and in Moonlight when seeking protection from magical or spiritual attack.

BURIAL AND RITUAL BREAKAGE

While demon bowls are traditionally meant to either be buried or ritually broken, there is no reason they cannot be beautiful. The outside of the bowl can be inscribed or decorated; in fact, the greater the energy you put into making your bowl, the better it will be. If you decide to bury it, I would suggest turning it upside-down or making two and placing them lip to lip. Bowls intended to be broken to expel evil can be pre-scored before the clay dries.

BIBLIOGRAPHY

Amulets and Magic Bowls: Aramaic Incantations of Late Antiquity by Joseph Naveh and Shaul Shaked.
Aramaic Bowl Spells: Jewish Babylonian Aramaic Bowls by Shaul Shaked, James Nathan Ford, and Siam Bhayro.

Dr. Jeremy Weiss presented a hands-on workshop on ancient and modern Jewish incantation bowls at the 2019 Hoodoo Heritage Festival at which participants made their own amulet bowls. The author of the divination book "Vulvamancy," he is a member of HP and AIRR and can be found online at Jewizard.com.

LOVE AND GLAMOUR MAGIC
Madame Nadia and Madame Pamita

WHAT IS GLAMOUR?

Originally, the Scots invented the word glamour to describe a magic spell that created any sort of illusion. The word was first seen in the early 18th century and was an alternative of the word "grammar" — showing its roots as magic that required an occult education and emphasizing the power of the word in spell work.

Today we specify glamour as magnetism – an air of mystery and an ineffable quality of seductiveness; a presentation that is better than everyday reality and the expression of effortless allure. Glamour magic can be used as a means of increasing one's self-confidence. It need not depend on natural beauty, instead it is a way of using our past experiences to create a persona or cast a veil of allure and magnetism over the eyes of those we wish to influence. It also can be used to dominate others in a professional or social setting — getting a high paying position, landing a lucrative part in a film, becoming the sought after friend or being the life of the party, for example.

Unlike other kinds of love work, glamour magic does not draw another person's heart to us. Rather it overwhelms the other's mind. They don't see us, but rather the enticing and entrancing cloak that we wrap ourselves in, drawing them like moths to the flickering flame or bees to the swaying flower.

TYPES OF GLAMOUR SPELLS

- **Beautifying:** Improving the perception of one's appearance.
- **Charismatic:** These spells used gain general attention in groups of people you wish to attract, whether they are lovers, fans, or followers.
- **Attracting a Specific New Lover:** Drawing a person toward you as a lover and admirer.
- **Getting a Commitment of Love:** Turning a casual relationship into a serious monogamous relationship.
- **Keeping or Binding Your Partner:** Causing your lover to focus on you and you alone can include anything from building a strong marriage to coercive binding and control work.

WHAT GLAMOUR SPELLS ARE NOT

Glamour spells are not:

- **Reconciliation:** You cannot fascinate someone who is finished with a relationship. Glamour requires a positive or at least neutral connection.
- **Fixing a Broken Relationship:** Seduction without addressing the underlying problems of a troubled relationship often creates more trouble.
- **Fidelity or Tying Nature:** Glamour rules by allure, not by control of another's sexuality.
- **Break Up Work:** Separation is the opposite of magnetism. Removing rivals is not seduction.
- **Sympathetic Magic:** Glamour is an immediate, first-hand experience; being in the presence of the target is essential. It is all about personal contact and conducting a magical exchange.
- **Changing Your Gender or Eye Colour:** When the term "glamour spell" is used in television shows and movies, it is accompanied by special effects and camera tricks. This has led many young people to think they can actually change their gender, eye colour, weight, or physical appearance with glamour spells.

THE KEY TO GLAMOUR MAGIC

The key to glamour magic is not chasing after someone but revealing just a tantalizing glimpse of yourself that entices, enchants, and powerfully draws the person to you on a subtle, energetic level.

FOUNDATION: DEMEANOUR AND ALLURE

Confidence and belief in your own magnetic power is essential. If you don't believe you are glamorous, no one else will either. Try these tricks to increase your sense of allure:

- **Dress a hand mirror with Look Me Over Oil.** Gaze into your own eyes and speak words of power, such as, "I am the most beautiful person in the room," "You find me irresistible," and "I love you."
- **Make a habit of taking candlelight baths.** Use special ingredients such as milk and honey, flower petals, or love and attraction oils.

PREPARATION: ADORNMENT AND BEAUTY

When you get ready to do your thing, you will want to leave your workaday world behind and prepare yourself to shine, like the woman in Psalms 45:13, about whom it was said, *"All glorious is the king's daughter within the palace; her raiment is of chequer work inwrought with gold."* Here are some little things you can do for yourself before you go to meet that special someone:

- **Wear flattering clothing:** Wash your clothes in Love Me or Follow Me Boy / Girl Bath Crystals.
- **Anoint your body:** Use Come To Me Oil, Kiss Me Now! Oil, or — for that extra edge — Jezebel Oil.
- **Splash your face:** Use Rosemary tea as a face-splash before applying your make-up.
- **Fix your hair products:** Use Look Me Over Oil and do up your hair, for as it says in scripture, a woman's hair is her glory (1 Corinthians 11:15). Yes, even an old grey head is a crown of glory if it was gained in righteousness (Proverbs 16:3).
- **Create a seductive mood:** Burn Fire of Love Incense in the home where you and your lover are to meet.

ACTION: MAGICAL EXCHANGE

The strongest glamour work involves a magical exchange of some sort. When you take something from or give something to the one you want, you are magically connecting that person to you. These contact spells may help you rope your target in:

- **Wear a love flower:** Pick a Rose, Red Clover, Orange blossom, or Lavender flower, dress it with your personal concerns, wear it, and then give it to your target when he or she notices it.
- **Deploy a pinch of a seductive herb:** Hide a pinch of a love or sex herb such as Damiana, Patchouli, Lovage, or Catnip in the pocket or shoe of your target.
- **Prepare food or drink:** Use edible love herbs or personal concerns and serve them to your target.
- **Get personal concerns from your target:** Use them in work such as making a doll-baby.
- **Collect the foot-track of your target:** Work with it on your altar or cast a spell within the foot track to be activated when he or she steps over it.
- **Give your target a tricked gift:** Offer a gift that you have secretly dressed with a love oil or sachet powder, smoked in a love incense, washed in a love bath, or fixed with your own personal concerns.

LOVE HERBS, ROOTS, AND CURIOS

- **Anise**
- **Calamus**
- **Catnip**
- **Cloves**
- **Couch Grass**
- **Cubeb Berries**
- **Dill Seeds**
- **Gentian Root**
- **Juniper Berries**
- **Lodestone**
- **Lovage Root**
- **Magnetic Sand sprayed with gold paint**
- **Master Root**
- **Patchouli Leaf**
- **Personal Concerns**
- **Poppy Seed**
- **Pyrite Grit for sparkle**
- **Queen Elizabeth Root**
- **Southern John Root**

As you work with herbs, oils, sachets, and curios, pray over them or speak your intention to them. See more love herbs in the spell recipe below.

A GLAMOUR SPELL TO DRINK

LOVE POTION NO. 9

Mix these edible love herbs in a muslin bag. As you put each herb in the bag, ask it to do your love work.

- **Cardamom**
- **Cinnamon Stick**
- **Coriander**
- **Damiana**
- **Ginger**
- **Lovage**
- **Peppermint**
- **Red Clover**
- **Red Rose Petals**

Soak the bag in wine or brandy for 9 days and use it as a tincture. Alternatively, steep it in boiled water for 9 minutes to make a tea, and add honey or sugar. Serve to your lover while gazing into his or her eyes.

This was a hand-out at the 2014 Hoodoo Heritage Festival. Madame Nadia is a member of AIRR and Hoodoo Psychics; she can be reached at MadameNadia.com. Madame Pamita is a member of AIRR and Hoodoo Psychics; she can be reached at MadamePamita.com.

GET WHAT YOU WANT IN LOVE AND MARRIAGE
Ms. Robin York

A HOODOO HOW-TO FOR LOVE

Love may be the most sought-after area in rootwork, whether aimed at romance, sex, or marriage. A broken partnership, a lonely bachelor- or spinsterhood, or just a lover who refuses to take it to the next level — all create the kind of pain it can be hard to move past. Every trick in the rootworker's conjure bag can be adapted to this difficult part of life.

ALWAYS BEGIN WITH CLEANSING

A number of clients want to jump straight into love work, but if you want to be successful, take the precaution of cleansing yourself of anything negative that you might bring into your relationship — or bed! Chinese Wash and spiritual baths are a necessity before moving to your next step, a love bath brewed with herbs and crystals.

A RED MOJO HAND FOR LOVE

A simple red bag of love herbs, hidden away on your person, can bring a clear advantage in love and romance. Make sure to spot it with personal concerns and a love oil of your choice.

MAGICAL CANDLELIGHT FOR ROMANCE

No one will be the wiser when the candles you light in the bedroom have been fixed with condition oils and herbs ahead of time. Set the mood for love and let the magic do its work.

LOVE UP YOUR DOLL-BABY

Figural candles in the shape of men and women (or even vulvæ and penises) can be baptized and used as doll-babies. Oil them up in the middle of the night when your target is sound asleep. Dreams of you are sure to follow.

SET TRICKS TO GET YOUR LOVER IN BED

No one ever turned down a massage — and no one needs to know that you've spiced up the massage oil with some magic. Choose your hoodoo oils both for their condition and for a pleasing and sensual experience.

CONJURE CONDITION FORMULAS

Whether as an oil, incense, sachet powders, or bath crystals, the scent of traditional hoodoo condition formulas never fails to delight the senses — and conjure up results! Here are some favourites which can be mixed and matched for added impact:

- **Adam and Eve:** To bring a "perfect" mate. Can create a physical bond difficult to break, or attract a lover "fated" in the stars.
- **Attraction:** If the one you love doesn't seem to know you exist, this will do the trick! Great with lodestone spells.
- **Bewitching:** Gives an extra "glamour" to your work and increases confidence in those who need a boost in self-esteem.
- **Chuparrosa:** The hummingbird, god of love for natives from Central and North America, sucks dishonesty from the flower of your love.
- **Cleo May:** Based on a perfume from the 1920s and used by working girls to sweeten clients.
- **Come To Me:** To turn an acquaintance into a friend or a friend into something more!
- **Dixie Love:** Down-home love's Southern recipe.
- **Fire of Love:** When you need to spice up your relationship or inspire a little passion.
- **Kiss Me Now!:** Get past the first hurdle and go in for the lip lock. Don't just grab that kiss: make it memorable!
- **Lavender Love Drops:** A formula for same-sex love and relationships.
- **Look Me Over:** To gain attention and admiring glances from all who see you.
- **Love Me:** An old-time favourite for all love jobs.
- **Marriage:** Bless a current marriage or call forth a proposal from your beloved.
- **Q:** The original in-the-closet oil for men and women of the "Q" persuasion.
- **Reconciliation:** For use when you've argued once too many times with the one you love.
- **Return To Me:** For re-establishing contact when geography intervenes.
- **Stay At Home:** Tired of your loved one going out on the town? That time and attention can be yours instead!
- **Stay With Me:** Suspect an affair of the heart? Prevent divorce and keep those interested glances from turning into something more.

HERBS AND ROOTS FOR LOVE

When we're stuffing a doll-baby, brewing a spiritual bath, fixing candles, or constructing a mojo bag, herbs are a primary ingredient, the roots that give rootworkers our name. Handed down through generations and even brought here from far-away continents, the plants of use in hoodoo are many and varied — perhaps none moreso than the herbs, roots, and seeds found suitable for love.

Our list is drawn primarily from *Hoodoo Herb and Root Magic: A Materia Magica of African-American Conjure* by Catherine Yronwode. Do not eat or drink herbs until you have researched their toxicity.

- **Balm of Gilead buds:** To heal relationships.
- **Cardamom Seed:** Super-sexy passion herb.
- **Catnip:** "Captivates" and "captures"!
- **Cherry Bark:** For sexual attraction.
- **Cinnamon:** Attractant for love or luck.
- **Coriander Seed:** For love and faithfulness.
- **Cubeb Berries:** Inspires fiery love, new or old.
- **Cumin Seed:** To keep your lover faithful.
- **Damiana:** For sexual love and lust situations.
- **Dill Leaf:** Used for those unlucky in love.
- **Dill Seed:** Adds irresistibility to glamour work.
- **Ginger Root:** To heat things up sexually.
- **Honeysuckle Flowers:** To tie your lover to you.
- **Hyssop:** Removes sin; helps lovers forgive.
- **Jasmine Flowers:** To enhance dreams of love.
- **Juniper Berries:** Lowers inhibitions.
- **Lavender Flowers:** Harmonious love.
- **Lemon Mint:** Attracts new love.
- **Licorice Root:** To change a person's mind.
- **Lotus Root:** For love and protection.
- **Lovage Root:** For passion with a lover of the opposite gender.
- **Patchouli Leaf:** To attract both love and money.
- **Poppy Seed:** Adds confusion to glamour work.
- **Queen Elizabeth Root:** Famous to attract men.
- **Raspberry Leaf:** To keep lovers from straying.
- **Red Clover:** For a happy marriage.
- **Rose Petal or Bud:** To draw and keep true love.
- **Safflower Petals:** Used by gay men to attract a dominant partner.
- **Senna Leaf:** To get love from one who doesn't notice you.
- **Skullcap:** To encourage fidelity.
- **Spikenard:** Love herb mentioned in The Bible.
- **Tonka Bean:** Makes love wishes come true.
- **Vanilla Bean:** Placed in sugar for love.
- **Violet Leaf:** To attract love, new or old.

TRADITIONAL TRICKS FOR FIDELITY

Finally, here are eight traditional workings to keep a relationship solid, so that you never lose what you have worked so hard to gain:

A Magnolia Leaf in the Mattress: To keep a faithful marriage bed, Southern women would sew Magnolia leaves into the mattress. Nowadays, it's easier to tuck a Magnolia leaf or two between the mattress and box springs.

A Wedding Ring in the Sugar Bowl: We all want our spouses to stay sweet on us. When quarrels arise, put your wedding ring in the sugar bowl, pray over it to bring back smiles and kisses, and put it back on.

Socks Buried in the Backyard: If you fear your partner is straying, bury their dirty sock in the backyard to keep them home. You can even tie one of your socks around it!

Pubic Hair in the Hatband: Keep 'em crazy for you by putting one of your pubic hairs in their hatband, as close to their brain as you can get!

Tie His Necktie Every Day: Tying his necktie for him will keep him thinking of you all day long. I suppose it can work just as well for women wearing power ties.

Menstrual Blood in the Coffee: If there was only one love spell, this would be it. Menstrual blood in coffee is the classic. Men can use a little chamber lye (urine) to effect the same purpose.

Pre-wear Underwear or Lingerie: Giving your partner some sexy underthings as a surprise gift? Make sure you wear them first, to hold them forever.

Step Over a Broom: While jumping the broom has returned to favour in marriage ceremonies, it's still useful long after. Every time you move to a new home, step over a broom as you first enter, sweeping out old hoodoo and guarding against future tricks.

Ms. Robin York presented this workshop at the 2018 Hoodoo Heritage Festival. She co-founded the Annual MISC Hoodoo Rootwork Workshops and is well known for her money spells, gambling spells, love spells, and curse spells. You can find her online at RobinsMojo.com or at the AIRR site.

SPELLS FOR A LOVER TO RETURN OR RECONCILE
Deacon Millett

MAIL A LETTER IN A HOLLOW TREE

If you and a friend knew each other when young, but drifted apart and became separated though time, you may write the person a letter "in the air." Keep it short and friendly, but ask the person to contact you if possible. Seal it and mail it in the hole in a hollow tree; the tree's leaves will bear the message on the wind. Try this three times only.

MIRROR, PHOTO, APPLE, CANDLE

Back in the 1930s, Madam Lindsey, a professional Spiritualist and root doctor of Algiers, Louisiana, told the folklorist Harry Hyatt this work of reconciliation:

"You get a brand-new mirror, a small ten-cent one will do. Put this person's photograph on the back, facing in. Prop the mirror so that their head is upside down. And you get a red candle and a red Apple. Write this person's name on parchment seven times, and stick it down into the red Apple. This is to make them think of you continually. As long as that Apple is fresh, they can't forget you. Put the red candle into the hole in the Apple and set it before the mirror. Whatever anger that person has for you, it'll fade away. Then you'll get to be the Apple of their eye again. Do this with seven different candles. If the candle burns the Apple, you'll have to get a fresh Apple and a fresh parchment paper and start again."

PSALMS FOR MARITAL PEACE

In the 1600s, a German immigrant in Pennsylvania, Johannes Gottfried Seelig, translated the medieval Jewish tract, *Shimmush Tehillim* (*The Magical Uses of the Psalms),* into German. It was later translated into English and republished as Godfrey Selig's *Secrets of the Psalms.* Here is a formula from this famous book:

"Whoever has a scolding wife, let him pronounce the 45th Psalm over pure Olive Oil, and anoint his body with it, when his wife, in the future will be more loveable and friendly. But if a man has innocently incurred the enmity of his wife, and desires a proper return of conjugal love and peace, let him pray the 46th Psalm over Olive Oil, and anoint his wife thoroughly with it, and, it is said, married love will again return."

SLEEPING WITH YOUR PHOTOS

In the 1930s, a Waycross, Georgia, worker told Harry Hyatt to take two photographs, one of yourself and one of the person you wish to draw back to you. Write the 23rd Psalm on the back of one and the 42nd Psalm on the back of the other. Place them face to face under your pillow and sleep with them there. Your lost love will shortly return.

END QUARRELS IN THE KITCHEN

If you and your mate always seem to be fussing in the kitchen while meals are being prepared, it may be that the room itself has a jinx on it. A traditional remedy for this is to sprinkle dried Basil on the floor and sweep it out the back door, because "Evil cannot stay where Basil has been."

NINE LUMPS OF SUGAR LAY A TRAIL

During the 1920s, Ruth Mason, a root doctor in New Orleans, told the folklorist Zora Neale Hurston how to draw a lover back, "Take the following mixture and sprinkle it over nine lumps of loaf sugar: essence of Van Van, essence of Geranium, essence of Lavender. Go nine blocks from the house and turn around and drop one lump of sugar in each block all the way back to the house, and he will make up with you."

NINE RED CANDLES FOR A RETURN

To reconcile a faltering marriage, if one party has walked out, Ruth Mason said you should take nine deep red or pink candles and write the absent person's name on each candle, using a needle. Then write the name three times on paper. Put the paper in a cup, pour Van Van Oil in the cup on the paper and dress all the candles with Van Van Oil. Burn one of these candles every day at the hours of seven, nine, or eleven. Call the name of the party three times as each candle is burned.

These spells are taken from Deacon Millett's 96-page book "Hoodoo Return and Reconciliation Spells," presented at the 2015 HHF. The complete book is available from the Lucky Mojo Curio Co. Find Deacon Millett at FourAltars.org

GAY AND LESBIAN LOVE SPELLS
Professor Charles Porterfield

BIRDS OF A FEATHER

Back in the days when being a gay man was an offense punishable by law, a coded term for a male couple was "birds of a feather," which refers to the old English maxim, "Birds of a feather flock together." This phrase can be found, for example, in Waymon "Sloppy" Henry's 1929 blues song "Say I Do It," where *two [men] could be seen, running hand in hand, in all kinds of weather, till the neighbours they began to signify, 'bout the birds that flock together."* What was once a cause of scandal can now be a source of pride: Take two bright and beautiful feathers — those from Parrots or Macaws are excellent — and name one for you and one for your lover or partner. Put a love-drop from each of you on the base of your named feather. Place the feathers in a bottle or bud vase, right out in plain sight. If you are a polyamorous man, you may add a new feather to your "flock" for every man you love, until you have created an entire bouquet of feathers. Be sure to get a drop of the love juice of each man on the base of each feather. The feathers should be individually identifiable, because each represents a specific person. These men will continue to stay in your life as long as their feathers stay in your collection. If someone has to go, remove his feather and cast it to the wind. If there are hard feelings upon parting, burn his feather to ashes and blow the ashes out of your life at a crossroads.

TO KEEP A FEMALE LOVER FAITHFUL

A lesbian or queer woman who wishes to keep her lover faithful will bind together two Queen Elizabeth Roots, one for herself and one for her lover, with red thread and dress it daily with Stay With Me Oil.

TRANSGENDERED ROOTS

A curio shop keeper who sorts and grades many pounds of roots often finds "transgendered" roots. A naturally formed John the Conqueror Root (a "male" root) that looks like a vulva or a Queen Elizabeth Root (a "female" root) in the shape of a penis are highly valued by intersex or transgendered people. Rare as they are, they are not easy to acquire, but if you befriend a curio shop keeper, and ask nicely, you may be offered one. Use it wisely!

TWO OLD QUEENS

If the term "two old queens" seems dated, that's because it is. This term for an elderly male couple dates to the era before same-sex marriage was legal. A simple playing card spell helps bring this about. You will need two Queens from a deck of cards. You can pick the favourite suit of each man, choose colour-coded cards (Spades or Clubs for a darker man and Diamonds or Hearts or a paler man), or you may determine the cards by astrological cues (Spades for an air sign, Clubs for a fire sign, Diamonds for an earth sign, and Hearts for a water sign). If the two of you pick the same card (two Queens of Hearts, for example), that is fine; you will just need two decks of cards to get them. Write your names and birthdates on the card backs. Use a bit of honey and your combined sexual fluids to "glue" the two Queens together, face to face. Place the bonded cards in a Bible and consider yourselves wed. May you happily grow old together!

TO MAKE A MAN FOLLOW YOU

If you are in a house party and see a man whom you would like to hook up with, this sneaky trick may work for you. You will need a bit of absorbent cloth or paper towel, and a glass. Go to the bathroom, wet the cloth or paper and wipe under your arms to get your sweat, then wring the water out into your empty drink glass. Offer to get the person a refill, take your two glasses away, refill the person's glass and drop your sweat-water into it. As the drink is consumed, he will begin to follow you. In 1939 a man in Sumter, South Carolina, told Rev. Hyatt that his mother, a woman of mingled Black and Native American heritage, had taught him this trick 40 years earlier because a bully boy was picking on him. He worked the trick, and it "conquered" the boy, who soon became his best friend and was still following him around to that day. Madame Lindsey, a conjure doctor of Algiers, Louisiana, also told this trick to Rev. Hyatt, the same year.

These spells come from Professor Porterfield's 's 96-page book "The Sporting Life" presented at his Hoodoo Heritage Festival workshop in 2016. The complete book is available from the Lucky Mojo Curio Co,

HOW TO ATTRACT NEW LOVE
Deacon Millett

A CLEAN SLATE

"New Love" work comes in two varieties — attracting a target of interest or opening oneself to love in general. The latter, which we'll explore today, invites God to bring us the "right" suitors, whomever they may be.

Starting fresh in such an endeavour is the only way forward. For a simple cleansing, recite Psalms 51:7-12 over a white candle each morning and night for nine days. You may anoint it with Road Opener Oil or accompany it with Block Buster Incense. If entering the dating game after a long time away, go ahead and take a 13 Herb Bath for thirteen days.

If you are still stuck on a previous lover, it is very difficult to bring a new one your way. Cut and Clear work, with or without a Black Walnut bath, may be needed to open your heart and mind to new possibilities. Many drag their feet on this vital step, wasting months and even years holding on to a long dead affair or infatuation.

THE LAW OF ATTRACTION

Have you ever noticed that, when you've just met a new love and all seems right with the world, suddenly everyone you meet is interested in you? It's the Law of Attraction. Simply put, like attracts like. Love attracts love, and the LACK of love, if that is your focus, will bring more of the same.

Do not make this fundamental mistake! Instead, light a vigil to attract love and KNOW that it is bringing you results! Visualize the perfect partner for you. DON'T base it on a real person, no! Instead imagine the qualities you most desire in a partner.

If sex is your primary need, and you are not looking for someone to also share your life with, then focus on the physical traits which most attract you. But, if you desire a lifelong commitment, seek instead loyalty, generosity of spirit, a sense of humour — the things that will bring ease in the coming years. Imagine the complement to your own personality, someone who will fill in your gaps while enjoying you for who you are!

SET YOUR EXPECTATIONS

I have had clients give up on love work after only months, because the perfect man didn't knock on their door bearing a ring. Go to the places your ideal mate would go, be it a bar, library, dance club, alumni event, amusement park, or church singles picnic. You must meet people, and lots of them.

Even if you believe we have many true loves in our lives, the Earth has 7.5 billion people on it! How many must you meet to find your diamond in the rough? Expect "bad" dates, and thank the Universe for saving you for someone better! Each "negative" experience refines what you wish to attract.

If a friend mentions someone you "just have to meet," don't hesitate, for (s)he who hesitates is lost. Many have delayed meeting a soulmate for lack of the right outfit — or waistline. Do not spend months on online chatting. If someone strikes your fancy, meet in person. It is vital that you bask in their aura and experience their scent.

SEEDS OF LOVE BATH BOMB

The past behind us, and expectations set, it's time to welcome the future. Before going out, take a love attraction bath by candlelight. Let go of any frenetic feelings or anxieties and instead invoke a spirit of luxury and self-fulfillment. Then assemble these simple ingredients:

1/2 cup citric acid
1/2 cup Epsom salts
1 cup baking soda
1 oz. of any Love or Attraction oils, your choice
1/4 cup dried Lavender buds or Rose petals

Directions: Combine all of the dry ingredients except the flowers. Whisk with a fork, adding oil VERY slowly to prevent any reaction. Test the mixture and, if it holds together when pressed in your hands, stop adding oil — it's ready. Add flowers and press into moulds (ice trays work well). Let dry for several hours, then remove from the moulds. Continue to let dry for a week before storing in an airtight jar.

NINE LOVE POTIONS

While the "classic" love potion is to compel a specified target, the following are more generalized to set the mood, whether for you alone, a date picking you up, or a party or other gathering. Use iced teas in Spring and Summer and hot teas or cocoa in Fall and Winter.

HEAL MY HEART LEMON LOVE BREW

Use a vegetable peeler to zest several Lemons and to shred a fresh ginger root. Dry in an oven on low heat until dehydrated, then finely dice. Add Hyssop flowers, Lavender buds, and Peppermint to the mixture, reciting Psalms 51. Keep in an airtight jar and brew one tablespoon to eight ounces water.

NEW MOON PASSION PUNCH

At the New Moon, simmer Hibiscus petals, a broken Cinnamon stick, and Orange peel for twenty minutes. Sprinkle with Damiana and Passionflowers midway. Strain and sweeten to taste.

WONDER WORKER

Using a black tea of your choice, add Ginseng (Wonder of the World), crushed Cardamom pods, and Cinnamon chips. Recite from the Song of Solomon as you let it steep. Perfect before a night on the town or to restore lost nature.

CARDAMOM ROSE COCOA

Toast two Cardamom pods in a dry saucepan for a few minutes. Break pods in two with a decisive phrase, such as "true love now!" Discard the pods but keep the seeds, adding two cups of milk. Warm over medium heat, while breaking a small chocolate bar into pieces. Add to the mixture, along with four tablespoons condensed milk and two tablespoons cocoa powder. Whisk until smooth. Remove from heat, add one tablespoon rosewater, and serve.

TRUE LOVE ELIXIR

Fill a mason jar three quarters full with Rose petals. Top off with brandy or vodka, and store in a cool dark place for at least two weeks. When the Rose petals have fully infused and lost their colour, strain. Add a drop or two to any appropriate beverage when a jolt of love is needed!

"BE MY" HONEY

Crush one heaping teaspoon of Rose petals into a coarse powder. Split one half a Vanilla bean and scrape out the black seeds inside. Combine with Rose blend in a half cup of raw honey, saying, "As this honey is sweet to the tongue, so shall my honey be sweet on me." Let infuse several days and use as desired to sweeten others. This blend can also be used as the base for a very nice honey jar. Just add your petition, photos, and personal concerns, ring with Rose petals on a white saucer, and burn a pink candle on top!

FAST LUCK IN LOVE COFFEE

In your drip coffee pot, add the following to fresh grounds for one cup of coffee: one whole Clove, one pinch Saffron (gay men might substitute Safflower), and one dash powdered Cardamom. Brew coffee and then addcRose water and cream as desired. This makes a perfect "perk me up" for Saint Expedite to help bring a new lover fast. Once Saint Expedite comes through for you, leave him another cup with pound cake and a vase of red Roses.

APHRODITE'S FRUITS OF THE EARTH

At the Full Moon, combine one cup dried Rose hips and one cup dried Hibiscus flowers. Add 1/2 cup each of freeze-dried Strawberries and Apples and 1/4 cup each of shredded Coconut and dried Orange peel. Mix well by hand, crumbling ingredients while calling on the goddess of love to deliver the right suitor to you. Mix with spring water in a large jar, and leave outdoors overnight to steep in the Full Moon's light. Chill and serve at any positive event.

VISIONS OF LOVE CHAI

Heat 3/4 cup water and 1/4 milk in a saucepan. Before it boils, add two cracked Cardamom pods, one Star anise, and a pinch each of Peppercorns (red or black), Cinnamon chips, Coriander seeds, and Cloves. Bring to a boil, remove from water, and add two teaspoons Assam or Ceylon tea. Steep two minutes, sweeten, and serve. A heady combination to help you envision your true love.

Candle minister, rootworker, and member of AIRR Deacon Millett is the author of "Hoodoo Honey and Sugar Spells" and "Hoodoo Return and Reconciliation Spells." His next book focuses on attracting and keeping new love. This workshop was presented in 2019.

TEN LITTLE FINGERS, TEN LITTLE TOES
Lady Muse

DIVINING CAUSES OF INFERTILITY

Precious Little Bundles of Joy are described in the Bible as "Olive plants round about thy table" (Psalms 128:3). Who would ever imagine being hindered from experiencing the miracle of childbirth? As a wise ol' saying goes, "You Ain't Never Stuck"! It is the belief of many that Prayer Changes Things! All we need is the Faith as a grain of a Mustard Seed, but let us not forget that Faith without Works is dead.

If think of the reasoning behind the hindrance or blockage of such a miracle, we may find that jealousy, envy, greed. or some good o'l fashion Pay Back is the root of such a crossed condition, mess, or juju ball. The question is not *if*, but *how* can the effects of this juju ball be reversed? Once the root is identified, it can be plucked up, bound, and cast into the abyss.

Protecting the delivered individual is also of great importance and should not be forgotten. The first step is to divine and consult with your Spirit guides on the situation to reveal pertinent information that relates to who, what, when, where, why. It is also crucial to get proper guidance as to how to execute the best course of action for the individual.

UNCROSSING INFERTILITY

The second step is a good ol' fashion Heavy Uncrossing. There are many different way to uncross the situation depending on your preferred tradition. Keep in mind that there are more ways than one to reach a goal, therefore in this type of rootwork, we must explore remediation for both women and men.

As a rule of thumb, it is always good to cleanse yourself, your work area, and your tools prior to beginning any type of rootwork or ritual, or the preparation of spiritual supplies for yourself or a client.

One effective method of uncrossing involves a strong Uncrossing Bath. This can also be thought of as a type of baptism. The bath can be prepared for the individual or it can be accomplished by utilizing an effigy to represent the individual that is crossed. Spiritual condition bath mixes can also be designed to be employed by way of laundry if necessary.

UNCROSSING BATH FOR WOMEN AND MEN

- **Hyssop**
- **Oak Bark**
- **Nettle**
- **Rue**
- **Quita Maldicion a.k.a. Gray Nickers, Fever Nut, Sea Pearl, Latakaranja, (*Cæsalpinia crista*) or Senna Leaf (*Senna spp.* in the *Cæsalpinioideæ*)**

CANDLE WORK TO UNCROSS INFERTILITY

One way to direct energy to the right person when doing rootwork is by using a candle that represents the astrological sign of the individual. Draw a triangle on your work space, using a mix of Agrimony, Lemon Grass, and Cascarilla. Place a white candle at the bottom right of the triangle, a black candle at the bottom left, and the Zodiac candle of the individual on the top tip of the triangle.

Write your petition and set it in the middle of the triangle. Next, on parchment paper, write the Name of God that represents spiritual cleansing (Mem Vav Mem). Place that on top of your petition paper. Place a clear quartz crystal on top of the name of God.

Start your three lights during a Waning Moon cycle on a Sunday night during the hour of the Sun and have the individual take an Uncrossing Bath. Do this for nine nights.

FOCUSSING ON FERTILITY

The third step in this process of Faith, Patience, and Perseverance is focusing on the fertility of the individual. This includes regulating menstrual cycles and or raising sperm counts. Spiritual condition teas and Baths can be used to deploy this intent as well.

FERTILITY BATH FOR BOTH WOMEN AND MEN

- **Queen's Root**
- **Unopened Pine cone**
- **Angelica (Dong Quai) Root**
- **Motherwort**
- **Maca Root**

FERTILITY TEA FOR WOMEN

- Nettle
- Red Clover
- Red Raspberry Leaves
- Motherwort
- Angelica (Dong Quai) Root
- Maca Root
- False Unicorn Root Tincture

PROTECTING THE PREGNANCY

As the womb is blessed with the little bundle, it is important to protect the mother and baby during the pregnancy. Speak into existence a mantra such as, "This unbreakable union is protected from the evil envious eyes of enemies known and unknown."

PROTECTION BATH FOR A MOTHER-TO-BE

- Squaw Vine
- Angelica Root
- White Clover
- Boldo Leaves

Preparing for the arrival of the miracle should include cleaning and anointing the home to word off negative energies and to build a concrete foundation of energy that gears the baby towards a blessed, positive and successful life.

EASING CHILDBIRTH

One common spell to ease childbirth is to place a pair of open scissors beneath the mother-to-be's bed, to "cut off her pains." Another custom is to untie every knot in the house, on aprons strings, curtain tie-backs, shoelaces, and more, in order to "unlock" the baby from the womb.

Once the baby has arrived and the afterbirth has been delivered, it is an old Native American custom to bathe the woman's genitals with a weak tea of Dixie John or Birth Root, also called Beth Root, either plain or mingled with Raspberry leaves, and to have her drink a cup of it as tea.

In many cultures it is understood that a baby born with a veil or caul will develop supernatural gifts, such as the gift of sight or prophecy, the ability to see ghosts, and a healing touch. It is also a special sign of good luck and protection. Often families will keep the caul to protect the child from drowning in water.

BLESSING THE BABY

During the final stages of this journey, as we are preparing for the arrival of Ten Little Fingers and Ten Little Toes, a powerful amulet anointed for protection, health, and success can be chosen to give to the baby during a Blessing ceremony. In doing this work, you can petition a deity, spirit, angel, or ancestor for protection of the mother and baby.

You may find yourself drawn to a specific Spirit revealed in a dream, vision, or divination. Learn about its sacred animals, foods, plants, stones, colours, numbers, day of the week, and taboos, if any.

Once the Spirit has been identified, honour it with offerings of welcome. These can be presented on an altar designed for the spirit or at a sacred place where the spirit presides. Ask the Spirit to connect to the amulet by praying over it. Promise that you will honour your relationship to the Spirit by reverencing special days and things sacred to it as you ask it to be a Guardian for the baby.

With so many amulets to choose among, unless your culture has specific traditions, a Guardian Angel amulet would be an excellent choice. The amulet can be the seal of the Angel or an image representing the Angel. This gift can be given by way of Teddy Bear.

After the precious miracle arrives and both the mother and baby are safe, perhaps after 30 days (or 40 days, in Jewish and Islamic tradition), it is time to bless the baby for Protection and Success. This blessing can be formal, meaning is done by a minister, or informal, conducted by the parents of the baby.

BABY BLESSING BATH

- Angelica Root
- Solomon Seal Root
- Motherwort
- Five Finger Grass
- Flax Seed

Ten little fingers, Ten little toes,
Ohhh, where does the time go?

Lady Muse is the Ordained Pastor of House of Self-Empowerment Spiritual Center. A prophet, teacher, Eclectic Spiritualist, rootworker, Palo Priestess, and member of HP and AIRR, she presented this workshop at the 2019 HHF.

NEW ORLEANS FAMILY AND LOVE SPELLS
Zora Neale Hurston, Ann Fleitman, Larry B. Wright, Anna Riva, cat yronwode

HOODOO'S OLDEST GRIMOIRE

Thirty hoodoo spells from New Orleans were published by Zora Neale Hurston in 1931. Other authors have since added to the collection, which goes under the title *"Genuine Black and White Magic of Marie Laveau."*

THE MAN WHOSE CHILDREN DO NOT HELP HIM

O mother, all my life I worked to aid and assist my wife and our children. Now I am grown old and my heart is breaking because my children come here no more. O mother, how can I draw my children back, that I may leave them my property with a loving heart?

My dear son, I understand your sorrowful plea. You will take the Root of Rattlesnake and Oil of Sassafras. The oil you will sprinkle on the root and make four bundles of it, and one of these you will put in each corner of the home so that the evil spirits of the four winds will not abide there. And you will put a picture of the Holy Saint Joseph in the room wherein you take your rest, and before it you will burn a Blue Candle every day until the spirit of God enters the hearts of your children. And as the candle burns, pray to Joseph to intercede for you in the hearts of your children so they will do those things which are their duty.

In the clothing of your children put the Essence of Influence, and if you cannot get to their clothing, write them a loving letter and sprinkle Powder of Influence onto the letter, so it will get on their hands as they open it. And you mix Holy Water with it the Oil of Cedar and Essence of Amber; this you will put on your clothes when you see your children, so that they can see your sorrow and they in their turn be sorry for you. And a great pity shall swell up in their hearts for you.

If you visit their house, burn Devil's Incense, a pinch every day for nine days, in your room there, and do not open the door until the smoke has penetrated into the four corners. But also remember at all times that you yourself must never lose the love you bear for your children, for if you do, then your sin will be even greater than theirs and you will not succeed in your undertaking, for no matter what they may do or say against you, still it is your duty to love and protect them even unto the last day of your life. So Be It.

THE MAN WHO CANNOT GET A SWEETHEART

O dear mother, I ask your good and wholesome advice, for I don't seem to have any luck to get a sweetheart. My heart yearns for a sweetheart and it would be my complete happiness if I could make one understand me and love me in return.

My son, I am glad you have come to me for advice, for many more good sons of mine come not to me and therefore are not happy. In order that you may be blessed, in the water in which you bathe you will put every day for three weeks five drops of the Black Cat Perfume Oil to attract to you the spirit of love, and it will help you to gain your desires.

And in your room you will burn John the Conqueror Incense every day. And you will get Peace Water and sprinkle it in front of the house wherein lives the lady of your choice. Sprinkle it in such a manner that she will step on it or over it. You will do this for three nights after dark when no one will see you, and be sure that you step over it when you go in to see her.

And when going to see her, you will sprinkle on your garments the Love Oil. And on your skin you will use the Love Powder, so that she will listen to your words. You will tell her how beautiful she is and how sweet is her voice when she speaks, and you will impress upon her mind that you think very much of her. And in case you cannot see her or speak to her, then you will sit yourself down and write her a letter praising her and speaking of her beauty, and before you seal this letter you will put a few drops of the Hoyt's Cologne around the edge of the paper.

And when you are well acquainted with her, but not before then, you will put some of the Kiss Me Now Powder on her garments so that her love for you will grow warmer and she will never turn from you or forget you. So my son, do all of these things to get the help of God and to attract the spirit of love, that your sweetheart will give you many happy days. So Be It.

These two spells are extracted from the 53 spells in the 96-page book "Genuine Black and White Magic of Marie Laveau," compiled and edited by me, cat yronwode, and presented at the 2019 Hoodoo Heritage Festival. The complete book is available from the Lucky Mojo Curio Co.

MONEY MAGIC
Ms. Robin York

MONEY ALTARS

Money altars have been around for a long time. Having a money altar can help you bring money to your home, small business, or company. As your altar grows, so does your bank account and prosperity. People also use their altars for help with gambling by putting items on them that they might use with games of chance, such as poker chips, cards, dice, racing forms, lottery tickets, or cards.

These are other things you can put on a money altar: paycheck stubs, pictures of homes, a client's business cards, and court papers involving lawsuits. You can use any kind of idol on your altar. I use a "fat man" or Hotei Lucky Buddha. I also put green and yellow candles on my altar. Lodestones and Pyrite are important to have as well. Large and small denomination bills, lucky elephants, green pyramid candles, and acrylic pyramids with lucky items inside are all good for a money altar. Some will use Mercury Dimes to help generate and draw money and luck. You can also use currency from different countries, because if you have customers from around the world, then you'll want their type of currency too.

Make sure that you put lucky and money drawing oils on your good luck charms. If you have a Buddha on your altar, be sure to oil his hands. Always use the Buddha that has his hands up so he can hold the money that you place on your altar.

Never put your money altar on the floor. This will bring you negative energy and drain away your money luck. Always keep money altars high up, like on a table, book shelf, or dresser.

FEEDING YOUR MONEY ALTAR

Some people use their own essence to feed their altar, putting their urine on their Lodestones and Pyrite. You can also sprinkle Magnetic Sand on your Lodestones to feed them and burn a candle on the altar at least once a month.

Some people put lucky food offerings on their altar, or use a particular kind of money drawing candle, or a certain type of whiskey.

MONEY ALTARS FOR BUSINESSES

Money altars help bring in positive money energy and prosperity power. Stores or restaurants that display altars draw customers without them even knowing it, and the altars have a calming effect on those who shop there. People of many cultures keep altars in their small businesses, among them Chinese, Vietnamese, Mexicans, and Italians.

One of the culture groups in Louisiana and Florida, the Italians, use altars to Saint Joseph in their small businesses. They also like to use special breads, cookies, cakes, and dried Fava Beans on their altars for good luck and prosperity.

The Chinese like to use fruit, such as Oranges, and they light incense on their altars. They also put tea, water, or rice wine in a cup to honour their ancestors and thus receive in return blessings, more business, and more money.

MONEY HERBS

If you are taking out a loan for a small business, then you would use Alfalfa or Gravel Root herb on your altar. If you have an altar for gambling, use Cinnamon, Fenugreek Seeds, and Patchouli Leaves. Before you go to the casino, put some Cinnamon in a white handkerchief, for a man or, for a woman, in the upper part of her right bra.

Tea has been associated with money and prosperity for centuries. It originated in China as far back as the Shang dynasty, and later was introduced to Europe and the Americas. Tea leaves are the cured leaves of a Camellia tree with green leaves and yellow flowers, resembling U.S. currency and gold coins. Tea has beneficial properties, including the ability to attract money, blessings, prosperity, good health, love, and luck. Herbs can also be added to your favourite tea to offer pleasant aromas, flavours, stimulation, and magical symbolism.

Many money herbs can be found right in your kitchen, such as Rosemary, Nutmeg, Ginger, Cinnamon, Chamomile, and Basil, to name but a few that are ideal for drawing in money productivity.

MONEY BONES

A dead human's bones, particularly the finger bones, added to Red Beans and sewn up in a green bag make for an excellent hand to use in any type of gambling that involves the hands, such as pulling the slots, throwing dice, and playing cards. Make sure you dress the bones with Hoyt's Cologne or an oil like Pay Me, Money Drawing, or Attraction.

Bones from other species of animals may also be lucky. Among these are a lucky Raccoon penis bone, a Black Cat bone, and a wish bone from a Chicken or a Turkey. You can also use a Rabbit's foot, Alligator foot, or Goat hooves to help draw money luck, just by putting these bones into a bag.

MONEY CHARMS

Some people, like President Obama, regularly carry lucky charms. When people use charms it makes them feel like they have the advantage over others. Some people use charms in spells along with their favourite sachet powders and oils. Anything can be used as a lucky charm. For creative examples check the front panels of slot machines or visit a bingo parlour.

In the ancient civilization of Egypt, charms played a significant role, not only for protection, but as status symbols. Pharaohs wore charm bracelets and necklaces dedicated to gods to show their status in the world and in the afterlife. Roman Christians used undergarments talismanically to identify themselves and gain entrance into secret and forbidden worship activities. People still use clothes as lucky charms at the casino, race track, or sporting games. These include socks, t-shirts, or underwear they have won in.

Jews, Muslims, and people of other cultures carry small slips of paper with portions of their scriptures inside metal or leather cases for protection and luck.

In the Middle Ages charms and amulets were used by knights and kings. They wore their charms on their belts to wreak havoc on their enemies and for protection in battle. Queen Victoria wore a charm bracelet. She had small beads of glass beneath which were displayed the family crest.

Charms still hold their magic as long as you believe in them. Please refer to The Black Folder, pages 105-107, for more about prosperity charms.

MONEY OILS

Many people use money oils to draw money to them by anointing hands and feet. Women put oils on their breasts, bellies, and purses, and men put them on their wallets. You can also anoint candles.

People come to a worker for different money problems. You need to know all of the oils and herbs. Sometimes you will use an oil that is meant to do something else, but it would work for your situation.

A lot of times I combine different oils and herbs to make one oil. This works all the time for me and my clients. By doing this you are making one of a kind oils that are designed for their situation. Do not be afraid to mix oils or herbs. You will come out with the right combination all the time.

MONEY OIL COMBINATIONS

Some of my favourite ways to make oil blends:

- **Money House Blessing and Pay Me Oil:** Dress the front door and altar to aid a home business.
- **Attraction, Money, Love, and Cleo May Oils:** A good combination to attract money from men.
- **Lucky Buddha and Money Drawing Oils:** if you use a Buddha on your altar you need to rub these on his head and tummy.
- **Money Drawing and Pay Me Oils**: Put these on your hands and ask for debts to be repaid.
- **Prosperity and Attraction Oils:** This is a good blend for your business and money altars.
- **Money Stay With Me and Boss Fix Oils:** This is good for rubbing on paycheck stubs to help with keeping a job.
- **Lucky 13 and Lady Luck Oils:** I like to blend these when I go to play bingo.
- **Prosperity and Money Stay With Me Oil:** Use these your bank card to help your money grow.
- **Money Drawing and Road Opener Oils:** Dress a gold and green candle to guide you to wealth.
- **Fast Luck Oil:** Add it to bring in luck in a hurry.
- **Five Finger Grass Oil:** Add it to bring success.
- **Lady Luck Oil:** Add good old Lady Luck if you want to have more power when playing cards.
- **Black Cat Oil:** When gambling luck changes for the worse, add this to reverse bad luck to good.

Ms. Robin York wrote this flyer for her 2015 "Money Magic" workshop. A member of AIRR, she can also be contacted via her RobinsMojo.com web site.

OUR FAVOURITE MONEY SPELLS
Ms. Melanie, Kast Excelsior, Miss Elvyra, Lou Florez, Miss Phœnix LeFæ, Ms. Robin

MONEY DRAWING OIL LAMP
BY MS. MELANIE

I use antique Oil Lamps, but you can buy one or make your own with a Mason jar. The main ingredients used are: Petition Paper, Bayberry, Irish Moss, a Pyrite chunk, Alfalfa, Allspice, Magnetic Sand, Two Dollar Bill (five-spotted with Money Drawing Oil), a silver Mercury Dime (minted no later than 1946), and Money Drawing Oil.

The Oil Lamp and Silver Dime are wiped down with either Ammonia or Chinese Wash to remove any negativity from previous handling and then set aside to air dry.

While they are drying, focus on writing your petition paper. Be very specific in what you want to draw in. The more specific the request, the more specific the answer will be. I five-spot the petition paper with Money Drawing Oil.

Once the Mercury Dime has dried, dress it with Money Drawing Oil and add to the Oil Lamp base along with the other ingredients listed above, praying over each as you drop it in. Next, add a few drops of Money Drawing Oil.

Now, you are ready to add the lamp oil. Pray Psalms 23 over the lamp and visualize the money rolling in. Light your lamp and give it to God to take care of.

JUPITER'S TRIPLE STACKED SPELL
BY KAST EXCELSIOR

I call this "Jupiter's Triple-Stacked Money Condition Petition Spell" because it calls in and "stacks" three distinct conditions in sequence to manifest a specific set of experiences in the life of the spell's target.

Start with the 4th Pentacle of Jupiter from the *Key of Solomon.* It should be about 4 inches in diameter. You can print or scan a copy out so that it fits on about a quarter-page of a standard letter-size paper, or, if you like, you can draw it yourself by copying an example in a book or online.

On the blank backside of the pentacle, write out in an unbroken cursive script around the outer edge:

"With opened road the money flows into my hands it grows and grows."

Then write the target's name (along with optional business name, bank, or investment account numbers) in the center. Anoint the outer edge of the circle with Road Opening Oil, anoint an inner circle with Money Drawing Oil, and anoint the very center point with Money Stay With Me Oil or Prosperity Oil.

This charm can then be smoked with the corresponding incenses and folded into mojo bags or burned underneath (or attached to the side of) dressed and fixed glass-encased vigil candles.

AVOCADO PIT MONEY SPELL
BY MISS ELVYRA

Make a tea with 1 teaspoon of powdered Yellow Dock Root in a cup of water.

Wash a cleansed Avocado pit in the Yellow Dock Root and roll the damp pit in a pinch of Magnetic Sand. Place the dressed Avocado pit and a small Lodestone on a Two Dollar Bill and wrap the bill around them, tying this bundle up with green sewing thread or embroidery floss.

On a large green plate make a spiral with 1 tablespoon of cornmeal.

Inscribe or carve the words "Money Come To Me" onto a 4" green altar candle. You can easily fit the words in if you carve them in a spiral stripe around the candle. Anoint the candle with Money Drawing Oil, then roll it in a couple of pinches of powdered Basil and put it into a candle holder.

Place the dressed candle in the center of the Cornmeal spiral on the plate, and set the wrapped Avocado pit and Lodestone bundle next to the candle. Burn the candle completely down.

The best time to do this spell is on the dark of the Moon or on a Thursday.

GIVE ME A RAISE MONEY MOJO
BY LOU FLOREZ

Here are the supplies you will need:

- **Calamus Root:** Utilized to achieve commanding influence and power over your boss.
- **Benzoin Resin:** To enhance good fortune and money luck; for steady employment.
- **Alkanet:** For money drawing, prosperity, and to be given the respect of "royalty."
- **Irish Moss:** To manifest continuous prosperity, good fortune, money drawing, and luck.
- **Cinnamon:** To add energy and "heat" to formulas involving good luck, money drawing, and fortune.
- **Orange Peel:** To aid in opening the road and bringing in possibilities with sweetness.
- **A Pinch of Gunpowder:** To add a spark of action and energy and help to clear away obstacles.
- **Bergamot Oil:** Be sure to use skin-safe essential oils, cut with a carrier oil. Alternatively, you could use Hoyt's Bergamot or any Bergamot Perfume.
- **Green Flannel Mojo Bag:** For money.

Write a petition to get the raise you want on a Two Dollar Bill with the "Success Sigil" ($$¢¢$$) in each corner. Pray over the petition and place it and the herbs in a green flannel bag. Anoint the mojo with the Bergamot Oil and spray it with whiskey. Work with it every Monday, Wednesday, and Friday.

VACATION MONEY ALTAR
BY MISS PHŒNIX LEFÆ

Create a dedicated altar space where you will draw in money to fund your vacation plans. It doesn't have to be large, but only use it for this working. As you work, visualize your destination and see yourself in the areas you will visit. Cleanse the surface and cover it with a green cloth. Put a Mercury Dime dressed with Money Drawing Oil in each corner as you state your wish. In the center, lay images of your vacation destination with your petition written on them.

Next, prepare a "money drawing box" to store your money. The first money in the box should be a $2.00 bill marked with the "Success Sigil" ($$¢¢$$). Beside the box, place a 7-knob green candle, on each knob of which you have carved the name of your vacation spot. Dress the candle with Money Drawing Oil and burn one knob per day. As you work at your altar, burn Crown of Success Incense. Any "extra" money goes in your box to fund your trip.

HOW TO DRESS A GAMBLING ALTAR
BY MS. ROBIN

You will need a "fat man" Hotei Lucky Buddha statue with arms raised and hands up. Lay out green or gold fabric to secure and personalize the space provided for your altar. Cleanse your Buddha with Chinese Wash or Van Van Oil. This method may also be used to cleanse and bless dice, chips, or any trinkets you would like to place on your altar to symbolize gambling success. Next you will need to gather herbs and oils:

- **Cloves, Whole:** For money luck and good times.
- **Nutmeg, Whole:** For money luck and health.
- **Bay Leaves:** To place your bets with wisdom.
- **Money Drawing Oil:** To attract money to you.
- **Pay Me Oil:** To get the casino to pay out to you.
- **Cinnamon Powder:** To dress a candle for money.
- **Nutmeg Powder:** To dress a candle for money.

Place the whole herbs and some money in the statue's hands for 24 hours. You can put any denomination of money into the hands of your Lucky Buddha, from $5.00 to $100.00. With a red pen, write "RTM" (Return To Me) on the money, signing with your initials. Dress the money lightly with the oils and place it horizontally across the hands of the statue.

After 24 hours, set the whole herbs around the base of the statue, along with your other trinkets, and light a green and gold vigil candle dressed with the powdered herbs and both oils. When you go to gamble, use the prepared money and, if you can, leave the vigil light burning at home to back you up.

Read more at our free page on Money Spells:
http://www.luckymojo.com/moneyspells.html

"Our Favourite Money Spells" was a hand-out at the 2014 Hoodoo Heritage Festival workshops. Ms. Melanie is the former proprietor of The Curio and Candle Shop. Kast Excelsior is a member of AIRR, a record producer, and a bone reader; he is available at ConjureHaus.com. Miss Elvyra is a member of AIRR and HP, a reader at MISC, and a teacher; she can be found via Elvyra.com. Lou Florez is reader, rootworker, and teacher; he can be contacted at LouFlorez.com. Miss Phœnix LeFœ is a member of HP amd AIRR, a teacher, and the proprietor of Milk and Honey; she is available via PhœnixLeFœ.com. Ms. Robin is a reader, rootworker, teacher, and member of AIRR; she can be reached at RobinsMojo.com.

NINE LUCKY HANDS
catherine yronwode

ALL-AROUND GOOD LUCK HAND

Tobacco Snuff, John the Conqueror Root, Black Cat hair, Cat's Eye Shells, and Lodestone, placed in a red bag and dressed with Black Cat Oil makes a strong mojo hand.

SEVEN-WAY ROOT BAG FOR MEN

A very strong mojo for male luck and power is made only with roots and no green herbs, contains a small piece each of Peony Root, High John the Conqueror Root, Lucky Hand Root, Bo' Hog Root, Sampson Snake Root, Master Root, and Black Snake Root. The seven roots are sewn into a brown leather bag which may be carried on one's person or hidden in the home or place of business.

SEVEN-WAY ROOT BAG FOR WOMEN

A very strong mojo for female luck and power, made only with roots and no green herbs, contains one piece each of Peony root, Queen Elizabeth Root, Lucky Hand Root, Angelica Root, Gentian root, Calamus root, and Blood Root. The seven roots are sewn into a brown leather bag which may be carried on one's person or hidden in the home or place of business.

LUCKY BEANS IN MOJO HANDS

Mojo Beans are often treated in the same way as other large brown botanical curios like Buckeye, Nutmeg, and High John the Conqueror — that is, they are oiled and carried in the pocket as a lucky piece or combined with other curios in a mojo bag or conjure hand. Deer's Eye Beans, Sea Hearts, and Sea Beans are handled in this way, and in addition to general good luck and gambling luck, the latter two, being sea-borne seeds, are also said to protect from death by drowning. Small red beans — especially *Abrus* and *Ormosia spp.* — are included in mojo bags for luck as well.

GENERAL PURPOSE LUCKY HAND

A very good general-purpose love-and-money-drawing mojo can be made with Dragon's Blood, Cinnamon chips, and three Tonka Beans. Add other ingredients as desired, and dress it with Fast Luck Oil.

THREE JOHNS TRIO HAND FOR LUCK

John the Conqueror, Little John to Chew, and Southern John Root, can be combined to make a famous trio hand for the Three Johns. Pray over each root separately: Psalms 23 *("The Lord is My Shepherd...")* over the John the Conqueror, Psalms 37 *("Fret not thyself because of evil-doers...")* over the Little John, and Psalms 136 *("O give thanks unto the Lord; for he is good...")* over the Southern John. Then carry them in a bag and dress the bag with Hoyt's Cologne. If you wish, this trio can also be made with chips of the roots, hair of the person, and the person's name on paper; then wrapped and wound in red thread to make a jack ball for divination as well as luck.

CROSSROADS AND GRAVEYARD DIRT

Rev. Harry Middleton Hyatt recorded this simple lucky jomo from a person known as Informant #1095 in Waycross, Georgia, in 1939: "[Go] to the forks of the road about twelve or one o'clock in the night and get some sand and put it in a bag and put it over your mantlepiece. Go to the graveyard and get some dirt and sew it up with that. And that would make you lucky — good a jomo as you'd want."

A LUCKY WISH-GRANTING MOJO

Write your secret desire on paper and cross it with your name written three times. Fold the name paper toward you around a small, whole Dandelion root. Dress it with Holy Oil and carry it in a red bag with three Mojo Beans and seven Job's Tears, to get your wish.

LUCK, LOVE, AND MONEY HAND

A Rabbit Foot for luck, a small Nutmeg for money, and three Tonka Beans for love will make a very strong, naturally sweet-smelling, and all-purpose luck-drawing trio. Carry them in a red flannel bag and dress the bag with Fast Luck Oil.

"The Art of Making Mojos" is a 96-pge book i presented at the 2018 HHF. This extract contains nine samples from the more than 100 hands that it contains. The entire volume is available from LuckyMojo.com.

BUSINESS MONEY SPELLS
Miss Phœnix LeFæ

SPELLS FOR SUCCESS IN BUSINESS

Starting a business can be an exciting adventure and also a scary financial investment. Whether it's an online shop, a consultancy, a brick and mortar store, or a home business, you will need money for everything from inventory, rent, utilities, advertising, shipping, and travel to uniforms, licenses, business cards, office supplies, and taxes. It takes luck to make money in business, and these spells can help.

CUT A PENNY IN TWO

In February 1939, Informant #995 in Saint Petersburg. Florida, told Harry Hyatt how to have luck in business: "You take a penny and cut that penny half in two, if you want to be lucky with money. You put one half in your left pocket and leave the other half home, and you're going to be lucky in getting money in any kind of business you go into. That's luck. I've tested that out. That's extreme luck."

LODESTONE NEST FOR A SHOP

Prepare a money-drawing Lodestone as described on page 36, and set it in a little nest with a folded two-dollar bill and coins of every denomination in your cash register. Be sure to include one coin from the nest — your trained hunting money — in the change you give to your first customer of the day. Replace the coin with another to keep the lodestone working.

ANNUAL SHOP CLEANING

Raise your shop's energy with an annual spiritual cleaning. Wash with hot water and Chinese Wash, from top to bottom and back to front. Seal each room with a prayer and light a white candle as you finish it.

MOVING MERCHANDISE

Every item you sell can be fixed to draw a paying customer. Depending on what they are made of, you can dress, dust, or smoke them with Look Me Over and Attraction Oils, Powders, or Incense. Do this both to new inventory and to unsold goods that are going on markdown sale.

MONEY MASTER JAR

Cleanse a Mason jar by swirling Florida Water inside and pouring it out. When the jar is dry, add Bayberry, Five Finger Grass, Cinnamon, Solomon Seal Root, Master of the Woods, Master Root, and a lodestone. Prepare an Alligator foot by placing a Mercury dime in it, and using green thread to wrap the paw and hold the coin in place. Tie the string off with three knots. Set the Alligator foot in the jar. Sprinkle Magnetic Sand over the items and feed the jar a drop of whiskey. Cap the jar and hide it near the front door of your business. Feed it a drop of whiskey daily.

DRESS A PHOTO TO SELL ONLINE

If you sell at an online site, you want your merchandise to get noticed. Print out a photo of each item that you have listed online. At the center of the image, write the dollar amount you want to sell the item for. Anoint the four corners and the center of the photo with Look Me Over Oil. Circle the image with the word *"sell"* written over and over again, without lifting your pen from the paper. Set a green glass-encased candle dressed with Crown of Success, Money Drawing, and Pay Me Oils on the photo and keep it burning as long as the item is for sale. If you list many items, print them out, dress each photo and put them in a keepsake box with the candle on top so that your online sales grow and increase.

DRESS YOURSELF FOR COMMISSIONS

If you sell on commission, you have to make a good impression on your customers. Every morning, dress yourself with Prosperity Oil. Wear it alone or add a couple of drops of it to Hoyt's cologne or your favourite perfume or aftershave. Put it on your wrists, behind your ears, and behind your knees. As you anoint yourself recite the Lord's Prayer or Psalms 23, followed by your goal or wish, something like: *"I will reach and exceed my sales goals. I will attract eager customers with money to spend. I am successful."*

"Cashbox Conjure" is a 96-page book by Miss Phœnix LeFæ featured at the 2018 HHF. The full book is available from LuckyMojo.com. Miss Phœnix is a member of AIRR and owner of Milk and Honey in Sebastopol, California.

OUR FAVOURITE GOOD LUCK SPELLS
Ms. Robin, Angela Marie Horner, Mama E., Papa Newt, Elle DuVall, catherine yronwode

MS. ROBIN'S LUCKY GAMBLING SPELL
BY MS. ROBIN

Sunday, March 13, 2005

Hello,

I would like tell you about the gambling spell I use when I go to bingo. It has worked every time now. This does not mean you will get rich, but it does make your pocket feel good.

It takes a little preparation:

The night before, take a bath in Pay Me Bath Crystals by Lucky Mojo. Air dry, don't towel dry yourself. Take a small bucket or a mug-size cup of your used bath water outdoors and throw it over your left shoulder to the West and don't look back.

Take all the money that you're going to play with and write, "Money, return to me" (or "RTM" for "Return To Me") and put your name (or your initials) on each bill of the money, then anoint each bill with three hoodoo oils: Lady Luck, Pay Me, and Alleged Money Drawing Oil. Finally, dust Pay Me powder on all the money.

Use two vigil candles; a Lady Luck and a Lucky 13 Candle. Put a little pinch of bath crystals in both candles. Put the prepared money under both candles, then light the candles and say, "Let this money bring me more money."

When you are done, put some Pay Me Powder on your chest or bosom and go to sleep that way.

Let the money stay under the candles until it's time to go to play, then take it out — and Good Luck to you.

This has worked for me five out of six times and the one time it didn't work it was because I did not do the work fully and I lost big time.

I went to bingo Saturday, March 12, 2005, and won $575.00. Last week, March 5, 2005, i won $1,300.00 and a DVD home theater, plus lots more money.

Love, Robin

SIGIL MAGIC ON A LUCK ALTAR
BY ANGELA MARIE HORNER

Copy the Spell Star insert between pages 64 and 65, paste it on green parchment, and outline it in gold. Draw or print the bind-runes in this book titled You Will Have Success; Your House Will Succeed; To Draw Money; Power Protection, and Plenty; and Carry This For Luck Over Land and Sea; the 1st, 2nd, and 7th Seals of Moses, the 5th Pentacle of Mercury; and the 4th pentacle of Jupiter. Write petitions on the back of each sigil. Place the runes clockwise in the above order at the points of the star. Place the Seals in the spaces between the points: 1st Seal, top left; 2nd Seal, top right; 7th Seal, middle bottom. Now the Pentacles: 5th lower left; 4th lower right. In your favourite magic script, write your wishes for luck along the lines that make the Star. Using the same script, circle the Star to bind the spell: "As I weave it, it comes into being, as I bind it so it comes to me, as i will it, so mote it be" Smoke all petitions in a mix of Abramelin, Black Arts and Lucky Spirit Black Incense, and Life Everlasting flowers.

Now make a sugar jar. Copy the 4th Pentacle of Jupiter and draw the bind rune To Draw Money in the spaces the sigil makes. On the back, in an unbroken circle, write, "Lady luck come live with me." Write your petition inside of this circle. Fold powdered money-luck herbs such as Allspice, Cloves, Cinnamon, and Nutmeg into the petition and dress it with Van Van Oil. Put it into the jar with pyrite, dollar bills, and top it with more sugar. On the outside of the jar fix your favourite sigil of luck with a petition written on the back in an unbroken inward spiral to fill the entire space, facing the glass. On the opposite side of the jar, fix a picture of your client or yourself, with the name and birth date on the inside, facing the glass. Place the jar in the middle center of the Spell Star. Light a green or gold candle on the jar every Friday.

Choose and name a medium or large Lodestone and set it in a green or gold glass or metal cup or bowl, on a bed of Gambler's Gold herbs. Add a silver Mercury dime and six rolled-up Chinese Spirit Dollars. Dress the rim of the cup or bowl with Van Van Oil, place it at the middle top of the Star, and feed the Lodestone with Magnetic Sand or Anvil Dust every Friday.

LUCKY CAT MOJO BAG SPELL
BY MAMA E.

On the back of your photo write your name seven times, stacked. Rotate the photo ¼ turn clockwise and write "Good Luck" seven times, stacked, across your name. Dab Lucky 7 Oil or Fast Luck Oil on the four corners and the center of the paper. Fold it in half three times, turning it clockwise each time. Place it under a metal dish.

Carve "Good Luck" across the front of a green Cat candle and your full name across the back. Dress it with Lucky 7 Oil or Fast Luck Oil and set it on the dish. Dress a golden dollar coin or a silver dime, a whole Nutmeg, and a High John Root with the oil. Place them in a triangle formation on the dish around the Cat candle with the coin at top and the High John Root and the Nutmeg on each side of the lower points. Light the candle and pray over it for good luck, asking the spirit of the lucky Cat to draw good fortune your way.

Once the candle has finished, place the Nutmeg, coin, and High John Root in a green flannel bag with a pinch of black Cat hair, your folded photo, and a pinch of the leftover candle wax. Hold the open bag by your lips and breathe into it, to give it life. Name your mojo in the Name of the Father, the Son, and the Holy Spirit. Tie it shut with three knots.

Dress your mojo bag with Lucky 7 Oil or Fast Luck Oil by dabbing it in a quincunx pattern (four corners and one in the center). Carry it with you against your skin for the first week so that it becomes accustomed to your energy. After that, you can carry it in your pocket or purse to continually draw money your way. Always keep it away hidden and do not let anyone see it or touch it. Feed it weekly.

Dispose of the leftover candle wax at a crossroads.

SAINT CAJETAN FOR GAMBLING LUCK
BY PAPA NEWT

Saint Cajetan (born Gætano dei Conti di Thiene; October 1, 1480 - August 7, 1547) is the patron saint of bankers, gamblers, gamers, unemployed people, job seekers, document controllers, and good fortune.

After praying to Saint Cajetan, bet him that he can't pull off a miracle and make you win at the casino. If you do win, donate a portion of the winnings to charity in his name.

GOOD LUCK, PROSPERITY, STRENGTH
BY ELLE DUVALL

Buy a potted Bamboo plant of any species. These be found at almost every plant nursery and at some hardware stores with nursery departments. Take the Bamboo out of the small container it comes in and untangle the roots gently. Wrap a piece of your hair inside, among the roots of the Bamboo. Place the plant a glass vase filled with pebbles and loose crossroads dirt. The roots will make their way to the bottom of the pebbles and dirt mix and drink water that is fed to it.

Place a small High John Root, a few Allspice berries and some Cinnamon bark chips near the top of the pebbles so that they do not sit in the water at the bottom, but will soak into it a little at a time as you water the plant. Keep the potted Bamboo in a spot that is seen often and gets great filtered light. Place it near where you get ready for the day, Every day, stroke it and ask it to bring you good luck and confidence. As you take care of the Bamboo and it grows, so does your luck, prosperity, and strength.

YOUR LUCKY NUMBER FOR THE YEAR
BY CATHERINE YRONWODE

To get your lucky number for the year, wait until your birthday, then convert the month and day of your birth, plus the current year, into numbers, add them together, and reduce the sum to a single digit (1 thorugh 9) or to a Master Number (11, 22, or 33), whichever comes first. That's your lucky number!

For example, my birthday this year is 5-12-2019 and 5 + 12 + 2019 = 2036. Reducing 2036, i find that 2 + 0 + 3 + 6 = 11, a Master Number. Thus 11 is my lucky number for the "personal year" that runs from my birthday in 2019 until the day before my birthday in 2020. Try it — and Good Luck to you!

"Our Favourite Good Luck Spells" was a hand-out at the 2019 Festival. Ms. Robin, the founder of AIRR, can be reached at RobinsMojo.com. Angela Marie Horner is a member of AIRR and HP and a reader at MISC; she is online at LotusRavynConjure.com. Mama E. is a member of AIRR and HP; she can be found via ConjureDoctor.com. Papa Newt is a member of AIRR and HP and is also online at PapaNewt.com. Elle DuVall is a member of AIRR and HP; she is available via WorkingWithSpirits.com. I am online at AIRR, HP, MISC, LuckyMojo.com, and the Lucky Mojo Forum at Forum.LuckyMojo.com.

MONEY AND LUCK SPELLS WITH PLAYING CARDS
Professor Charles Porterfield

A DECK OF CARDS FOR MAGIC

A deck of playing cards need not be used for divination alone. They are magical in themselves, and there are numerous songs, stories, and myths about them. They have been employed as declarations of love, threats of war, carriers of confession, curses, and blessings.

In ancient times all of the items used for sortilege were also considered to be objects of power, and playing cards continue to retain their talismanic nature. A deck of cards or even an individual card still carries great magical imagery, symbolism, and intent.

WHY USE PLAYING CARDS IN MAGIC?

After we learn to work with playing cards to divine the future, we can then begin to find more complex uses for them, but we are left facing a simple question: why playing cards?

There are several arguments for the use of playing cards as components of spell work in hoodoo and conjure. A few of them are:

- **Access:** Playing cards are ubiquitous in America. Most stores carry them, from gas stations to grocers, and they can be found easily without the need of a specialty seller.
- **Cost:** Compared to the average cost of even a cheap deck of tarot cards, standard playing cards are far more affordable.
- **Disposability:** Due to lack of expense and ease of procurement, it is a simple matter to employ playing cards in spell work that might mark, tear, or burn them, as opposed to using more expensive and harder to obtain Tarot cards, which are treasured and kept by their owners.
- **Symbolism:** Playing cards are a rich part of American society, appearing in stories, songs, plays, and movies. Their images are deeply rooted in our thinking and culture.
- **Traditionalism:** Tarot cards were uncommon in hoodoo until the mid-20th century. If we wish to take a more traditional stance in our practice, then regular playing cards are in line with what older practitioners had at their disposal to use.

CARD SPELLS FOR MONEY AND LUCK

FOUR AND JACK FOR WORKING GIRLS

If you wish to increase your prospects and attract generous clients, working girls dress the Four of Diamonds and Jack of Diamonds with Cleo May Oil for tips from men. If you are working a harder line, dress them with Jezebel Oil. Use Q Oil to attract gay customers. A man who escorts women can use Mandrake Oil. Tie the fixed cards around a red glass-encased vigil candle dressed with Attraction Oil. Light the candle and pray Psalms 18:19. Place the candle in a window or near the door of where you work.

THE PROFESSOR'S 777 GAMBLING HAND

For luck at games, take the Seven of Hearts, Seven of Diamonds, and Seven of Clubs from a new deck of cards, and dress them with Hoyt's Cologne. Next, dress a pair of bone Dice, a Rabbit's foot, and a Mercury Dime with Van Van Oil. Finally, dress a Lucky Hand Root, a Buckeye nut, and a bit of Irish Moss with whiskey. Place all of these in a green flannel bag, and breathe into it before tying it shut with seven knots. Feed the bag with Hoyt's Cologne or whiskey and carry it on you when gambling.

RED PEPPER RESTORES LUCK TO A DECK

In the 1930s, an old practitioner from Illinois told Rev. Hyatt that you can sprinkle Red Pepper on playing cards to "burn bad luck off them."

DIAMONDS AND CLUBS FOR BUSINESS

To aid business, take the Nine of Diamonds, Nine of Clubs, and Eight of Clubs from a new deck. Across the Nine of Diamonds write "My Bank," across the Nine of Clubs write the "Success Sigil" ($$¢¢$$), and "My Shop," and across the Eight of Clubs write your own name and birth date. Dress the Nine of Diamonds with Money Stay With Me Oil, the Nine of Clubs with Prosperity Oil, and the Eight of Clubs with Attraction Oil. Place the Nine of Diamonds in your wallet while praying Luke 11:9, and keep it there. Tack the Nine and Eight of Clubs up in your shop near the front door or cash register after praying Psalms 90:17 over them.

SEWN CARDS TO GET A JOB

In 1970, Prophet Warkiee Sarheed of Saint Petersburg, Florida, shared this spell with Rev. Harry Hyatt: Write the name of the man who can give you a job on a piece of paper. Sprinkle bluestone on it, fold it up and put it between the Five and Six of Diamonds taken out of a new deck. Sew the cards together with a needle and thread (either black or white; it doesn't matter). Wear this in your shoe and you will be hired within five days. Note that Bluestone is toxic; crumbled dry laundry blueing is safer.

SEVEN DIAMONDS FOR STEADY WORK

For steady work or keep an existing job, take the Seven of Spades from a new deck of cards, turn it face down, and place it under a flat stone. Take the Ace through Seven of Diamonds and pin each card to one knob of a green 7-knob candle. Pin the Ace to the top knob, the Two to the second knob, and so on, working your way around and down the candle in a spiral. Write the job you desire on a clean piece of paper and place it on top of the rock along with a one dollar bill, as you say the following: "I have paid the price through my misfortunes. Grant me this job, I pray, O Lord." Dress the candle with seven drops of Steady Work Oil as you read the 76th Psalm over it, and burn the candle on the papers, one knob each day until it is done.

SIX DECKS OF CARDS TO BRING TRADE

In 1939, Rev. Hyatt interviewed a retired medicine show performer and professional root doctor in Sumter, South Carolina. This man, born in 1874, was widely travelled, well read, and an expert at what he called "hoodooism." He told how playing cards draw business to a beer garden or piccolo joint (which, outside of the Carolinas, would be known as a juke joint), and he repeatedly used the old word "paire" to refer to a deck of cards: If another fellow opens up right next to you to beat you out of business, and you want the trade to come into your business instead and to be successful, just buy yourself six paire of cards, real gambling cards, and burn up three paire of them. Hide the ashes of the three burnt-up paires under your counter. Place the three unburnt paires on top of the ashes, side by side, and on top of each paire place a silver coin. You need three pieces of silver, even if it is just three dimes. This will help to draw trade to your business. But, remember when you go to sweep out your business, never sweep those ashes or cards out. Just leave them where you hid them.

ACE OF SPADES FOR GAMBLING LUCK

In 1939, a professional rootworker from Waycross, Georgia, told Rev. Hyatt how to rip up and burn the Ace of Spades to ashes, mix the ashes with salt and sugar, and dress your cards for luck. After that, he said, you put the remnant ashes in a pouch in your pocket. Then, while at the card room, you take a ring from your finger, drop it into the ashes, pull it out and place it back on your finger. If you touch someone with that hand, they will have to leave the game and you can sit in and have good luck with your fixed deck.

THREE CARDS AND A DIME LUCKY HAND

In 1938, a professional conjure doctor from Mobile, Alabama, gave his way to make a gambling hand to Rev. Hyatt: "Now for gambling, you take three playing cards; take the Ace of Spades, the Jack of Clubs, and the King of Diamonds. You tear just a small tip [the index] off those three cards. Take the small tip off those three cards, and after you do that, get you a file. You take this file and file a silver dime in half. You take this dust now, from the dime, and you save it. Then get you a piece of Lodestone [grit], and get you a piece of red flannel. You put the pinch of card [the index] from the Ace of Spades on the flannel, and then you place the first half of the dime on the flannel. After you put the one half on the red flannel, you place a pinch of card [the index] from the Jack of Clubs, and the other half of the dime, like a sandwich. Then you put the other piece on top, [the index] from the King of Diamonds, and put this dust, the filings from the silver dime, on top of that. You put the piece of Lodestone [grit] in there with that on this piece of flannel. Put it in there with that, and you dress it with Hoyt's Cologne; just a little Hoyt's Cologne, and you dampen this, you see. And after you dampen this, you fold it. But before you sew it up, you take a pin, a straight pin, and cut the head off it. Cut the head off the pin, and put the head inside of the flannel. When you fold it up, pin this other part of the pin in the flannel. Then you sew it up. After you sew it up, then you wear it, and when your luck seems to be changing a little, you dress it with Hoyt's Cologne. That's to keep the Lodestone growing."

"A Deck of Spells: Hoodoo Playing Card Magic in Rootwork and Conjure" is a 96-page book by Professor Porterfield that was given away at his 2015 Hoodoo Heritage Festival workshop. This is a sample; the full book is available from LuckyMojo.com.

SIX CONJURE CURSES
Miss Aida

CURSING TO HARM OR KILL

URINE IN THE FIREPLACE

During the 1930s, all along the East Coast, from New York City through Albermarle, Virginia; Wilson, North Carolina; Brunswick, Georgia; and down to Saint Petersburg, Florida, the folklorist Harry Hyatt met workers who told him a very old curse that consists of throwing your victim's urine into a fireplace. Some said it would run you crazy, others said it would give you urinary problems, and a few said that if it was done right, it would kill you. Most folks told Hyatt to just to throw the urine loose into the flames, but a few said to confine it in a bottle. Mrs. Baker, born in Albermarle, told it this way, "They get some of your water in a bottle and cork it up, dig a hole in the corner of the chimney and bury this upside down; and when this water would boil, you die."

KIDNEY FAILURE

One of the most common ailments people get is kidney stones, also known as gravel. To bring on a bout of this painful affliction, obtain an animal kidney. Beef is the easiest to obtain, but any species will do. Dissolve a packet of Destruction Bath Crystals in water, and prepare a number of petition papers with the command, "Kidney Failure." Make several slits into the kidney and fill the slits with small stones of all sizes and wedge in the folded papers. Stab three Coffin Nails through the kidney. Place the kidney in a container, and fill it with the dissolved Destruction Bath Crystals over it. Place the lid on and freeze.

TO SICKEN AND KILL YOUR SPOUSE

Go to the grave of someone who died of an infectious disease, gather a small amount of dirt and pay for it with 13 pennies. Back home, separate it into 13 tiny portions as you curse your no-good mate 13 times under your breath, stating everything that he has done to you, saying, for example, *"John Doe, you have sinned against our marriage, and now you will sicken and die by my hand."* For the next 13 days, sprinkle one portion of the graveyard dirt into food that you have prepared for him, being very careful not to eat any of the food yourself.

CURSING TO BRING UNHAPPINESS

SPOILED MILK TO RUIN A PARTY

My horrid neighbours planned to have a HUGE party in their front yard. This would have meant an extension of the party into my front yard. A couple of hours before the party, I laid spoiled milk all along our mutual property line, where they would step in it, and demanded that their party be spoiled. Without any meteorological forewarnings (it was predicted to be a beautiful day), a sudden gust of forceful wind came through. This was followed by a sudden drop in temperature and a horrendous rain storm.

It warmed my heart to watch these terrible neighbours frantically move table, chairs, and decorations into their garage, which could barely hold half of their invited guests. The party was a flop!

BREAK A MIRROR
TO GIVE SEVEN YEARS OF BAD LUCK

Dress a picture of your enemy with a cursing oil, place it face-in toward a mirror, and wrap it all in black cloth. At night, take this, with a hammer, to a crossroads. Lay it in the middle of the roads and smash it while calling down seven years of bad luck on your foe. Leave it there and walk away.

A SHITTY LITTLE
CHICKEN-HEARTED NOBODY

To cause an enemy to lose his courage, obtain a Chicken heart, three needles, and fresh Dog feces. Print out a copy of the Three of Swords tarot card, write the enemy's name on it, and around the name write, *"You are a shitty little Chicken-hearted nobody."* Slit the heart open and fill its chambers with feces, wrap it in the copy of the tarot card, and stab the three needles through it as shown on the card. Put it in a glass jar and freeze it.

This is an extract from "Cursing and Crossing: Hoodoo Spells to Torment, Jinx, and Take Revenge on Your Enemies" a 96-page book by Miss Aida that was given away to participants at the 2017 HHF workshops. The full book is available from LuckyMojo.com.

NORSE SPELLS OF DESTRUCTION
Dr. Johannes Gårdbäck

FÖRGÖRA: DESTRUCTIVE SPELLS

To get revenge, hurt, torment, kill, or curse is called *förgöra* (to destroy). The victim is *förgjord* (destroyed) or *förtrollad* (betrolled) and may be *modstulen* if his courage was stolen or *maktstulen* if his power was taken. Long distance destruction spells are *sänningar* (sendings).

THE VIRGIN MARY'S THEFT OF COURAGE
(Sweden, early 20th century)

Jesus went on a road. There he met the Virgin Mary. "Where are you going?" "I am going to the farmer's land to steal the courage of all my enemies through three names, God the Father, Son, and the Holy Spirit."

Jesus gick vägen fram, då mötte han jungfru Maria. "Vart ska du gå?" "Jag skall gå till bondens gård och modstjäla mina ovänner genom tre namn, Gud Fader, Son, och Den Helige Ande."

Read three times into alcohol and then spit three times in a bottle of alcohol. Then give it to your enemy to drink and he will be modstulen.

This is an unusual adaptation of a common troll formula. The Virgin Mary is often called upon in matters of childbirth, fertility, and pregnancy, but here, she is far from the timid maiden or sorrowing mother. The reason the northern Virgin Mary acts against enemies is that she inherited the traits of the older Norse goddesses as well as those of the Völvas, the living seers and troll women who act much like the Norns of mythology.

A DOLL TO FÖRGÖRA A PERSON
(Sweden, 18th century)

A doll to destroy a person can be made of mud and communion wine.

AN ETTERSHOT (POISONOUS TROLLSHOT)
(Denmark, 19th century)

Take a wasp's stinger and insert it into the enemy's clothes or the threshold of her bedroom with the words:

Rise swiftly, Devil's force, and sting!

Stig hastigt op, Djævelskraft for at stikke!

SEND TORMENT TO AN ENEMY IN ALCOHOL
(Sweden, early 20th century)

If you, N.N., are my enemy, then I send you to the lowest stair, to the burning lake. And there you shall whine and there you will be tormented, in the name of God the Father and Son and the Holy Spirit.

Är du, N.N. min ovän, så visar jag dig till den nedersta trappa, till den brinnande sjö. Och där skall du kvida och där skall du plågas i Guds Faderns och Sonens och Den Helige Andes namn.

Read three times into alcohol. The alcohol is then given to the enemy.

FÖRGÖRA A PERSON TO BE SICK FOR LIFE
(Sweden, early 20th century)

I command you, N.N., in the name of the blood of Jesus Christ, the Son of God, in the name of God the Father and the Holy Spirit, that you shall be sick as long as you live.

Jag befaller dig N.N., i Jesu Kristi Guds Sons blod, i Guds Faders och Den Helige Andes namn, att du måtte vara sjuk så länge du lever.

Read three times over an enemy while looking into his eyes.

It takes guts and quite a lot of hatred to perform this kind of spell. However, most practitioners say it might occasionally be justified.

FÖRGÖRA AN ENEMY USING A MATCH
(Sweden, early 20th century)

To destroy an enemy, take some of his hairs and wrap them around a sulphur stick (a common match) and throw it into the fire. You can also wrap the hairs around a fingernail of the person and throw it into fire.

This is an extract from the 288-page book "Trolldom: Spells and Methods of the Norse Folk Magic Tradition," by the Swedish root doctor and AIRR member Johannes Björn Gårdbäck. Johannes gave a workshop on Trolldom at the 2014 Festival; the book was published in 2015 by the Yronwode Institution for the Preservation and Popularization of Indigenous Ethnomagicology.

HOT FOOT FOODS
Ladies Auxiliary of Missionary Independent Spiritual Church

TEXAS HOT FOOT CHILI

2 pounds grass-fed ground beef (substance)
1 jalapeño pepper, seeded and diced
    (drive away enemies)
1 serrano pepper, seeded and diced
    (drive away enemies)
1 poblano pepper, seeded and diced
    (drive away enemies)
2 cans green chilies, 4 oz. each
    (drive away enemies)
Gebhardt Chili Powder, to taste
    (drive away enemies)
1 yellow onion, diced (luck)
2 cloves of garlic, minced (protection)
4 cans Ro-Tel Diced Tomatoes and Green Chilies
    (female protection)
Turmeric powder, to taste (health, protection)
Cayenne powder, to taste (drive off enemies)
Pinch of black mustard seeds (protection)
Black pepper, ground, to taste (protection)
13 black peppercorns (protection)
Pinch of salt (protection)

Set stove to medium-high. Sauté peppers, onion, and garlic in a splash of olive oil until peppers are soft and onions are clear. Add ground beef and cook until half done. Add chili powder, spices, tomatoes, and salt. Bring to a boil, then reduce heat to low. Stir counter-clockwise, calling the names of those you want to hot foot and telling them to get the F@#* away from you, out of your life, and out of your business.

Serve hot with cornbread that has been spiked with a dash of cayenne and green chili. Where are the beans? This is Texas chili, and traditional Texas chilis do not have beans. If you can't live without beans in your chili, just add them.

To drive off your enemies and get them to leave you alone, the chili is both spice-hot and stove-hot. However, you also want it to be inviting and tasty. This is great to use at a church potluck or office function. Leave it out anonymously so that your target will eat it.

— Briana Saussy, Texas, MilagroRoots.com

PICKLED PENIS PARTY PICK-UPS

1 jar dill pickles (male members)
1 pound thin sliced Havarti cheese
    (the appearance of nurturance)
1 pound thin sliced honey ham
    (the appearance of luck)
1 jar sweet hot mustard in squeeze bottle
    (protective sweetness)
1 box plastic sword party toothpicks
    (stab! stab! stab!)

Select a pickle from the jar to represent a male enemy's penis. As you make the sign of the cross over the pickle, give it the name of your rival, saying, "Joe you are, and Joe you shall be, to me." Dry the pickle with a paper towel and, setting it on a cutting board, slice it into lengthwise quarters (or spears). Use quiet focus here, like a surgeon. Repeat with each pickle. You can name each for the same person, or call a number of names into the work.

Lay out the slices of cheese. On each slice, write "I Can, U Can't" in mustard, using a squeeze bottle. The special decorating bottles are particularly good for this, but any will do. Place a thin slice of ham over each message and spit your curse lightly on it, then add the pickle spear at one edge. Roll the ham and cheese around the pickle, making a tube. Using the plastic party swords, stab them into the pickle tube, each time uttering a curse. Stab them one bite apart — every inch or so. Lastly, with hard chopping motions, dismember the bites into individual appetizers and serve. All those who partake are sharing in your curse work — including your rival himself.

Among my favourite mustards are Kosciusko Spicy Brown, Honeycup Uniquely Sharp, Koops Dusseldorf, Colman's Original English, and Beaver Sweet Hot.

— Deacon Millett, FourAltars.org

These two magical recipes are samples from the 96-page book "Hoodoo Food! The Best of the Conjure Cook-Off and Rootwork Recipe Round-Up" by the Ladies Auxiliary of Missionary Independent Spiritual Church, published by MISC and distributed at the 2014 Hoodoo Heritage Festival.

SIX BREAK UP SPELLS
Miss Aida

TO DRIVE PEOPLE APART

DOG AND CAT HAIR ASHES IN THEIR PATH

Write each person's name on the opposite ends of a piece of paper. Tear the paper in half. Burn it with black Dog and black Cat hair while demanding that the couple break up. Scatter the ashes over the path that they will walk, while again verbally commanding that they break up.

SKULL CANDLES FOR REPULSION

This spell is to make two people antagonistic toward one another. It is used when you do not seek favour from either one, and simply wish for them to hate one another. Acquire two black skull candles. Bore holes in the mouths, eye sockets, and frontal regions of both. In a small bowl, mix Deer's Tongue herb, Poppy seeds, Black Mustard seeds, Red Pepper flakes, and Restless Incense. Load this into the mouths of both candles, so that they will speak irrationally to one another. Seal the mouth-holes with wax. Load the frontal regions with a small petition stating, "*[Name] talks shit and is shit.*" Each skull candle will condemn the other. Seal with wax. Leave the eye sockets unsealed. Anoint both candles with Restless Oil, then roll them in Restless Incense. Name and baptize the candles. Smear both of their faces with Dog feces. Place them on your altar, facing one another. Light the candles and talk to them as much as possible while encouraging them to fight.

SPOIL A RELATIONSHIP WITH SPOILED MILK

Not only can you pour spoiled milk in the path of an illegitimate couple while commanding that the relationship spoil, but you can place their name papers, pictures, and personal concerns into a jar that contains spoiled milk and seal it tight. Be advised that spoiled milk has an awful odour, so prepare it outside. Shake the jar as often as possible while demanding that the relationship spoil. Remember that spoiling milk produces gases, so fill the container no more than two-thirds full to prevent leakage or explosions — unless you want to see the relationship explode.

TO DRIVE PEOPLE AWAY

CO-WORKER BE GONE HOT SAUCE BOTTLE

To separate a bad-hearted person from your job site, take the person's business card or hand-written signature, roll it up tight, and insert it into a bottle of hot sauce. Pray Psalms 1 over it with conviction, for the ungodly person to "leave the congregation." Fish the paper out and place the prayed-over bottle in the break room at work, for all to use.

CAUSING A FOOL TO WANDER

This spell causes your foe to wander aimlessly in confusion. Therefore, ensure that special attention is paid to stuffing the head. Fill the doll-baby with Spanish Moss, a couple of vials of Red Ants, Red Pepper flakes, Poppy seeds, Vandal Root, Restless Incense, Inflammatory Confusion Incense, and personal concerns. Include name papers, petition papers, and pictures anointed with Restless Oil. After sealing the doll, name and baptize it. Anoint the outer portion of the doll with Inflammatory Confusion Oil and Restless Oil. Your command ought to be consistent with the intention of the doll, therefore, to create confused foolishness, you can say, "*You don't know what you want and you don't know where you're going, so, like a fool, you will ramble and wander forever.*" To send the person away, throw the doll into a river or a sewer, or mail it to a foreign post office far away and do not disclose your return address.

GRAVEYARD DIRT BANISHING SPELL

Mix graveyard dirt with Banishing Oil and a small personal concern, such as a hair or fingernail of the person. Wrap this in a small square of black cloth and tie it up with a black thread or string. Bury it far away from the person's house so that the enemy will likewise have to go far away.

This is an extract from "Destroying Relationships: Hoodoo Spells to Break Up, Separate, Hot Foot, and Drive Off Your Foes and Rivals," a 96-page book by Miss Aida that was given away to participants at the 2018 Festival in a workshop presented by Deacon Millett. The full book is available from LuckyMojo.com.

OUR FAVOURITE COURT CASE SPELLS
Ms. Robin, Miss Michæle, Angela Marie Horner, Co. Meadows, Candelo Kimbisa, Ambrozine LaGare

HEAR SPEAK SEE NO EVIL IN COURT
BY MS. ROBIN YORK

To help close the ears, eyes, and mouths of those against you in court, make three unstuffed doll-babies or poppets using brown material, and place them in a jar to which you have added Vinegar, Red Pepper Seed, and Goofer Dust. Cap the jar, and soak the dolls for seven days, starting on a Sunday at midnight. Burn one 4" brown candle atop the jar each night for those seven nights.

Remove the dolls from the jar and fill their bodies with Spanish Moss, Goofer Dust, and Sulphur. Sew up each doll. Open up the head of one doll and fill it with Poppy Seed, Black Mustard Seed, and graveyard dirt, then sew it closed. Cut two small strips of black electrical tape. Place one strip over the mouth of the next doll, and place the second strip of tape over the eyes of the last doll.

Using Spanish Moss, wrap all three dolls together with their backs to each other, and seal them in a box along with nine Coffin Nails. Bury the box in a cemetery nine days before court. Remove the box when your court case is over, and dispose of it by throwing it into the ocean or into running water.

SWAYING THE SYSTEM
BY MISS MICHÆLE

When justice is on your side, but the full might of law and government is arrayed against you, take a series of seven baths with a mix of Court Case, King Solomon Wisdom, Do As I Say, and Victory Bath Crystals. Recite Psalms 35, Psalms 65, and Psalms 20 during each bath. Use the oils from these same products to dress your shoe soles so you track them into your lawyer's office and into court.

For your opponents, mix Black Mustard Seed and Poppy Seed with Inflammatory Confusion, Do As I Say, and Double Cross Powders, and a few drops of Castor Oil. Pray Psalms 1 and Psalms 9. Use this mixture to dress purple candles as well as legal documents sent to your opponent. On the day of the trial, as you walk to your seat, drop some of the seed from your hand where they must walk.

LOWERING THE BAIL
BY ANGELA MARIE HORNER

To get mercy for a client who needs reduced bail, start by drawing a Spell Star — a pentagram with a circle at each point, to hold small sigils, and a double circle all around it to receive a written petition.

These sigils go in the circles, clockwise from the top:

- **The Tetragrammaton:** At the upmost point to connect the works to Spirit as well as Earth.
- **Victory in Battle Galdrbok sigil:** For the client's lawyer; cross the lawyer's name over the judge's.
- **Road Opener sigil:** To open communication between the defense and a stubborn judge.
- **Fourth Pentacle of Jupiter:** To bring about a lower bail so the client can await trial at home.
- **Win in Court Galdrbok sigil:** For success.

These images go between the points, clockwise:

- **Chief Pushmataha, top left:** A great negotiator, to help the lawyer present an eloquent argument.
- **Mary Ellen Pleasant, top right:** The 19th century "Mother of Human Rights in California," who defended Black men and women in San Francisco.
- **Saint Jude, lower right:** For help; on the back, cross the client's name over the judge's name.
- **Justice tarot card, bottom:** Remind the judge she is non-biased and should not be too harsh.
- **Our Lady of Mercy, lower left:** On the back, cover the judge's name with the command, "Give Mercy."

Inside the double circle, use red ink to write Psalms 14:17 for freedom from slander, Psalms 19:22 to prevent protracted confinement, and Psalms 32:32 to receive grace and mercy. The 7th Pentacle of the Sun with the client's picture atop it goes at the center to aid in release from jail. On the back of the Spell Star write a petition for your desired outcome. Smoke the paper with Court Case and Our Lady of Perpetual Help Incense, as you ask the spirits to plead for the client's rights. Set it on a reflective surface, such as a silver tray. If the client is guilty, scatter Sumac berries over all.

Once the matter is resolved, burn the paper to ash and dispose of it at a crossroads or graveyard.

CHANGE THE JUDGE'S MIND
BY CO. MEADOWS

To sway the mind of a judge to rule in your favour, first carve the judge's name onto the forehead of a brown Skull Candle using a new needle. Dress the needle with Compelling Oil, then say, *"Your focus is unfocussed, your direction I will direct."* Aggressively stab the needle into the back of the skull's head and proclaim, *"I direct your mind."* Dress the candle with Compelling Oil, then place Compelling Powder into your left palm. Blow it onto the skull from four directions, but before each blow you must speak the desired outcome, beginning with, *"My mind is made up. I grant you [your desire]."* Finally, burn the ends of three pieces of Licorice Root, one at a time, placing the first in one ear while stating, *"The change is made; [name of the favoured] has won."* Place the second root in the right eye and say, *"The change is made; you can't uproot."* Place the last root in the mouth, commanding, *"The change is made; it's fated to be."*

Burn the candle in sections for 9 days leading up to the court date, and on the day of the trial drop the remains of the Licorice Roots inside the court room.

AID SOMEONE'S RELEASE
BY CANDELO KIMBISA

To help someone accused go free, first get hold of a suit of clothing that they have worn for 2 to 3 days. If they are still in jail, try to get the clothing they were arrested in. Burn the clothing to ash. Rub the ashes thoroughly onto a 2 to 3 foot length of good chain. Lock the ends of the chain together with a padlock, forming a circle. Obtain some dirt from around the jail and the court house, and rub the dirt over the chain. Write the names of the presiding judge, the lawyers, and all others on the prosecution's side of the case on parchment, burn it to ash, and rub the ash onto the chain. Break up High John the Conquer Root and rub it over the chain as you say, *"In the name of the Father, the Son, and the Holy Sprit, I consecrate this in the name of [the defendant]. He WILL be free!"*

Christen a baby doll stuffed with the accused's clothing and personal concerns. Set the doll inside the circle of locked chain. Recite aloud Psalms 23, and then use a pickaxe to break the chain open at the lock or by breaking a link. You may have to strike it more than once. Snatch the broken chain away, and place the doll in the home to which the accused will return.

STOP OR DELAY EVICTION
BY AMBROZINE LEGARE

TO WORK THE LANDLORD

As soon as you suspect that your landlord has taken legal action against you, collect the names of all parties representing him. Write a petition on a piece of brown paper bag that includes the names of your landlord, his attorney, and the law firm, in which you ask for this process to be delayed as long as possible or stopped altogether. In the center of the paper place some Poppy Seed and Alum, and five-spot the paper with Confusion Oil. Fold the paper away from you, then wrap it in red string while praying that *"all parties set against me to remove me from my home be confused, confounded, slow to act, slow to speak, careless with their legal paperwork, and tied so that they may not move me."*

Place the wrapped packet into a jar of molasses. Shake the molasses jar hard once in the morning after you wake up and again at night before you go to bed, each time praying that those set to evict you fail. Burn a new tea light on top of the molasses jar after each time you shake and pray over it.

TO WORK THE JUDGE OR MEDIATOR

Fill a small jar with sugar, a pinch of Cinnamon, and a paper with the judge's name written on it three times. Burn a tea light on this jar twice a day, praying each time that the judge favours you, grants you additional time, or throws out your case entirely.

Carry a small bit of the sugar and Cinnamon from the jar with you each time that you must appear in court for your case. Just before you enter the courtroom, place a pinch of the mixture in your mouth. Sprinkle the remaining mixture discretely on the courtroom floor. Once your case is done, dispose of these items by emptying the remaining contents of the jar into a river or at a crossroads. Dispose of the empty jar in your recycling garbage bin. Good luck!

"Favourite Court Case Spells" was a hand-out at the 2017 HHF panel discussion. AIRR member Ms. Robin is reachable at RobinsMojo.com. AIRR member AIRR member Miss Michæle is online at HoodooFoundry.com. Angela Marie Horner is at AngelaMarieHorner.com. Co. Meadows is at CoMeadows.com. Candelo Kimbisa is available at Kimbisa.org. AIRR member AIRR member Ambrozine LeGare is at AmbrozineLeGare.com.

THE NINE STAGES OF COURT CASE WORK
Ms. Robin

THE INNOCENT AND THE GUILTY

Court Case work is done by the number Nine. There ere are nine stages. Each stage is in two parts:

A) To protect the Innocent from injustice.
B) To get the Guilty charged and punished.

CANDLES FOR COURT AND LEGAL WORK

Whether a free-standing taper or a glass vigil light, all legal matters must start with a basic brown candle.

NINE COURT AND LEGAL FORMULAS

Use these products to anoint the body, dress candles, burn as incense, make sprays, or carry.

- **Law Keep Away:** To stop legal interference.
- **Court Case:** To do well in any court of law.
- **Just Judge:** To gain the mercy of the judge.
- **King of Solomon:** For the judge's wisdom.
- **Essence of Bend-Over:** To get your way.
- **Crown of Success:** To achieve your goals.
- **Protection:** To be shielded from attacks.
- **Victory:** To be vindicated or win a settlement.
- **Reversing:** To get a conviction overturned.

NINE HERB COURT AND LEGAL CASE MIX

Take a pinch each of these nine herbs and tie them into a cloth to make a charm packet or "mini-mojo."

- **Deer's Tongue:** For eloquent speech.
- **Sumac Berries:** For mercy of the court.
- **Oregano:** To keep interferring people away.
- **Little John to Chew:** To win in court.
- **Tobacco:** For victory in court.
- **Lemon Balm:** To break up bad conditions.
- **Flax Seed:** To gently move away bad energies.
- **Calamus:** To control what others say or do.
- **Licorice:** To rule and control others.

NINE PSALMS FOR COURT CASES

Become familiar with these Psalms. They can help.

A) Aid the Innocent: Psalms 3, 5, 17, 35, 37, 59.
B) Condemn the Guilty: Psalms 37, 58, 59.

1) THE POLICE STOP

A) Keep off the law's attention.
Bay Leaf; Agar-Agar, Arrow Root Powder. Law Keep Away, Protection.

B) Attract the attention of police to a criminal.
Clarity, Damnation, Goofer Dust.

2) THE ARREST

A) No charges; be let go with a fine or warning.
Make and use this spray: Law Keep Away, Blessing, Florida Water, Chinese Wash, water (or use Van Van Oil without water instead of Chinese Wash).

B) Ensure the arrest of a criminal.
Do As I Say, Damnation, Destruction, Essense of Bend-Over, Confusion, Inflammatory Confusion.

3) THE ARRAIGNMENT OR HEARING

A) Get charges dropped at the hearing.
Nine days before the court date, brew some of the Nine Herb Court Case Mix into a tea. Use it to bathe downward. Step out of the tub backward, and throw the bath water over your left shoulder to the West. Place all court papers on your working space and dust with Court Case Powders. Make a sugar or honey jar with more of the Herb Mix, set it on the paperwork, and burn brown candles on the jar. You can use various types of candles, like a figure candle or a regular brown jumbo candle. Load figurals and jumbos from the bottom with personal items and powdered herbs. Inscribe a petition on your jumbo or figural candle and dress it with oil. Or, instead of a sweet jar, you can dress a brown vigil candle with Court Case Oil for the innocent party, and place that on the court papers. Poke your holes at the top in the inside and add crushed or powdered herbs and three drops of oil.

B) Ensure that charges are filed against a criminal and that bail is high.
Make a vinegar jar for the guilty person, with Red Pepper, Black Pepper, Knotweed Vandal root, and Couch Grass to tie them down. Place it on the court papers and top it with a black candle dresed with with Damnation or Destruction Oil.

4) MAKING A PLEA DEAL

A) Get low bail and a good plea deal
Continue your sugar or honey jar, but add Sumac Berries for mercy of the court. Make an Ammonia jar to turn the situation upside down. Write the petition on a piece of paper wide enough to go around the whole inside of the jar. Write it in the present tense, describing what is wrong because you're going to "turn it upside-down." Tape the petition in the jar written-side-inwards. Put in a stone of your choice that pertains to the case. For instance, Black Tourmaline to reverse evil. Turn the jar upside down.

B) The criminal remains in detention.
Baptize a back wax figural candle for the criminal, put it into a birdcage, wrap chains around it, lock it in, and bind the key in the lock so it cannot be opened.

5) THE TRIAL

A) Be found innocent at trial.
Put the names of bad witnesses into a Beef tongue with Poppy Seeds and Red Pepper. Tie it with twine, cook it, and eat it all to eat their lying words. For each bad witness or police officer, name an individual black figural candle, put a hole in the head and fill it with Poppy Seeds and Confusion Powder. Put a hole in the mouth. Fill it with Red Pepper powder and Alum powder, and seal it with glue. If you have photos of the people, put Red Pepper and Alum powder on their mouth, and lay a strip of duct tape across it. Put duct tape across their eyes. Place each photo underneath its candle. The candles may be burned when the trial starts or wrapped up and buried with the photos, preferably in a Porta-Potty. At the trial, chew Little John Root in the court room and discreetly spit out the juice. Trace your right foot on paper and on it write the names of the 12 Apostles: Simon Peter (The Rock), Andrew, James Zebedee (The Greater), John Zebedee, Phillip, Jude Thaddeus, Bartholomew, Thomas Didymus, Matthew the Levite, Simon the Zealot, James the Lesser, and Mathias who replaced Judas Iscariot. Trace your left foot and on it put the name Judas Iscariot. Wear these in your shoes. When the bad witnesses talk, tap your left foot, and when the good witnesses talk, tap your right foot.

B) Ensure that the criminal is found guilty.
Put the criminal's name and the criminal's lawyer's name into a Beef tongue with Poppy Seeds and Red Pepper. Tie the tongue shut with twine, cook it, and eat it to consume false words before they are spoken.

6) FOUND GUILTY: THE SENTENCING

A) Get the lightest possible sentence.
Dress a white skull candle for the sentencing judge with King Solomon Wisdom or Just Judge Oil, surrounding it by a circle of Sumac Berries.

B) Ensure that the maximum fine or fee is paid.
Put a photo of the jail or prison where the prisoner is to be sent under the birdcage with a black figural candle, as per Stage 4. Or wrap a black candle with chains, pour Damnation Oil on it, and burn it over the photo of the jail or prison.

7) IN JAIL OR PRISON: THE APPEAL

A) Get released on appeal.
Make an Ammonia jar as per Stage 4.

B) Deny the criminal's appeal.
Baptize a black candle for the person, put it in a box upside-down, and bury it.

8) THE PAROLE OR PARDON

A) Get early parole, work release, or a pardon.
Get the official title of the parole board; Sugar Jar.

B) No parole, full sentence, even an execution.
Continue Stage 7B. Hang, shoot, or electrocute the black candle according to the customs of your state or nation. Add D.U.M.E. Oil if death is required.

9) TIME SERVED: THE AFTERMATH

A) Have the record expunged or sealed.
Take Hyssop baths, recite Psalms 51, make a mojo with Hyssop, Solomon's Seal Root, Flax Seed, and Yellow Mustard Seed. Feed it with Reversing Oil.

B) The criminal has a permanent record
Get his photo in a prison uniform or from mugshots.com, nail it with 5 nails to a piece of wood, place it between two inward-facing mirrors, front and back, wrap it in black cloth, and tie it with black thread, cursing as you go. Hide it where it will never be found.

Ms. Robin founded the Hoodoo Heritage Festival in 2008 and has presented workshops and panel discussions almost every year for our 12-year run. She was also the person who first proposed the creation of AIRR in 2008. This workshop was presented at the 2019 Festival.

OUR FAVOURITE SOCIAL JUSTICE SPELLS

Beverley Smith, Sister Girl, Papa Lou, Miss Michæle, Candelo Kimbisa, Angela Marie Horner, Professor Charles Porterfield

SOCIAL JUSTICE AND THE IMPORTANCE OF SELF-CARE
BY BEVERLEY SMITH

Many rootworkers are involved in social justice and restorative justice work because they want to make a difference in the world. They have a wonderful, rich heritage, and a wealth of skills and knowledge passed down from their Elders.

As a rootworker, I feel a responsibility to use my magic for the greater good. I feel that my ancestors are honoured when I employ the wisdom that they carefully crafted for the betterment and empowerment of my people. Black people who have descended from enslaved Africans have a responsibility to work against oppression and to level the playing field in any meaningful way. By doing rootwork and conjure to increase fairness and opportunity in our lives, we fight against bigotry and state-sponsored double standards, violence, and inequality.

Those that work for social justice are often under a great deal of stress and anxiety. They frequently feel others' pain acutely. People who are called to restorative justice work can be full of empathy and concern and experience tension and anxiety. Many times emotional stress evolves into physical ailments and disease. It's crucial to somehow stay involved, continuing to speak one's truth as an advocate, yet also take care of yourself. It is difficult to avoid stories, videos, and images of injustice when you are involved in equality movements. So it is important to use the tools available to us as rootworkers to protect our emotional, mental, and physical health.

"Self care" is a fancy way of saying taking care of one's self. Sometimes when you are driven by a need to confront injustice and bring about change you may become overwhelmed by the strain. You can become depressed and withdrawn. I have experienced terrible bouts of depression and hopelessness in the course of my efforts as an advocate. What follows are some suggestions on ways a rootworker can incorporate self-care into their social justice activism.

MASSAGE OILS

To make magical massage oils put several drops of a condition oil, such as Clarity, Peaceful Home, Healing, or Victory, in a base of Almond oil and use it as a massage oil. Massage helps us relax and connect again with our bodies and feel more comfortable during times of stress and anxiety.

BATHS

Leisurely soaks in Epsom Salts, essential oils, freshor dried herbs or herbal tea, condition oils, or prepared magical bath salts should be a regular part of your self-care regime. Unlike a spiritual bath, which is traditionally poured over one's head and body while standing, I suggest a soak in a bathtub full of water as hot as you can stand. A deep, hot bath relaxes muscles, draws out toxins, improves circulation, and complexion, and helps you recuperate after exertion.

A bath to promote healing could include Eucalyptus, Coriander, Plantain, Dill, Lemon Balm, Goldenseal, and Burdock.

An old recipe for a protective bath is a tea made of Nettles, Mugwort, Rue, Feverfew, and Yarrow.

A bath for relaxation would include Chamomile, Lavender, and Hops, for example. A bath for bravery would include Mullein and Borage.

A bath of Bergamot, Devil's Shoe Strings, and Oregano will help ward off the law and keep the police at bay.

Basil, along with Catnip and Chaney root in the bath help to promote joy and happiness. Basil tea can also be an effective floor wash against evil.

Dried or fresh herbs can be tied into cheesecloth and tossed in the tub making for easy clean-up.

Salt is often used as protection against evil. Table, Kosher, or Epsom Salt can be used alone, or mixed with herbs for the desired results. Packaged bath salts like Law Keep Away, Fiery Wall of Protection, Clarity, Psychic Vision, Crucible of Courage, and Mastery are an alternative to homemade herbal bath formulas.

TEAS

Teas are a lovely way to enjoy healing and nourishing herbs. There are many tasty commercial blends available, marketed for various conditions such as anxiety, insomnia, stomach upset, etc. It's fun and easy to blend your own formulas for specific goals like mental health, protection, courage, energy, and strength.

For fiery protection, Ginger tea is ideal as a warm beverage and as a face or hand wash.

For a protective and soothing tea use a blend of Mint, Rose hips, and Chamomile.

AROMATHERAPY

The science and therapy of aromas is a wonderful addition to self-care. Aromas can change your mood and mindset as well as aid in mental, emotional, and physical healing. Aromatherapy helps with bad moments of despair and grief. It has been shown that scent can bring about certain emotions and states of being.

Using a diffuser is a good way to experience essential oils like Frankincense for mental well-being, Neroli for lifting one's spirits, and Basil for focus and alertness. Incense is available in resin, powder, and stick form. Myrrh can be burned for physical strength and endurance, or Benzoin and Frankincense resins for mental well-being and restful sleep. Sandalwood aids in peaceful vibes in the home and promotes healing.

Well-known commercial blends like Law Keep Away, Controlling, Victory, Run Devil Run, Tranquility, and Peaceful Home round out your incense supplies.

MOJO BAGS

Mojo bags are well known and important amulets that can also help with self-care by working to protect and heal.

To conquer fear women can carry whole Angelica roots in mojo bags. Angelica root powder sprinkled around the home also helps to purify and protect.

A mojo bag for protection might include such items as Five-Finger Grass, Devil's Shoe Strings, Devil Pod, Frankincense, Master Root, Sandalwood, Burdock, and a silver Mercury dime.

PROTECTION AND SECURITY SPELL
BY SISTER GIRL

When trying to achieve social justice one may feel one's personal security is in jeopardy. This spell is for personal protection and to ensure safety and security. For this work you will need:

- **1 white glass-encased vigil candle or 1 white 9" jumbo candle**
- **Ammonia**
- **A paper towel**
- **1 bottle of Uncrossing Oil**
- **1 chunk of Camphor or a tub of Vick's Vaporub**
- **Bay Leaves**
- **Salt**
- **A skewer, needle, or other tool for the candle**
- **A piece of brown paper bag paper**
- **A candle holder or a plate**

If you choose to use a white glass-encased candle, wipe it down with a paper towel moistened with Ammonia. With a skewer, make three holes in the wax of the candle from the top down. Into these holes dribble a few drops of Uncrossing Oil. Finally, add a small amount of crumbled Bay Leaf, a pinch of Salt, and a pinch of crumbled Camphor or small dab of Vick's Vaporub into the top of the candle.

If you are using a free-standing jumbo candle, wipe it down with a paper towel moistened with Ammonia, then engrave a few words of your petition into the wax and anoint it with Uncrossing Oil, rubbing it downward and away from yourself. You may either sprinkle the Camphor, Bay leaves, and Salt around the base of the jumbo candle or, if you know how to prepare rolled candles, you may melt white wax, add the herbs and resin (or Vick's Vaporub) and roll the candle in this to fix it.

If you have a specific situation in mind or there is a specific outcome you desire, write a petition paper on a piece of brown paper bag and place it under the candle holder or plate.

Hold the candle up to God and pray with all your might for your protection, stability, safety, and security. Speak in your own words and claim it in the name of God. Finish by holding the candle to your heart and saying either Psalms 91 for protection or Psalms 121 for stability and security. Then light the candle and place it in the holder or on the plate.

GOOD COP - BAD COP SPELL
BY PAPA LOU

This spell is to strengthen officers who take their jobs seriously and do them fairly, while stripping away protection from those who break their oaths and terrorize the communities they are sworn to protect.

For this work you'll need:

- 2 toy police badges
- 2 taper candles (1-black, 1-white)
- King of Spades and King of Hearts
- 1/2 ounce Blessed Salt
- 1/2 ounce Graveyard Dirt
- Dark Arts incense

Since this work accomplishes two things simultaneously it should be done at a half moon. Take the taper candles and prepare them as follows. The white candle is to have the words "Law man," "Protector," "Honourable," and "Matthew 5:9" inscribed on them. This last verse is recited over the candles as you prepare them. The black candle is prepared by scratching "Oathbreaker," "Weak," "Powerless," or any name known onto it followed by "Ecclesiastes 5:4-6." This verse is recited over the black candle in full.

Sit the toy badges down on the ground. Heat the bottom of the candles until they become tacky and affix them to the badges. The badges will become a base supporting the candles. Insert the King of Hearts into the white candle by a corner, and do the same with the black candle and the King of Spades. Ring the white candle in blessed salt and the black in graveyard dirt. Light Black Arts incense and recite Proverbs 8:34 and Ezekiel 33:6.

Let the candles burn down, wrap the entire mess up in a paper bag, and leave it at a railroad track.

A SIMPLE JUSTICE ALTAR
BY MISS MICHÆLE

The simplest way to begin a justice altar is with a white candle, a glass of water, and at least one picture of a justice worker who has passed on to the right hand of God (because where else would they be?). When you see a news story that concerns you, print it out and write your prayer right on top of the text. Place it under the white candle. Pray appropriate Psalms for justice over it.

GUARDIAN ANGELS FOR JUSTICE
BY CANDELO KIMBISA

This spell is to beseech a target's Guardian Angels to work for you against them for justice. You will need the following:

- 3 normal household clear water glasses
- Dirt from 3 unkempt graves
- Saltpeter, Sulphur, or Gunpowder
- 3 small arrows, needles, or Coffin Nails
- A candle
- Some Honey

Place the three clear water glasses in the shape of a "V," with two in front closest to you and one in the back middle. Christen the three water glasses in the name of the target's guardian angels, for example, "I christen this glass in the name of 'target's' guardian angel." Inscribe your target's name onto the candle, and christen the candle in the name of your target. The candle will sit closest to you, in line with the back center water glass.

Next, take the graveyard dirt and form three lines that meet at the back glass. One line will run straight from the back glass to the center of the candle. One line will run from the back glass to the left-hand glass, touch the glass, and then curve to the side of the candle. The third line will run from the back glass to the right-hand glass, touch the glass, and then curve to the other side of the candle.

In the same pattern on top of the graveyard dirt place the Sulphur, Saltpeter, or Gunpowder. Place the three arrows (or needles or nails), one on each of the three lines, pointing toward the target candle.

Take the Honey and drizzle it around the top of the glasses individually, then around all the glasses in a larger circle. Light the candle, pick it up, and petition the guardian angels to send them after your target. If the target is a male, for instance, tell them, "You see how I have given you light and sweetness, something this man has not done. He has broken his vows to you and to society." Place the candle back in front where the lines meet, and then, using a cigar, match, or lighter, light the lines where they all meet at the back center glass. The fire will race along the Sulphur, Saltpeter, or Gunpowder like a three-pronged attack — a blitzkrieg. If the target realizes he is being attacked and stops one, there will still be two more.

TO WARD OFF BULLYING
BY ANGELA MARIE HORNER

To ward off evil attentions and push negative influences away from you, write the first line of each of the following Psalms, in numerical order, in an outgoing spiral on a piece of paper:

- **Psalms 7:** To overcome enemies
- **Psalms 12:** To overcome persecuting influences
- **Psalms 13:** To protect from bodily suffering
- **Psalms 14:** To become free from slander
- **Psalms 20:** For relief from danger and suffering
- **Psalms 44:** To become safe from enemies

Place a small pinch of the following herbs on the center of the prayer paper you have created:

- **Calamus Root:** Control people and break jinxes.
- **Basil:** For protection from evil.
- **Chia Seeds:** To stop gossip.
- **2 whole Cloves:** To promote friendship.
- **4 Red Lentils:** To draw friends close.
- **Pyrite Grit:** To bring luck.
- **Lodestone Grit:** To attract people.
- **A drop of Honey:** To sweeten people to you.

Fold the paper toward you, turning it clockwise with each fold, until it is small enough to fit inside a locket. Bind the locket closed with black thread (for protection). Anoint a white candle with Protection Oil and burn it for the locket while praying Psalms 23.

MAKING JUSTICE TRACKS
BY MISS MICHÆLE

If you live in your state capital or are visiting it for a vacation or for business, sign up for a tour of the buildings where your state's legislature meets to make laws. As you dress that day, wear a Bay Leaf on your person so that you slide right in under everybody's radar. When you arrive for the tour, duck into the nearest bathroom for privacy.

Dress the outside of your shoe soles with an appropriate oil or oil blend. For example, try Just Judge and Do As I Say on the right shoe, and Run Devil Run, perhaps with D.U.M.E. on the left.

Take your tour with the appropriate manifestations of wide-eyed, innocent, patriotic wonder, while tracking justice, accountability, and righteous retribution through the corridors of power.

THE SPIRITS OF ACTIVISTS
BY PROFESSOR CHARLES PORTERFIELD

The spirits, ashes, and graveyard dirt of those who laboured and fought in the battle for justice, equality, freedom are potent and powerful aids to we who come behind and continue the good battles that they were involved with, and sometimes died for.

After the famous labour activist, songwriter, and member of the Industrial Workers of the World, Joe Hill was executed by firing squad in 1915, his body was cremated and his ashes were placed into 600 small envelopes bearing the caption "Joe Hill murdered by the capitalist class, Nov. 19, 1915." These were sent around the world to IWW locals and to sympathizers of the Workers Movement worldwide with instructions that they all be released to the winds on May Day, 1916. The example of Joe Hill's ashes is a small, although well known, example of the remains of a noted Social Justice leader being used in honour and acknowledgement of the continuation of the work they were dedicated to in life.

The graveyard dirt of such noted individuals as W.E.B. Du Bois, Harriet Tubman, Roger Nash Baldwin, Frederick Douglass, Woody Guthrie, Martin Luther King, Jr., Sojourner Truth, Jackie Robinson, Rosa Parks, and others offers us an active connection not only to their spirits, but also the ability to call upon and request their aid, comfort, and righteous power in our own works for social justice. The spirits of these justice workers can be called upon in prayer, their graveyard dirt incorporated into protective charms and mojo hands, and their names added to our petitions for justice.

"Our Favourite Social Justice Spells" was a hand-out at the 2016 Hoodoo Heritage Festival workshops. Beverley Smith is a voice over actor and conjure worker; she can be reached at Facebook.com/beverley.m.smith. Kast Excelsior is a member of AIRR, a record producer, and a bone reader; he is available at ConjureHaus.com. Sister Girl is a member of AIRR and Hoodoo Psychics; she can be found via SisterGirlConjure.com. Papa Lou is a spiritual consultant and rootworker; he can be contacted via Twitter.com/papalouwwts. Miss Michæle is a member of AIRR; her web site is HoodooFoundry.com. Candelo Kimbisa, a Palero, can be reached via Kimbisa.org. Angela Marie Horner is a card reader, massage therapist, candle server, and reader at MISC, AIRR, and HP; she is available via LotusRavynConjure.com. Professor Porterfield is online at ProfessorPortfield.com.

OVERCOMING OBSTACLES AND OPPOSITION
Apollo Dark

KNOW YOUR OBSTACLES

Any obstacles you face are there for a reason. Once you know why an obstacle is in your way, you will know how to overcome it. Let's say you want to fall in love or you want money. Each of these goals potentially has its own typical obstacles, but the way you know what's stopping you is the same for both. You attempt your goal and see what happens. In each case the block will be shown.

THE POWER TO CHANGE

Don't let anything daunt you. Giving up or not believing you can defeat the opposition will stop you before you try. Belief in your ability to remove this obstacle is a key starting point for your work. Don't let anything stop you before you try. You can be the change you want to have, and the first step is faith in yourself.

Sometimes just changing the way you address the obstacle allows you to overcome it. Dress nicely, display decorum, work hard, have confidence, and show your value. These things can enable you to overcome a lot of obstacles, but sometimes nothing seems to work.

KNOWING WHAT TO CHANGE

Before proceeding, you may want advice. This is the time have a reading. Pull cards, look into a crystal ball, or use a pendulum for yourself, or reach out to a professional to read for you. If you work with a reader, ask for straightforward and to-the-point information about what's stopping you. In this reading there are two key questions to ask. First: What does my path to success look like? In the answer to this question, obstacles will show themselves. Second: What does overcoming the obstacles look like? This will give you a direction and a method in which to work.

SPELL WORK

Many kinds of spells are employed to overcome obstacles. Road Opener and Block Buster spells are two of the most positive types.

ROAD OPENING

The name "Road Opener" was taught to me as having developed on the East Coast, with roots in Puerto Rico, Cuba, and other Latin and South American traditions. It is known as "Abre Camino" (literally "Road Opener") in Spanish, but it long ago entered hoodoo and acquired an English name. Road Opener work is appropriate when dealing with obstacles that are circumstantial or natural in cause. It has been said that opening a road is like cutting away the brush on an overgrown path.

For instance, if you are trying to get a raise at work, but the boss hasn't noticed you, Road Opener and Boss Fix are a good choice, because the problem is a circumstantial obstacle. Perform Road Opener work when you want to find love, but you can't seem to find a good match. This is also circumstantial, so blend some Road Opener with Attraction and Look Me Over, and you will have a good basis to proceed with your spell work. You can also combine Road Opener products with Influence and Crown of Success to achieve a specific effect.

BLOCK BUSTING

The term "Block Buster" is more deeply rooted in African-American folk magic, where it generally refers to removing obstacles that have been thrown in front of you. For instance, if someone is speaking ill of you, or has put a jinx on you, your situation can be metaphorically compared to a road that was blocked when an enemy dynamited the hills above your path. They caused boulders to block your road, and you too can use dynamite to clear the road.

For example, if you are trying to get a raise at work, but someone is using that stuff to get the boss to dislike you, so that all your efforts fail, you could use Block Buster products to blow away the jinx. Mixing Block Buster with Stop Gossip and Compelling is a good combination for this situation. Next, say you are trying to find love, but nothing is working and no one seems to even like you. In this case a reading might show that someone has jinxed your love life. Try using Block Buster with Uncrossing and Jinx Killer to get rid of that nasty mess; then start your Love Me work.

ROAD OPENER CANDLE SPELL

This spell was taught to me by Miss catherine yronwode. Because it resembles a crossroads, you may work on up to four wishes — either four different ones or the same one four times. You will need:

- Four 4" candles in colours appropriate to your wishes: red for love, green for money, etc.
- Four 4" candle holders (Lucky Mojo Curio Co. sells nice little stamped metal star holders)
- One Road Opener Glass-Encased Vigil Candle
- One packet of Road Opener Sachet Powder
- One bottle of Road Opener Oil

First, dress the vigil candle. At some candle shops, this can be done for you by the staff. If you wish to do it yourself, you will want to use these items in this order: Road Opener Oil, Lemon Grass, Mint, Master of the Woods, Five-Finger Grass, gold glitter flakes, gold glitter stars. Remember, less is more. You don't want your candle to burn black, and it will if you use too much oil or too many herbs to dress it.

Now, pray over the vigil candle. Psalms 23 is appropriate, as is Numbers 13:30 *("...Let us go up at once, and possess it; for we are well able to overcome it.")*, Joshua 1:8 *("This book of the law shall not depart out of thy mouth; but thou shalt meditate therein day and night, that thou mayest observe to do according to all that is written therein: for then thou shalt make thy way prosperous, and then thou shalt have good success")*, or 2 Samuel 22:33 *("God is my strength and power: and he maketh my way perfect")*.

Next, dress the 4" candles with Road Opener Oil. Pray the desires associated with each candle: "May my road be clear to love." "May my road be clear to money." "May my road be clear to success."

Place the four 4" candles in their holders and set them up in a half-circle around the vigil candle. Take the Road Opener Sachet Powder and make three arrows pointing out between the 4" candles. Alternatively, make a four-way crossroads of them and point the arrows outward.

Light the 4" candles counter-clockwise (or, if you prefer, East, South, West, North), then light the vigil candle. Over the next hour, move the four 4" candles away from the vigil candle every 15 minutes. They will burn out after about an hour and a half. Let the vigil candle complete its burn over the next several days.

BLOCK BUSTER BURNING SPELL

This spell I came up with myself. It was adapted from traditions taught to me as I grew up. You'll need:

- **A small cauldron (3" to 4" would be ideal)**
- **A black pen and parchment or brown paper**
- **A self-lighting charcoal tablet**
- **A small amount of powdered sugar**
- **Lemon Grass**
- **Mint**
- **Matches**

This spell employs fire, so work in a fire-safe area. Do not perform this spell near flammable items.

Write out the name of your obstacles. In Block Buster work this can be the full name and birth date of the person who caused your obstacles, or you can state what your obstacles are: "No one hires me," "No one loves me," "I have no hope."

Light the charcoal and place it in the cauldron. Sprinkle Lemon Grass and Mint onto it to make a nice amount of smoke. Hold the paper and say "I burn this away from me. It is gone and never to return. This opposition is cast away." Hold the paper by a lower corner (the lower right if you are left-handed and lower left if you are right-handed). With a lit match, set the paper on fire at the upper opposite corner from where you are holding it. Place it gently on the charcoal.

Now take a small pinch of the powdered sugar and lightly toss it on the flame of the burning paper. Say "This Block is Busted Away." Recite Psalms 144. There will be a small fireball, and the spell is done.

MAINTAINING A CLEAR ROAD

Prayer is a powerful tool, so use it as often as you can. With a good prayer at night and in the morning, you will set up a nice sustainable guard on your path to success. I leave you with a written spell.

As you read this, may your road be clear. Your path to your goals is paved with prosperity. Joy and happiness flood to you. Success is yours, and your desires manifest. Fears and doubts fade from you. All the good in the world is for you, and may the years to come be ones of achievement and abundance. Amen.

This was a hand-out at the 2014 Hoodoo Heritage Festival. Apollo Dark can be reached at his web site, Apollo-Dark.com.

HOW CAN WE REMEMBER?: HARRY HYATT AND HOODOO
catherine yronwode

REV. HARRY MIDDLETON HYATT

Harry Middleton Hyatt was an Anglican minister who collected folklore as a hobby. Raised in Quincy, Illinois, he received his M.A. and D.D. at Kenyon College and Oxford University. He served as assistant rector at the Church of the Holy Spirit in New York City from 1951 to 1965. After his retirement in 1965, he returned to his hometown of Quincy, Illinois.

As a folklorist, Hyatt began this work in his own hometown and then proceeded onward to collect magical spells throughout the South. His two major works in this field were *Folklore From Adams County Illinois* (1935) and *Hoodoo - Conjuration - Witchcraft - Rootwork* (1970-1978). In addition, Hyatt was also a genealogist who published two books on his own family, *The Millers of Millersburg Kentucky* (1929) and *Descendants of John Walton of Baltimore Co. Maryland and Harrison Co. Kentucky* (1950).

FOLKLORE FROM ADAMS COUNTY ILLINOIS

Folklore From Adams County Illinois (FACI) contains hundreds of spells, magical beliefs, herb-based medical remedies, riddling rhymes, and tales. It consists of 10,949 entries on 723 pages, including an index. It was published in two editions, the first in 1935, and the second in 1965, both released under the imprint "Memoirs of the Alma C. Hyatt Foundation." Alma C. Hyatt was his wife. The second edition contains a lengthy illustrated appreciation of the then-late Alma Hyatt, in which Mr. Hyatt tells the world what an inspiration she was to him.

The section of *FACI* that deals with witchcraft is the most useful part of the book. It is comprised of brief quotes from unnamed folks to whom Hyatt assigned cultural ascriptions (e.g. "Irish," "German," "Negro," etc.) so that one can place the speakers in the traditions from which they came. Unfortunately, as Hyatt explained in his preface, the material was edited and "omission of Negro dialect means that coloured folk speak the same language as their white neighbours" with the exception of "a small vocabulary peculiar to themselves [of which] examples occur frequently in the text."

Even more inexplicably, all "lore definitely Jewish was excluded [and] the same is true of three or four Indian [Native American] sayings." Furthermore, Greeks and Italians living in the area, according to Hyatt, "are newcomers, and have not been approached for folk-lore." Such egregious editorial deletions blemish what would otherwise be a balanced representation of folk magical practices in Illinois at that time, but if one keeps these exclusions in mind, *FACI* is still a valuable document. The lengthy section on African-American hoodoo spells, and the unique quality of these spells, is what led Hyatt to undertake his later, more massive, work of hoodoo folk magic collection in the South.

FACI represents the largest attempt to catalogue ALL the beliefs of ALL the people living in one region (Adams County, Illinois, like the title says) and although Hyatt refused to collect material from Jews or Native Americans, for reasons that defy rationality at this point, there were plenty of Black people in Adams County, and Hyatt collected all of their beliefs, spells, and practices, and labelled them "Negro" for ease of extraction by researchers.

I am often asked what the differences are between the 1935 and 1965 editions of *FACI*. Basically — they are different, period.

The 1935 edition is easier to read (it is a typeset octavo volume), but the 1965 edition is MASSIVE — presented in typewriter type, like the later *Hoodoo - Conjuration - Witchcraft - Rootwork* books, and matching them in size and binding.

Additionally, the 1965 *FACI* is the only place where you can learn more about Hyatt himself. In a special insert section printed on glossy paper and illustrated with photographs, he describes his life and his relationship with his wife Alma, who was his muse and financial supporter throughout his long years of dedicated folklore collecting.

The other question often asked is "Why do i need to read FACI when it is not about hoodoo?"

False premise!

A great deal of FACI is in fact about hoodoo.

HOODOO - CONJURATION - WITCHCRAFT - ROOTWORK

It was Hyatt's realization that Negro magical beliefs differed greatly from his own English-American culture's beliefs that led him to go South and work on *Hoodoo - Conjuration - Witchcraft - Rootwork,* the largest collection of folklore from one cultural group in America. But *FACI* is not only important because it served as Hyatt's introduction to hoodoo — it is also the most thorough and factual record of Irish, English, German, and other White European magical beliefs in America ever assembled, and, as such, it deserves a place on the shelf of any American Neo-Pagan, Wiccan, Fam-Trad, or Pow Wow Magic practitioner.

Hoodoo - Conjuration - Witchcraft - Rootwork (HCWR) is a 5-volume, 4766-page collection of folkloric material gathered by Hyatt in Alabama, Arkansas, Florida, Georgia, Illinois, Louisiana, Maryland, Mississippi, North Carolina, South Carolina, Tennessee, and Virginia between 1936 and 1940. Supplementary interviews were conducted in Florida in 1970.

The collection consists of 13,458 separate magic spells and folkloric beliefs, plus lengthy interviews with professional root doctors, conjures, and hoodoos. The spells are organized by the form taken by the work (such as mojo hands), by the intention of the job (such as business luck), or by major ingredients (such as salt or blood).

All but one of Hyatt's 1605 informants were African-Americans, although a few narrations by European-Americans (collected for his earlier book, *FACI)* were also included. He gave each informant a unique number and entered it in his "Numbers Book," along with the person's name. Unfortunately, the Numbers Book went missing during a move, rendering most of the informants nameless, a loss that Hyatt deeply regretted.

Hyatt recorded the material on Edison cylinders and a device called a Telediphone, often without the full knowledge of the participants. He then transcribed and annotated it for publication. Occasionally his equipment failed or was not available and he took hand-written notes instead. The 1930s field recordings have since been destroyed, with the exception of a few cylinders that Hyatt had pressed onto 78 rpm records. The Florida interviews of 1970, recorded on cassette tapes, have survived.

As if to overcome the ham-fisted linguistic editing of Negro dialect that marred *Folklore From Adams County Illinois,* this time Hyatt transcribed the speech of his informants semi-phonetically. What may look to modern eyes like "racial stereotyping" or making fun of Southerners was actually his sincere attempt to catalogue variant regional pronunciations.

If you read several spells, you will see that he did NOT impose upon his informants one single stereotyped "Black dialect" or "Southern dialect" but in fact conveyed, as accurately as he could, the true sound of each person's speech. Reading the spells aloud and noting the location where each informant lived will help you comprehend this. I do not intend to apologize for Hyatt's technique, and i hope that future scholars will not do so either.

The publication of Hyatt's HCWR material was accomplished between 1970 and 1978, again under the imprint "Memoirs of the Alma C. Hyatt Foundation." The first two volumes were issued as a set in 1970, and said to be complete, but then, after a few years, three more volumes were released. Hyatt died before the sixth volume, an index, was prepared.

I have roughly indexed the contents of *Hoodoo - Conjuration - Witchcraft - Rootwork* at **http://luckymojo.com/hyatt.html**

In order to address the complexities of the material and the loss of the Numbers Book, and for the convenience of those interested in the broader areas of African-American genealogy and material culture during the 1930s, i have also placed online an index to the names and residential locations of informants for whom such data could be found. Via this "Hyatt Informants" page, interviews that were broken apart for use as individual "spells" can be reassembled, restoring a spiritual sense of the speakers' knowledge and style. I offer thanks to those who have helped me with this longterm project, which is online at **http://luckymojo.com/hyattinformants.html**

This flyer was abridged from my web page on Harry M. Hyatt at http://luckymojo.com/hyatt.html for use at the first "Voices of Hyatt" performance in 2015. This event featured Ambrozine LaGare, Sister Girl, and Khi Armand portraying a series of rootwork practitioner-informants, with Professor Porterfield in the role of Harry M. Hyatt, all speaking their parts aloud, directly from Hyatt's transcriptions.

VOICES OF HYATT: HARRY HYATT AND HOODOO
catherine yronwode

WHAT'S INSIDE THE HYATT BOOKS

Here's an outline of what's contained inside Harry Hyatt's *Hoodoo - Conjuration - Witchcraft - Rootwork*:

Volume One (1970):
- Introduction (i - xliii)
- Cultural Beliefs
  - General Description of Beliefs (1-19)
  - Belief in Spirits, Ghosts, the Devil, and the Like (19 -164)
- How Rootworkers Operate
  - Testimony From Laymen (165 - 217)
  - Comparisons Between Medical Doctors and Root Doctors (217 - 269)
  - Typical Methods Used by Root Doctors (269 - 349)
  - Timing of Spells and Recurrence of the Effects of Spells Over Time (349 - 361)
- Folk Medicine
  - Principles of Healing (361 - 410)
  - Alphabetic List of Ingredients (410 - 519)
- Mojo Hands
  - Alphabetical, by Major Ingredient (519 - 669)
- Spells for Business Luck
  - Alphabetical, by Major Ingredient (669 - 744)
- Shrines
  - Altars (Primarily New Orleans) (744 - 797)
  - Candles (Primarily New Orleans) (797 - 862)
  - Saints (Primarily New Orleans) (862 - 888)
- More Laymen Testimonies (888 - 931)

Volume Two (1970):
- Map of Fieldwork (932)
- Interviews with Root Doctors (933 - 1843)
- Illustrations: Photos and Documents (1844 - 1858)

Volume Three (1973):
- More Interviews with Root Doctors (1844 - 2339)
- Conjure with Human Body Parts and Waste
  - Sexual Fluids, Sex Magic, and Impotence (2341 - 2509)
  - Blood ("Everyday Blood" and "Her Private Time") (2509 - 2540)
  - Urine (2540 - 2618)
  - Excrement (2618 - 2636)
  - Sweat (2636 - 2781)
- Illustrations: Photos and Documents (2782 - 2800)

Volume Four (1974):
- Introduction (i - iv)
- More Work Utilising Human Body Parts and Waste
  - Shoes (2801 - 2818)
  - Foot Tracks (2818 - 2936)
  - Hair (2936 - 3049)
  - Fingernails, Toenails, Footskin (3049 - 3077)
- Systemic Body Ailments
  - "Live Things in You" (3077 - 3109)
  - Cures For Disease (3109 - 3155)
  - Alcoholism (3155 - 3166)
  - To Keep Persons Asleep (3166 - 3185)
- More Interviews with Root Doctors (3185 - 3241)
- Murder
  - How a Murderer Can Escape (3241 - 3258)
  - How a Murderer is Caught (3258 - 3293)
- Death, Burial, and Graveyard Dirt
  - Obtaining Graveyard Dirt (3293 - 3419)
  - Working with Graveyard Dirt (3348 - 3385)
  - Coffins and Bones of the Dead (3385 - 3419)
- Body Substitutes
  - Photographs (3419 - 3497)
  - Names and Handwriting (3497 - 3589)
  - Handwriting (3589 - 3610)
- Theft Cases (3610 - 3633)
- Court Cases (3633 - 3714)
- Hens' Eggs (3717 - 3776)
- Illustration; First Sexual Spell, 1936 (3778)

Volume Five (1978):
- Introduction (i - x)
- Salt and Its Combinations (3779 - 3830)
- Nails, Needles, Pins, Tacks (3830 - 3876)
- More Frogs and Toads (3876 - 3913)
- More Black Cat Bones (3913 - 3951)
- More Candle Rites (3951 - 3971)
- More Sex and Impotence (3971 - 3994)
- More Hag and Witch (3994 - 4003)
- Sell Self to the Devil (4003 - 4013)
- Leather-wing Bat (4013 - 4027)
- Miscellaneous Spells (4027 - 4492)
- Florida Root Doctors, 1970 (4493 - 4754)
- Illustrations; Police Permits, 1930s (4755 - 4759)

Volume Six (Unpublished):
- The index was in preparation when Hyatt died and was never released, leading to the frustrating condition of the material as it now stands. The above index was all that was published.

BIG DATA

Harry Hyatt's *Hoodoo - Conjuration - Witchcraft - Rootwork (HCWR)* is one of the largest collections of folklore ever assembled. It is also one of the most chaotic, which is not so much a failure on the author's part as it is the result of the fact that he did not have the funds to hire a professional indexer or even to have the work typeset before it was printed. What you see in these books is 42 years of Hyatt's field notes, dating from 1936 to 1978, presented in the form of hand-typed pages. In total, there are 1,600 interviews in the 4,760 pages of the 5 volumes. The amount of expense, travel time, and labour it took to collect, preserve, and publish the material is a testimony to the phenomenal interest that Harry Hyatt had in his subjects and their spiritual lives.

The interviews conducted with professional root doctors are word-for-word transcripts, not indexed in any way. All of them are presented in semi-phonetic form, in order to assist linguists in understanding the regional dialects of the subjects and to help in understanding the class or education level they presented. In addition to these impenetrable walls of typewriter type, there are thousands of semi-indexed fragments of interviews, both with professionals and with regular practitioners and laypeople, consisting of 13,458 separate magic spells sorted into rough groups, some by situation or intention, some by ingredients, and some just "miscellaneous."

CRITICISM OF PHONETIC TECHNIQUE

Criticism has been levelled at Hyatt for his use of phonetics to individuate the speech patterns of his subjects. However, without those vocal cues we would not be able to bring to life the voices of his interviewees in a personal, identifiable manner. In my opinion, any attempt to force a narrow political view — the false idea that he was somehow "disrespecting" Black people by printing their words phonetically — stems from a misunderstanding of what he was doing.

Hyatt made a conscious choice to serve linguists as well as folklorists, but the technology of the times — and the expenses of buying wax cylinders for his recording devices — required that, once transcribed, each cylinder had to be returned to the manufacturer for re-surfacing, so that it could be used again. There were no permanent audio files; thus the transcribers' phonetic spelling was the only way the voices of the speakers could be indicated with accuracy.

CRITICISM OF THE INFORMANTS

In recent years, a well-known Southern White folk magic teacher has opined in print that Hyatt was an ignorant Northerner who was fooled or gulled by Southern Black liars, and that a great part of the spells in *HCWR* are "just nonsense" and "plain laughable" (direct quotes) and therefore unworthy of study or practice. The basis for the author's claim is personal gnosis and self-appointed authority, for she wrote, "I feel in my heart that some of these folks just made things up so they could have the money" (direct quote) and "I would say that about 60% of those writings are junk. Common sense tells me this, along with what I know as fact."

It would be low to point to White covetousness of personal attention as an obvious commercial factor that may affect the making of such accusations against deceased Black hoodoo practitioners. It would also be easy to broach the topic of racism when a Southern White author says, "I know the mindset of the blacks" (direct quote) and tells us that "most of these blacks were share croppers or just worked for white folks," despite the fact that Federal Census records reveal actual informant occupations ranging from oystermen, barrel makers, waiters, Pullman porters, and auto mechanics to prostitutes, bootleggers, retired housewives, ministers, fortune tellers, and rootworkers.

But, leaving that aside and speaking from a frame of mind that embraces compassion, i choose to interpret these claims as a manifestation of White-privileged BLINDNESS to Black America. I also think i can demonstrate the source of this blindness, in the specific cultural context of how folklore studies and their academic publications intersect with the celebration of actual family traditions in the age of internet accessibility.

CULTURE OVER GEOGRAPHY

In the introduction to Volume One of *HCWR*, Hyatt discoursed at great length about the differences between *HCWR* and his earlier book *Folk-Lore from Adams County, Illinois (FACI)*. As he explained, *FACI* was a geographical survey of folklore and folk magic beliefs, while *HCWR* was a look at the folklore and folk magic beliefs of one then-segregated population, no matter where geographically located. In other words, in *HCWR* he chose to look at Black culture, not at Southern culture.

DEMOGRAPHY A DETERMINANT

In describing why he chose a geographic tactic for the compilation of *HCWR,* Hyatt explained that although he was only collecting from African-American informants, he was well aware that Anglo-Americans also have folk magic practices and that the two cultures interacted, despite the segregation laws that were in place during the time of his work.

He then quoted many paragraphs by his professional root doctor informants (as distinguished from his "person on the street" informants) in which they replied to his questions about demography:

- What percentage of Negroes believe in hoodoo?
- What percentage of Whites?
- Do you serve Negro clients?
- Do you serve White clients?

Some of his professional informants told him that they specialized in serving a White clientele (and Hyatt noted that this would have been more profitable to Black spiritual workers than limiting themselves to serving genrally poorer Black clients). He also compiled accounts in which Black clients described the race of their own personal root doctors — Black or White. Some Blacks did patronize White root doctors, but Hyatt did not follow through and interview those White rootworkers, for reasons explained below.

From his demographic data, Hyatt drew the conclusion that most Black root doctors averred that about 90% of Negroes "believed in" hoodoo at the time he was collecting, and that these same Black professionals figured that 40% - 60% of White people also "believed in" hoodoo (as performed by Black workers for White clients) or in some other form of folk magic. He then applied a cost-benefit ratio analysis to his proposed folklore collecting project and decided that the percentage of respondents would be higher per mile travelled and week spent on the road if he limited his work to Blacks. In other words, he CHOSE not to interview Southern Whites, but to collect Black folk magic only. He said this, and explained why, precisely and clearly.

That decision on Hyatt's part — to ignore Southern White folklore — leaves a lot of White newcomers to hoodoo confused and feeling disenfranchised. "My momma did some of this, too, and WE weren't Black" is the burden of their refrain of complaint when they encounter the Hyatt interviews.

DEALING WITH HURT WHITE FEELINGS

So, how can White Southern authors reconcile the differences between the White Southern folklore of their ethnic heritage and the Black Southern folklore so massively displayed by Harry Hyatt? And how can they feel "included" in the current online interest in African-American hoodoo? The obvious answer would be for them to start on the solid basis of understanding their own culture first, before looking into hoodoo. We could help them out by telling them to ask their own families, their White neighbours, and their White friends, about Anglo-European folk magic. We could suggest that they read the Foxfire books of the 1970s and consult the earler works of Vance Randolph, B. A. Botkin, and Wayland Hand.

But that may not be good enough for some of them. Hoodoo suddenly got popular on the internet and they want their share of the fame and interest, so they resort to explaining the differences between their family's White Southern folklore and Hyatt's collected Black Southern folklore by attempting to discredit both Hyatt AND his Black informants. If all of the differences are discounted as "useless junk" (a direct quote) and are made to go away, then what remains will be only the similarities, the folklore that they know, namely White Southern folk magic, which they believe to be the only right, proper, and authentic form of folk magic. In other words, they are displaying a fundamental ignorance of, and disrespect for, Black culture by trying to claim hoodoo as their own through the avenue of discrediting Hyatt's interview subjects.

The injured sense of identity that leads White Southern interpreters of folk magic to tilt at the windmill of Hyatt's collection can be found in statements like, "I have never felt the need to defend myself because I think most of the stuff Harry M Hyatt wrote is bullshit. That doesn't make me a racist it makes me a person who knows HER heritage."

After that it is only a short step farther to remove Black folk magic from contact with the White South. To paraphrase Pierre Damien Mvuyekure (in *The African Diaspora: African Origins and New World Identities,* University of Indiana Press, 1999) they "break, reconfigure, refashion, and weld" Black folk magic into a fabulous and fantastic construct of Haitian Voodoo and Cuban Santeria with Catholic overtones, re-exoticizing it as the magic of the "Other" so they can claim the re-enchantment of their own White culture under the popular names of hoodoo and conjure.

WHY SINGLE OUT HARRY HYATT?

I believe that one reason Hyatt's work has been attacked is because, as is quite apparent, these White authors are not familiar with earlier collections of Black folklore, either academic or anecdotal. As one wrote, "There is not a lot of written information out there except for the work gathered by Mr. Harry M. Hyatt." This is manifestly untrue, but the writer is not engaged in primary exploration of present day Black culture and is evidently unfamiliar with alternative, non-academically-mediated sources of historical Black folk magic information, such as the WPA Slave Narratives and the texts of 1920s-1930s blues lyrics.

Of course Hyatt's work is the largest collection of African-American folk magic ever assembled, but academics do not calculate a source's value by its size alone. They also ask, "Can this data be independently confirmed?" And in Hyatt's case, it can be. The same material can be found in the earlier works of Leonora Herron, Alice Bacon, Mary Alicia Owen, Helen Pitkin, Newbell Niles Puckett, and Zora Neale Hurston, as well as in the songs of Arnold Wiley, Jim Towel, and the Memphis Jug Band. To discredit Hyatt's 1,605 African-American informants as "a dangerous crock" (direct quote) accomplishes nothing in the end, because researchers can read the exact same spells in a transcription of the lyrics to Sara Martin's 1925 recording of the blues song "I'm Gonna Hoodoo You."

To one who falsely views Hyatt as the sole collector of Black folklore, it may seem that he was publishing Southern folklore, falsely identifying it as "Negro," and including within it practices not of "[THEIR] heritage," which, therefore, would be untenable. By discrediting the veracity or knowledge-base of Hyatt's Black interviewees, they may think they can stop up the free flow of information about African-American culture and appoint themselves the gatekeeper-interpreters of all Southern folk magic. Furthermore, by denying their reliance on written texts that describe specifically BLACK folklore, they might aspire to become the inheritors of their own WHITE "grandmother stories," to use Chas Clifton's term. (See Clifton's 2006 book *Her Hidden Children; The Rise of Wicca and Paganism in America*, AltaMira Press, 2006, especially Chapter 5, on "self-invention.")

Ultimately, given the number of independent data points collected by Hyatt in so many cities for so many years, the attempt to categorize the material as "foolishness" (direct quote) is not sustainable.

THE GREAT CONSPIRACY

Wrote the Southern White critic of Hyatt's informants, "I for the life of me can't see black folks in that day and time telling some white man their business, even if he did have black guys as go between men." These "go between men" (Hyatt called them "contact men") were employees who travelled with Hyatt, pre-interviewed root doctors, rejected unsuitable prospects, and drove interviewees to their meetings. For the record, they were, from 1936 - 1940:

- **Julia [-]:** Alma Hyatt's housekeeper in New York.
- **Jerry Williams:** Ocean City, MD, related to Julia.
- **Walter J. Maddox:** Princess Anne, MD, the head waiter at a hotel.
- **Mr. [-] Gavin:** Wilmington, NC; his wife Carrie was Julia's sister, she too was related to Jerry Williams.
- **Mr. [-] Carter:** Norfolk or Fredericksburg, VA, a chauffeur for hire who drove Hyatt down into SC.
- **Edward Bufford, Jr.:** Mobile, AL, an auto mechanic and chauffeur for hire.
- **Mack Berryhill:** New Orleans, LA, a taxi driver.
- **Marshall [-]:** New Orleans, LA, a taxi driver (who may be the same as Mack Berryhill).

1,605 Black people from 9 states told Hyatt similar spells. If they all told the same lies to fool a White man, they must have been in secret communication with one another. Perhaps the contact men coached them on what to say. But what about Sara Martin, back in 1925? Surely she had no idea that Hyatt's informants in Quincy, Illinois, planned a massive bamboozlement in 1935 — or did she? Do you see where this logic leads? If Black people lied to Hyatt from 1935 - 1978, they must have lied to Puckett from 1925 - 1926, and to Hurston from 1928 - 1930 as well. We find ourselves looking at a conspiracy theory in which an army of taxi drivers secretly spent decades synchronizing Black lies about hoodoo.

The only way to stop this madness is to listen to the Voices of Hyatt, that is, to the speakers themselves.

This flyer is abridged from my web pages on Harry M. Hyatt at http://luckymojo.com/hyatt.html and from the Lucky Mojo Forum for use at the second Voices of Hyatt performance in 2016. This performance again featured Professor Porterfield as Hyatt, with Ambrozine LeGare and Kast Excelsior voicing a second series of informants who tell the stories of their work in conjure, directly from the pages of "Hoodoo - Conjuration - Witchcraft - Rootwork."

A CLOSING CIRCLE
catherine yronwode

THE SOCIAL NETWORK

The Hoodoo Heritage Festival is an unusual gathering, held for the benefit of friends and community members. Although it is always open to the general public, it has, for all the years of its existence, attracted a small, dedicated group of professional root workers, practitioners, readers, and shop keepers who wish to teach and learn more about the practice of conjure in a low-key, non-commercial setting. Additionally, because it is held at the conclusion of a week-long session of hands-on apprenticeship training for professional practitioners, the Festival tends to attract people who are not coming out to buy some lifestyle clothes or to learn a few tricks; instead it serves as a gathering place for those who wish to make hoodoo a serious personal practice or even a profession.

With so many people in attendance, and such tight scheduling as we move from workshop to workshop, the major times we get to hang out with one another are at lunch and after the day's activities are finished. For the past few years we have formalized the end of our yearly event with a closing circle, where we can solidify the transient connections we make during the days of activity. At this circle, business cards are exchanged, web site URLs are scribbled on Post-Its, promises of Facebook friendship are extended, and folks hug or shake hands, as if they were parting for the week at church.

But what is our social network, really? And how does our knowing each other help us to improve our practice of rootwork and our ability to turn our passion for folk magic into a way of living, even to the extent of earning our daily bread by it.

In what follows, i would like to give you all some advice — the recommendations of someone who has worked as a reader, root doctor, and shop keeper for many years — on what it takes to be a success in this field, and to do so in an organic, naturally unfolding way, through the development of a social network, both in-person and electronic. To do this requires almost no financial investment, but it does require time, and an understanding of what people want, and why they seek you out,

MODALITIES OF OUTREACH

To best utilize a social network, you first need to understand these three avenues of communication:

TOP DOWN: The teacher, the emcee, the author, the presenter, the artist, the celebrity, the guru.
> **Method:** Communication flows from you to your audience.
> **Advantages:** You control the message; if you are dynamic, you will accumulate fans.
> **Disadvantages:** You receive no feedback; you must always generate new content; you must control distribution of your content.

BOTTOM UP: The fan, the devotee, the student, the radio show caller, the reviewer.
> **Method:** An audience members reacts by contacting the teacher, author, or celebrity.
> **Advantages:** Good feedback cheers you; suggestions help you expand your offerings.
> **Disadvantages:** You leave yourself open to haters and jealous rivals posting spurious negative reviews; you may lose your focus.

PEER-TO-PEER: A gathering of equals, a party, a panel talk, an interest-group, a self-help group.
> **Method:** Communication flows freely among equals, with no single point-source of origin.
> **Advantages:** More minds bring more data and life experience to the discussion.
> **Disadvantages:** Ignorant people, haters, or those with strong opinions can dominate and derail unmoderated conversations.

How you feel about these communication forms and where you find your own comfort zone when navigating them will ultimately have an impact on the way in which you achieve success as a fortune teller or root worker. If you are so unassuming that bottom-up communication is your preferred state, you may remain a perpetual student or fan. If you want to always be in charge, you may become a guru or top-down celebrity. If you like to share, you may join forces with your comrades, but abjure personal fame. And, of course, you can blend methods — you can be an accessible celebrity, a collaborative teacher, or a fannish forum moderator. The choices are yours.

A GUIDE TO NETWORKING

Once you understand which modality of outreach suits your personality, you can enter into social networks well prepared to take on the role you want.

THE SOCIAL NETWORK OF FACE-TO-FACE

Business cards are your best way to make an impression face-to-face. Always have your cards on you and be ready to give them out, either peer-to-peer, or top-down. If you wear several hats, have a card for each service you offer. Printing both sides is slick, but i recommend having some cards that are blank on the back so you can write notes on them with URLs, dates, locations, or prices. Never write on the front of your card; use the back for that. I carry double-sided and blank-backed card at all times. Avoid the elegantly austere card. Your name, company name, telephone number, fax number, street address, email address, web site URL, social media URL, and a description of your services will fit on one side of a card.

THE SOCIAL NETWORK OF SALES LITERATURE

If you sell via mail order or in a storefront, be sure to create some giveaway sales literature and free information sheets. This is top-down work, but It is also traditional in conjure shops that the hand-out sheets include a spell, so every sales sheet is also a collectible gift. Create several spell pages for different conditions, each on a different colour of paper, and key them to products purchased by each customer.

THE SOCIAL NETWORK OF SOCIAL MEDIA

Facebook, Twitter, Instagram, and other social media sites are peer-to-peer networks, but you can also use them for top-down presentation of current events. Remember that social media is not the place to air your dirty laundry or to grouse about your hangover; it may seem to be peer-to-peer, but you will also have fans, followers, clients, and customers to whom you must always appear in a professional light.

THE SOCIAL NETWORK OF A WEB SITE

Owning your own domain is essential for self-branding. It is the best way to make top-down social contact. However, if you add web form-mail to the site, you actually must answer it promptly; don't give the false impression of accessibility and then fail to follow through on the implicit promise of a response.

THE SOCIAL NETWORK OF A NEWSLETTER

Email newsletters are a good top-down method for staying in touch with customers, but don't spam them with too-frequent email blasts. Discount coupons keep folks interested. Constant Contact and Mail Chimp offer online archiving. Don't forget to announce each new issue in your social media platforms.

THE SOCIAL NETWORK OF A BLOG

A blog is easier to create than a full-blown web site but it is not an effective way to brand yourself. It is top-down, but if folks can leave comments, you must monitor the pages perpetually for spam and haters.

THE SOCIAL NETWORK OF INTERNET RADIO

If you like to talk, try Blog Talk Radio, archive your shows, and when people download the podcasts you may even get a little money back. Top-Down shows and peer-to-peer shows are both well-received. Announce each new podcast via social media.

THE SOCIAL NETWORK OF INTERNET VIDEO

If you feel comfortable on camera (or just don't give a damn about how you look), try posting a series of instructional videos on Youtube. This service will automatically create a channel to archive your shows and you can earn cash if you allow ads. You will want to either disable comments (a bit unfriendly and top-down looking) or regularly monitor the comments to remove posts from spammers and haters. Announce each new video via social media.

THE SOCIAL NETWORK OF AN ONLINE FORUM

Running a phpBB style forum is lot of work but a great community-builder. It works both peer-to-peer and as a top-down way to introduce yourself to clients. You will also accumulate lurkers, bottom-up followers who never post. Be prepared to immediately remove all spam, troll, and hater posts. You will need to check your forum daily and if it becomes large, you may need help running it (i offer store credit to my Forum moderators). If you can't create your own forum, consider joining mine at Forum.LuckyMojo.com!

I wrote this flyer for the 2016 Hoodoo Heritage Festival workshops. I am a member of Hoodoo Psychics and the Association of Independent Readers and Rootworkers and i can also be contacted for readings or spiritual work via my own LuckyMojo.com web site.